IMAGES
of America

BROWN COUNTY

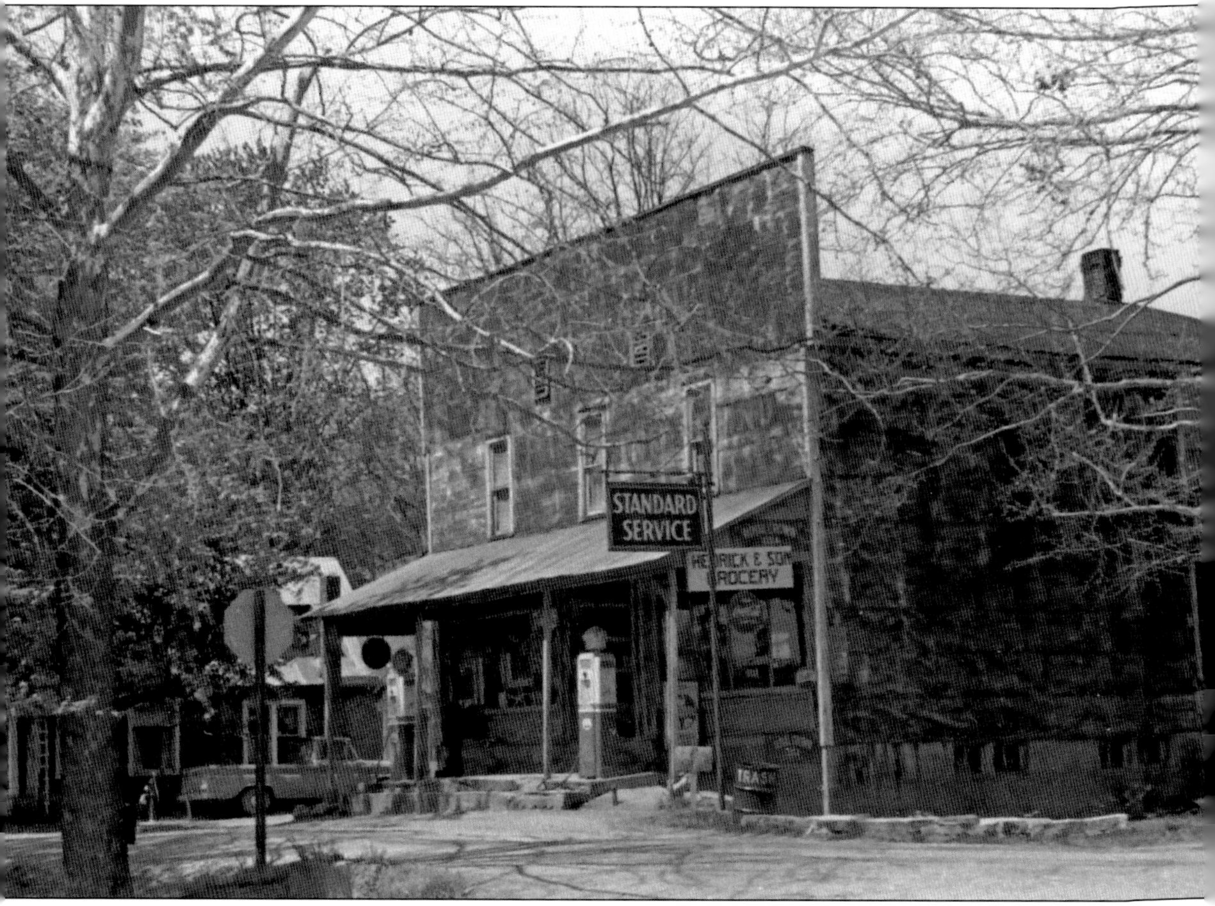

Nine years before Abraham Lincoln was elected president, Story, Indiana, came into being. In 1851, Pres. Millard Fillmore granted a land patent to Dr. George Story for the creation of this little village. Story was one of the largest settlements in Brown County, but now the population is down to four and horses (there are five) outnumber people. The Story General Store, which opened in the 1850s and was rebuilt after a fire in the early 1900s, is now the Story Inn, a restaurant and bed and breakfast. (Story Inn.)

On the cover: A favorite of both tourists and artists who came to the area was the Pittman Inn in Nashville. The flavor of Brown County is captured succinctly in this 1900 quote from artist Adolph Shulz, written after he had first explored the county by horse and buggy, "Never before had I been so thrilled by any region; it seemed like a fairyland with its narrow winding roads leading the traveler down into the creek beds through the water pools and up over the hills." (Brown County Historical Society.)

IMAGES
of America

BROWN COUNTY

Rick Hofstetter and Jane Ammeson

ARCADIA
PUBLISHING

ISBN 978-0-7385-7725-8

Published by Arcadia Publishing
Charleston, South Carolina

Printed in the United States of America

Library of Congress Control Number: 2009928805

For all general information contact Arcadia Publishing at:
Telephone 843-853-2070
Fax 843-853-0044
E-mail sales@arcadiapublishing.com
For customer service and orders:
Toll-Free 1-888-313-2665

Visit us on the Internet at www.arcadiapublishing.com

To our families for all their support.

Contents

ACKNOWLEDGMENTS

Besides its beauty, there is another reason why Brown County, Indiana, is so popular, and that is because of the warmth and generosity of the people who live there. Their help was essential in creating this book, and we would like to extend warm thanks to Cherry Williams, curator of manuscripts at Indiana University's Lilly Library, for allowing us access to their wonderful collection of Frank Hohenberger photographs and for their use in this book. Another big thank you goes to Debbie Dunbar, director of marketing and communications for the Brown County Convention and Visitors Bureau, who helped point us in the right direction at the very beginning of the project. Another thank you goes to Nancy and Ron Coulter, archivists at the Brown County Historical Society, who were willing to put in long extra hours helping find and identify photographs and providing historical context for many of the images found in this book.

Then there is a special thanks to Mike Kelley, owner of the House at Stone Head, who not only provided us with photographs and the history of his wonderful house, now more than a century old, but helped coordinate access to other photographs of the wonderfully named community of Stone Head. Suzannah Zody, Annie May, and Sarah May, all descendents of the original owners of the House at Stone Head, lent us their valuable family photographs to include in this book.

Carol Lucas Cummins, whose family is from Elkinsville, spent time recounting the stories of life in that small community before the waters of Lake Monroe made much of what she knew vanish.

Nelson Price, that great raconteur and host of WICR 88.7 FM's *Hoosier History Live*, also took time to share his vast knowledge of Brown County. Journalist Jackie Sheckler Finch shared stories of the county's history, and in Gnaw Bone, thanks go to Pat and Bill Watkins for their photographs and tales.

I'd also like to thank the authors of such books as *The Dusty Road Leads to Elkinsville*, by Robert Cross; *Brown County Remembers*, compiled and edited by Dorothy Biney Bailey and indexed by Nancy Coulter; *Brown County Folks*, by Richard Reed; *The Stuff of Legends: Tales of Van Buren Township of Brown County's People*, by Helen Ayers; and such Web sites as ourbrowncounty.com and the Brown County Rotary (www.browncountyrotary.org), because without their dedication to the preservation of Brown County history so much would have been lost.

Introduction

The lure of Brown County, with its winding roads that meander over streams through groves of trees and hollows, attracts both visitors and artists who revel in the charm of its small towns, covered bridges, wooded hillsides, and quaint names such as Stone Head, Stoney Lonesome, Bean Blossom, Schooner Valley, Needmore, and Gnaw Bone.

The story of Brown County is the story of people attracted to its isolation and beauty who wanted to capture it through such mediums of photography, clay, or paint and the story of hardworking "hill" people sometimes just eking out a living. In some ways, it seems as though these two groups might never coincide. Cartoonist Kin Hubbard highlighted the eccentricities of rural Brown County natives in his wildly popular *Abe Martin* cartoons, which were syndicated nationally. But despite this layer of fun, there was respect for those who lived here and an acknowledgement of their way of life.

One such man who earned the respect of the "inners," as they were known, was photographer Frank Hohenberger, whose beautiful, haunting, and visually compelling black-and-white photographs of Brown County captured life back in the early to mid-1900s. Many of Hohenberger's images are available at Lilly Library at Indiana University in Bloomington, and they kindly shared some for this book. Hohenberger moved to the area from Indianapolis after he developed film for a customer who had taken photographs of Brown County. Intrigued, Hohenberger looked up the area on a map.

"I was interested in character and types," Hohenberger told writer Webb Waldron for an article that appeared in *American Magazine* in October 1933. "And I had a hunch that there was something down here that I could do well. I had about twenty-five dollars saved up. I quit my job, took a train to the nearest station and came across the hills to Nashville with Daddy Woods, the mail man."

It took a while for Brown County folk to accept him, but they did. And his photographs, which he described as showing "the way character stood out in the faces of these people," helped propel both Hohenberger and Brown County to further fame.

There were other artists here too. In 1907, noted artist T. C. Steele moved with his wife, Selma, to a rise that overlooked the valleys and hills of Brown County. His dedication to the place attracted more artists. Steele's home, studio, and gardens are now a historical site open to visitors, and it is possible to stand on the porch of his house and see the same lovely view that he did so many years ago.

When the Steeles first moved here, travel was difficult. The roads, still unpaved, often were impassable, and the area's rural character was such that Selma Steele's player piano was eyed with suspicion by those who worked from dawn to dusk (and probably much later) trying to make a living out of the land. Modernity would come late to Brown County, and the hardness of their lives can be seen in photographs taken at that time—pictures of weathered but interesting faces and cabins that seemed to be mere strips of wood barely held together. But even in the black-and-white photographs, the natural beauty of Brown County stands out.

The first car appeared in 1913, and electricity arrived even later. For some of the more rural villages, such as Story and Elkinsville, electricity did not arrive until the late 1940s, more than a half century from when Thomas Alva Edison started his Edison Electric Light Company in 1878. At the time, Edison said, "We will make electricity so cheap that only the rich will burn candles," but it was poverty that kept the incandescent lightbulbs from burning in the hills and valleys of Brown County. Indeed, there is a tale of an older woman in Story who taped over her electrical outlets because she did not want the juice to leak out and cost her extra.

The hills here are full of history. There is the town of Elkinsville, whose residents were forced to abandon it to make way for Lake Monroe with just a few homes and remnants of buildings remaining. But whereas Elkinsville is almost a ghost town, Story, founded in 1851 and once one of the largest communities in Brown County with its own school, church, mill, and general store, barely escaped that fate. The lights at the general store—and from the crown-topped gas pumps that are more than six decades old—now glow in the soft evenings as the Story Inn, a destination bed and breakfast and restaurant. Old houses have been historically renovated and now serve as guest quarters as does an old mill. Story is considered to be one of the best representations of a pre–Civil War Indiana town, a picture-perfect place for visitors willing to travel off the beaten path.

Covered bridges still carry travelers across streams here in Brown County. The oldest covered bridge in Indiana, and the only covered two-lane bridge in the state, is located right off of State Route 46 at the north entrance to Brown County State Park. The bridge was built in 1838 to cross Ramp Creek in Fincastle, Indiana, and was moved to the park in 1932 where, after renovation, it now spans Salt Creek. The Bean Blossom Covered Bridge still carries traffic across Bean Blossom Creek. Though cars, and not horse and buggies, move across the wooden floors of these bridges, they still in some ways transport people across time.

The stone head marker that stands where the road divides, west to Story or east to Pike's Peak (the founder of that town wanted to make it to Colorado but only got this far and thus settled by naming the town after his ultimate destination), has always been a tourist attraction. There once was a community here called Stone Head, and now there is just one of the original houses, built in 1891. The marker dates back to 1851 and tells the mileage to various places, but more than that it is a reminder of how little has changed over the last century or so in this pastoral wonderland.

One

NASHVILLE

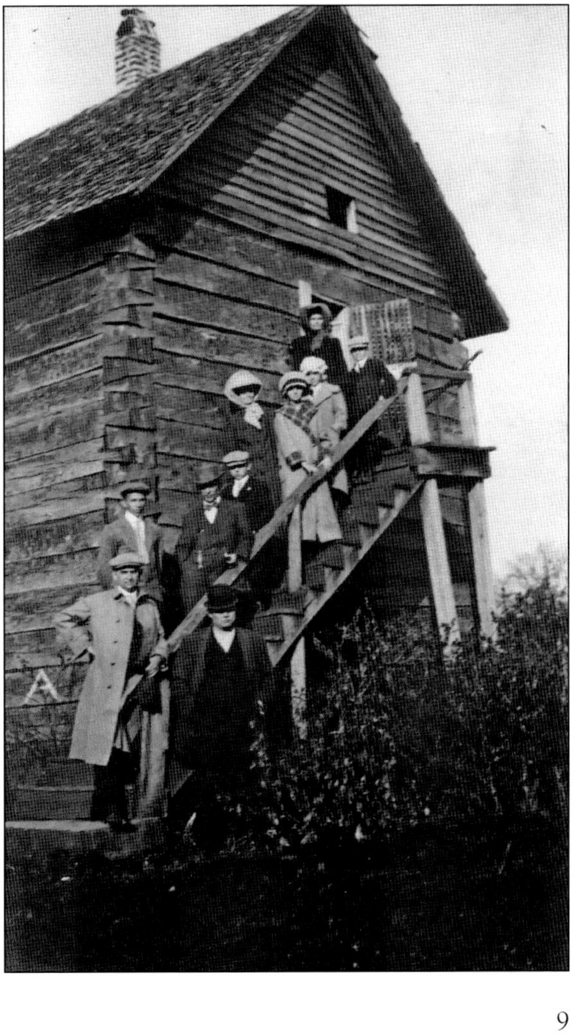

By the 1910s, the old log jail, built in 1879, had become a Nashville tourist attraction but during its day was used frequently, as at times Nashville could be a rowdy place. According to www.genealogytrails.com, "William S. Roberts was one of the first Justices of the Peace of this township. His old docket exhibits many amusing items. In 1839, Stephen Gibson was fined $1.50 for an assault and battery on Samuel Parsley." (Brown County Historical Society.)

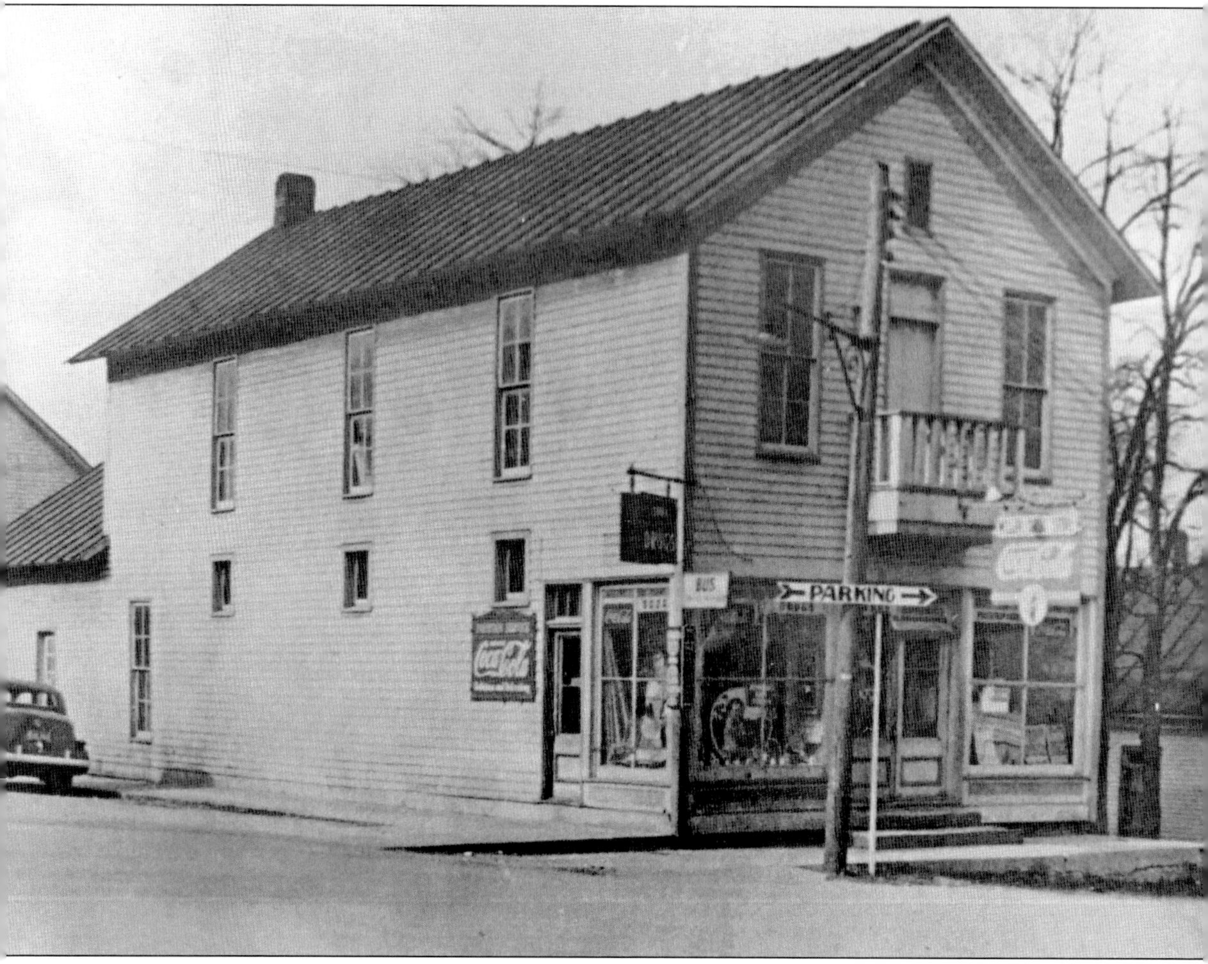

A perfect spot to gather for coffee or a meal, the Hob Nob Restaurant, located on the corner of Van Buren and Main Streets in the heart of Nashville, is the oldest commercial establishment in Brown County. Since being built in 1873 by the Taggart Family, it has housed several businesses, including an ice cream parlor on the second floor and Miller's Drug Store, named after the family that bought the building in 1925. (Brown County Historical Society.)

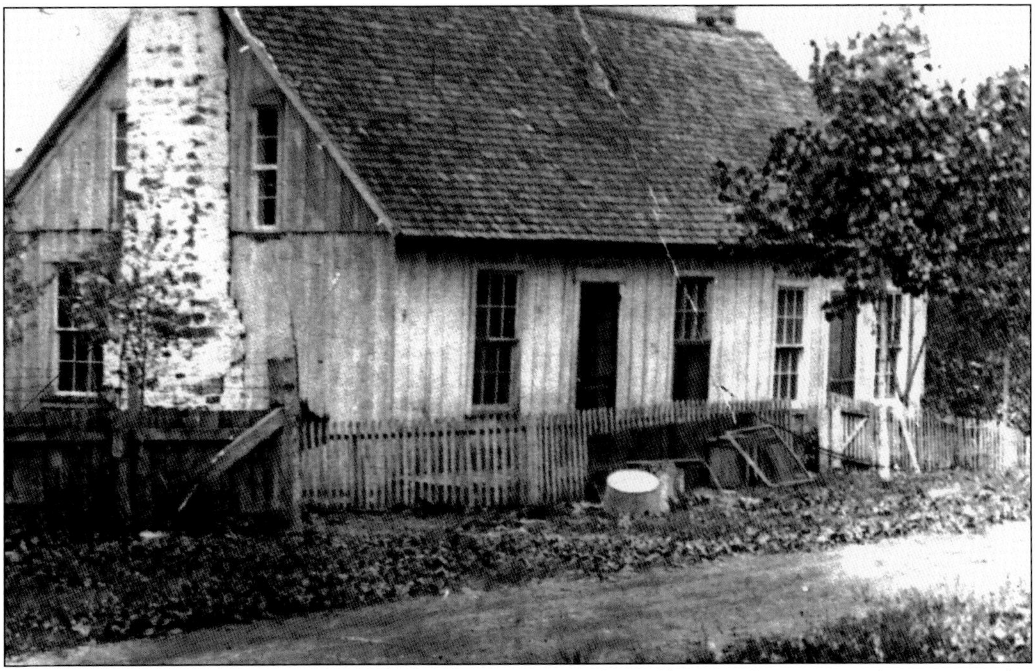

In 1835, Banner C. Brummet built the first house in the village and two years later opened a liquor and grocery store. The home, which still stands in Nashville, was sold in 1850 to a Miss Pettgrew and then in 1871 to Mollie Lucas, who owned it until 1932 and ran it as a boardinghouse for "genteel young ladies." (Brown County Historical Society.)

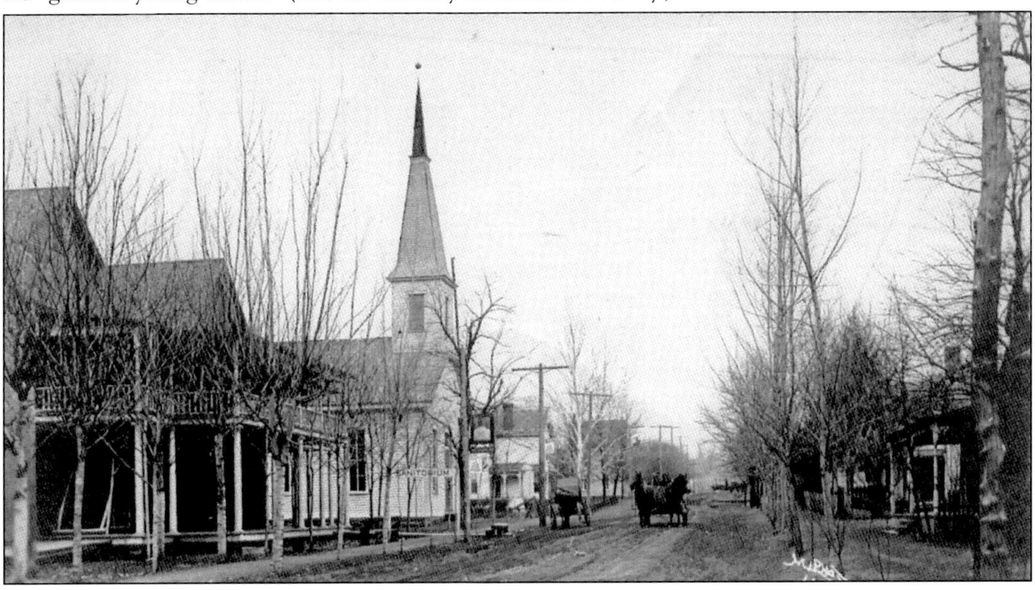

This is an early scene of Nashville showing the Pittman Inn and the Christian church; it was charming scenes like this that attracted artists like T. C. Steele and Adolph Shulz. In 1824, William Snider cleared land and built a log cabin in what would become Nashville. Two years later, county agent Banner Brummet laid out the town, calling it Jacksonburg in honor of Pres. Andrew Jackson. Since there was already a Jacksonburg, Indiana, the name was later changed to Nashville after Brummet's hometown in Tennessee. (Brown County Historical Society.)

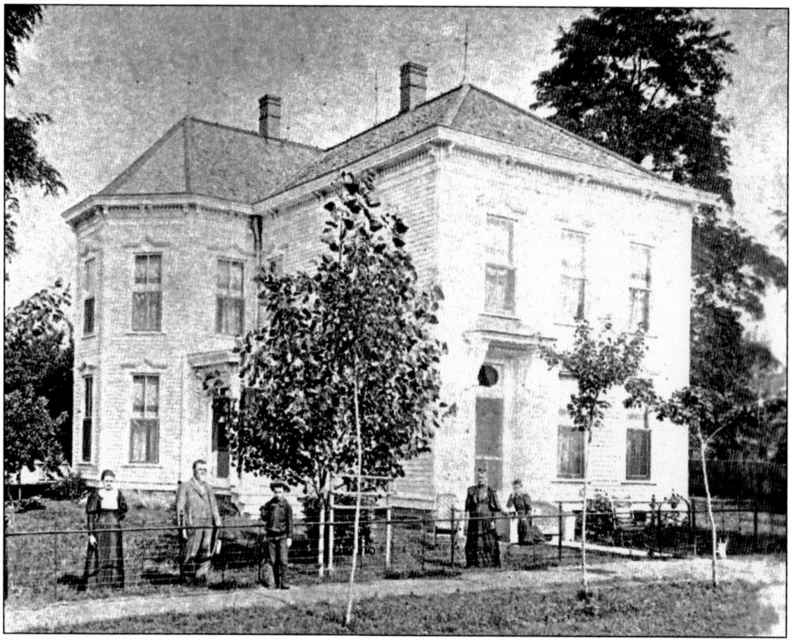

This 1895 photograph shows the home of Alonzo Allison Sr., which was built in 1865. Allison, who came to Nashville in 1870, purchased the *Brown County Democrat* in 1885 and ran it until his death in 1926. (Brown County Historical Society.)

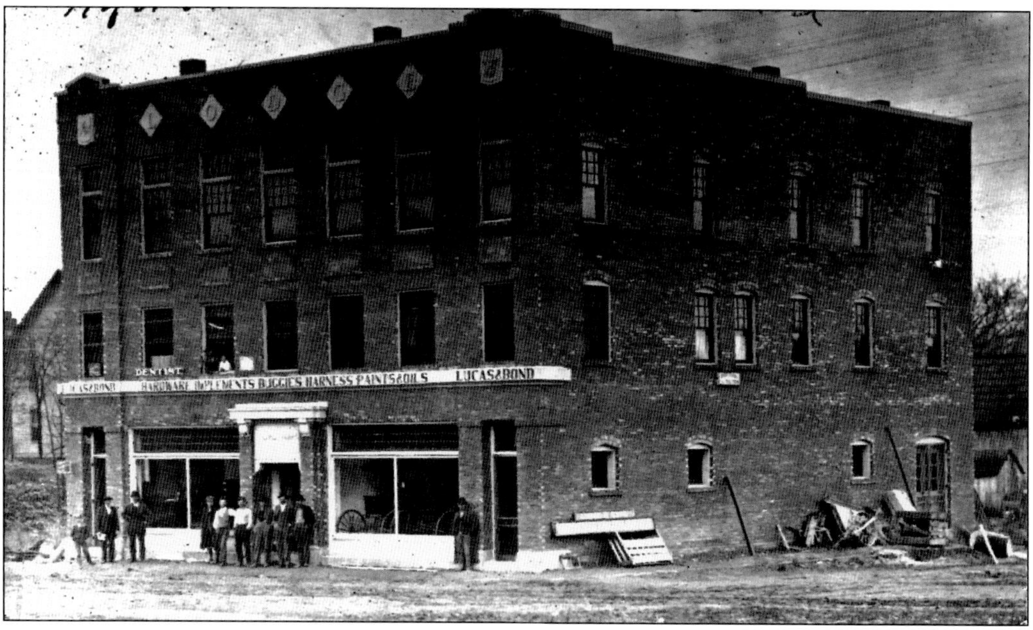

Completed in 1910, at the time this photograph was taken, this three-story brick building, which now houses shops, was the Nashville Masonic Lodge, founded in 1851. In *Brown County Remembers*, Harold Adams recalls, "[E]very fall the Masons held an oyster supper and all members and families were invited. . . . Long tables were set up with white tablecloths. Tables were decorated with big dishes of celery and great bowls of crackers and large bowls to put oyster soup in." In earlier years, there was a hardware store on the first floor and doctors' offices on the second. (Brown County Historical Society.)

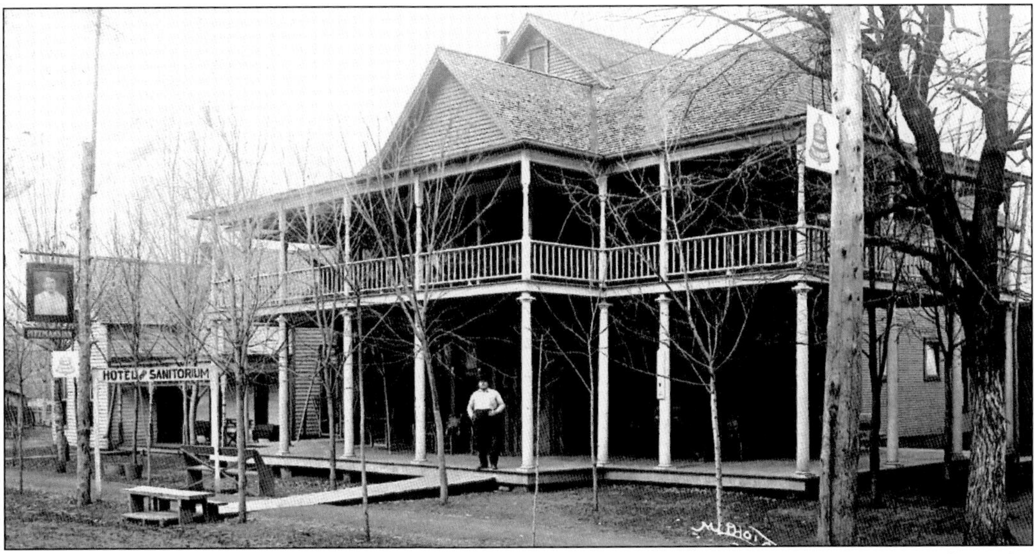

Billy Pittman would stand in front of the Pittman Sanitorium on Van Buren Street when the hack from the railroad carrying passengers arrived as can be seen in this 1910 photograph. "Who can forget Billy with his congenial smile and his mouth full of brightly shining gold teeth?" Wayne Guthrie stated in *Brown County Remembers*. Passengers would ask if there was room, and Pittman responded, "We'll make room." (Brown County Historical Society.)

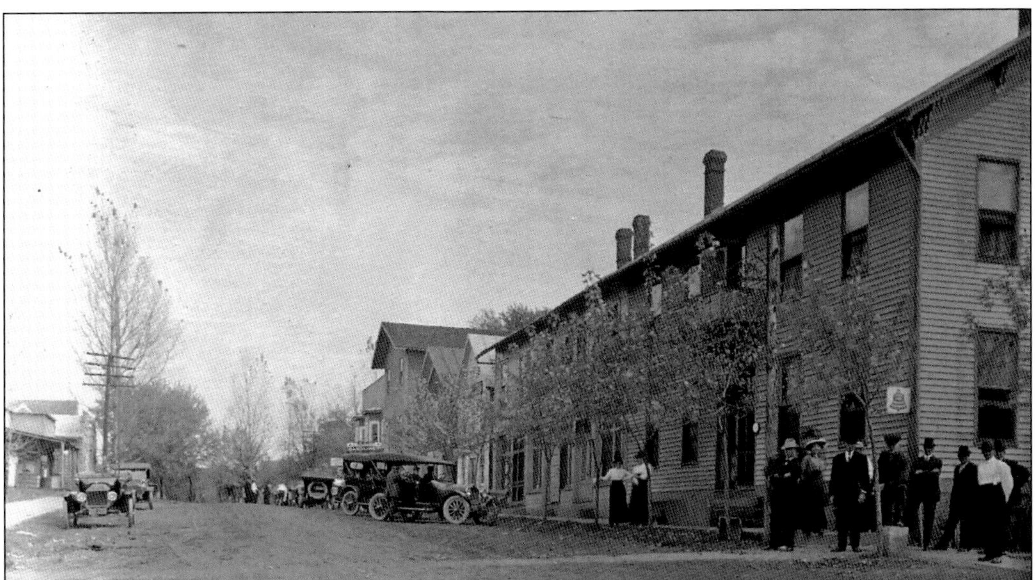

The original Nashville House is shown here in 1915 on the corner of Van Buren and Main Streets in downtown Nashville. To this day, though this building burned down and was replaced, the Nashville House continues to be a landmark in Brown County. The man with his arms folded, standing next to the pole, is Herman Burns. Taylor Wilson recalls that many people in the outlying communities thought of Nashville as being a Sodom and Gomorrah. (Brown County Historical Society.)

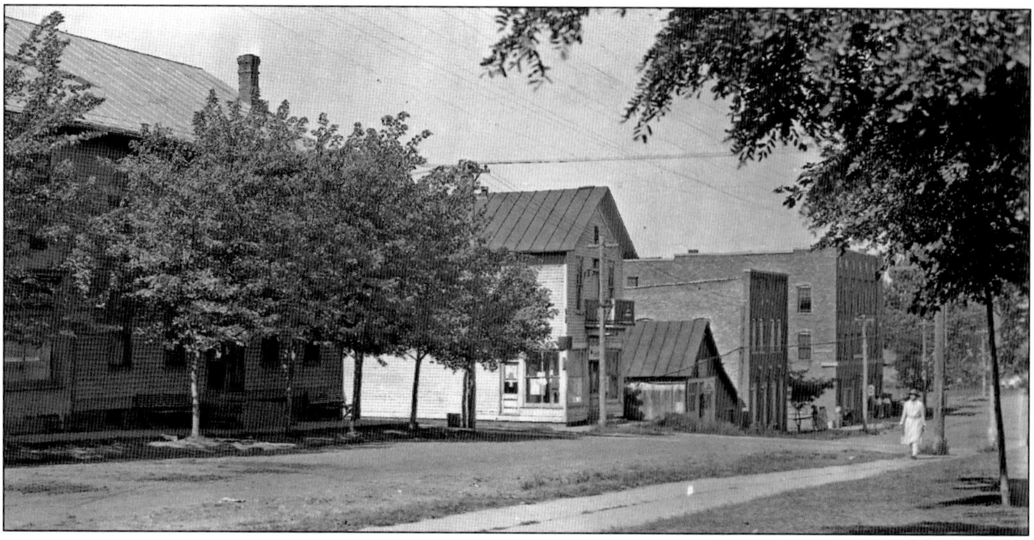

By the time this photograph was taken in 1918, despite its lack of paved roads and rural remoteness, Brown County and Nashville were becoming a popular destination for tourists and artists who were drawn to its rural beauty. Note the white, two-story building on the left. That is now the Hob Nob Restaurant but in the past housed a butcher shop and grocery store. (Brown County Historical Society.)

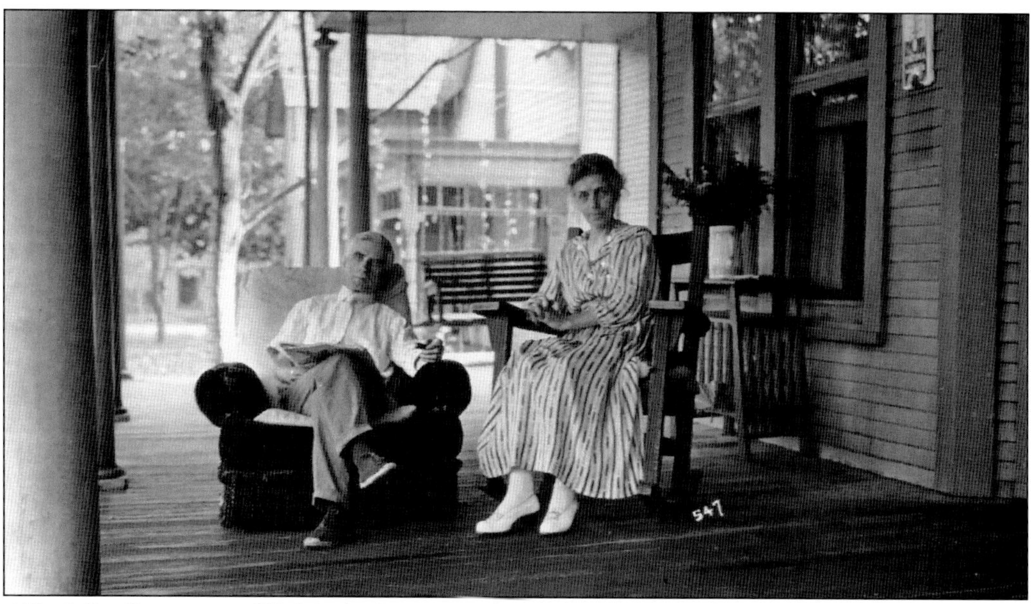

Alfred Gindle, owner of Ye Maple Arms Hotel, is pictured on Van Buren Street in 1918. "When I was a boy the town of Nashville was just as quaint as pictures show it," recalled Taylor Wilson in *Brown County Remembers*. "The streets were dirt and gravel and graded up like a country road with side ditches." (Photograph by Bruno Lundren; Brown County Historical Society.)

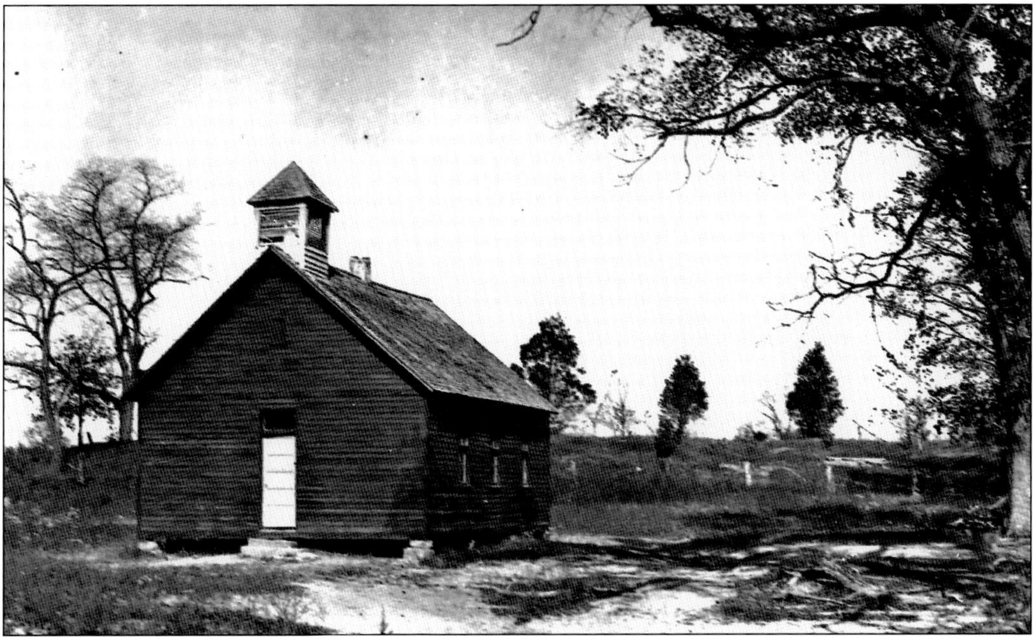

Nashville School is pictured here in 1918. According to Taylor Wilson in *Brown County Remembers*, the foxhunters' meet was so important that school was dismissed on Thursday and Friday for an event. The first schools in Brown County were built of logs, but by 1872 one-room frame schoolhouses dotted the county; in 1900, there were 73. (Brown County Historical Society.)

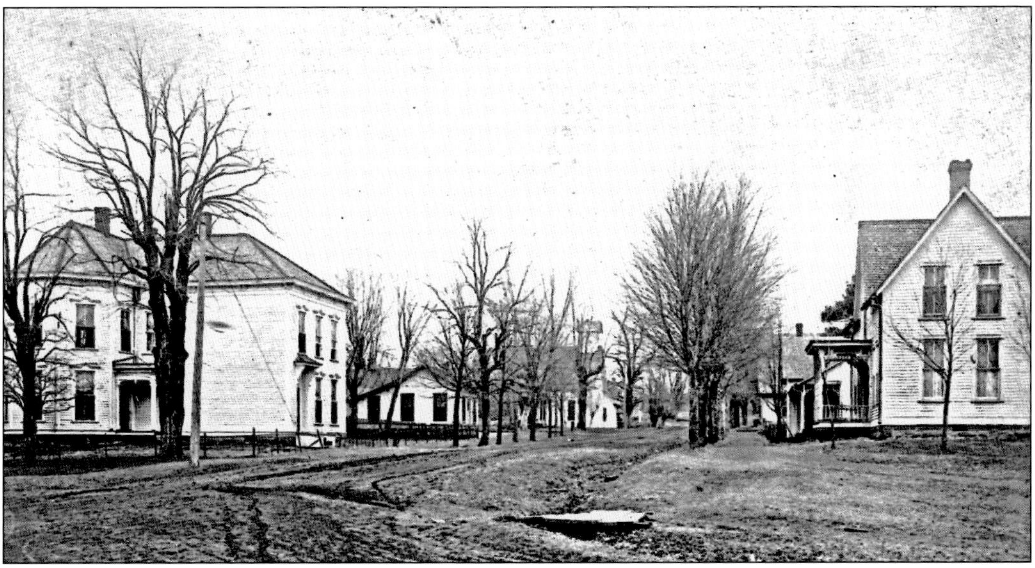

Famed photographer Frank Hohenberger captured the beauty of this area in his black-and-white photographs in the early 1900s. According to an article written by Webb Waldron in 1933, "[Nashville] was a place with only about 300 population, with two groceries, a livery stable, a drug store, and a boarding house; a village far off the railroad, with no industries, entirely dependent on the trade of the hill folk." This postcard, taken around 1920, shows the Taggart, Seitz, and Tilton homes. (Brown County Historical Society.)

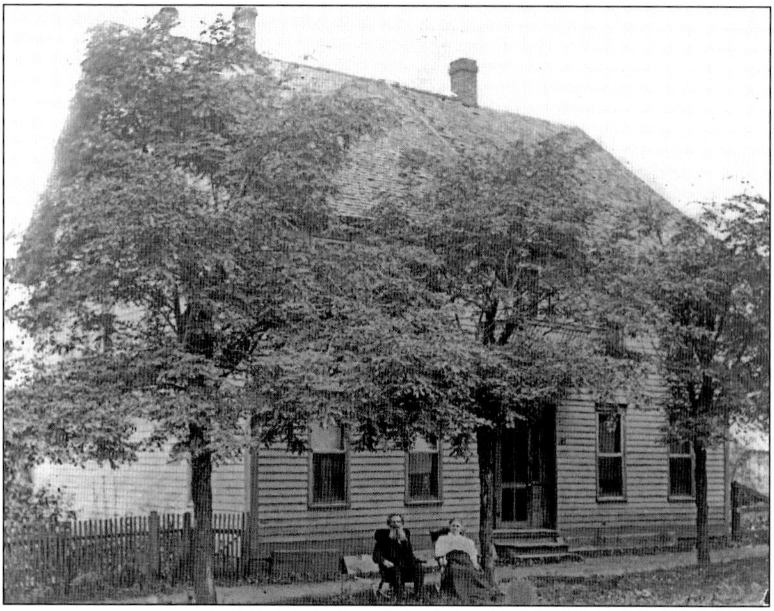

The Minor House was built in 1893 by Robert (1825–1908) and Rachel Minor (1833–1912). Located at 48 South Van Buren Street in downtown Nashville, it is now the home of the Brown County Art Guild and, according to Betty Shickley of the Brown County Art Guild, was extensively renovated over a three-year period starting in 1975. (Brown County Historical Society.)

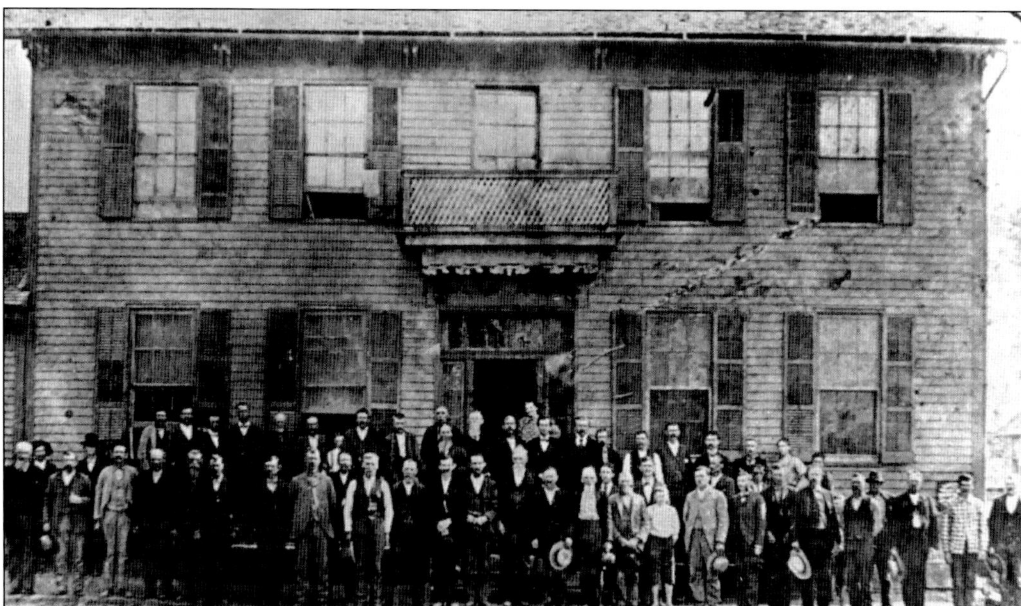

Though there are mostly men standing in front of the Minor House in this old photograph, according to Barbara Judd of Nashville at one time this was a ladies' hotel. Children of the women who lived in the hills of Brown County would stay during the week in the winter so they could attend school, as the roads were often impassable. By 1916, the Minor House was used as a dormitory for high school girls. (Brown County Historical Society.)

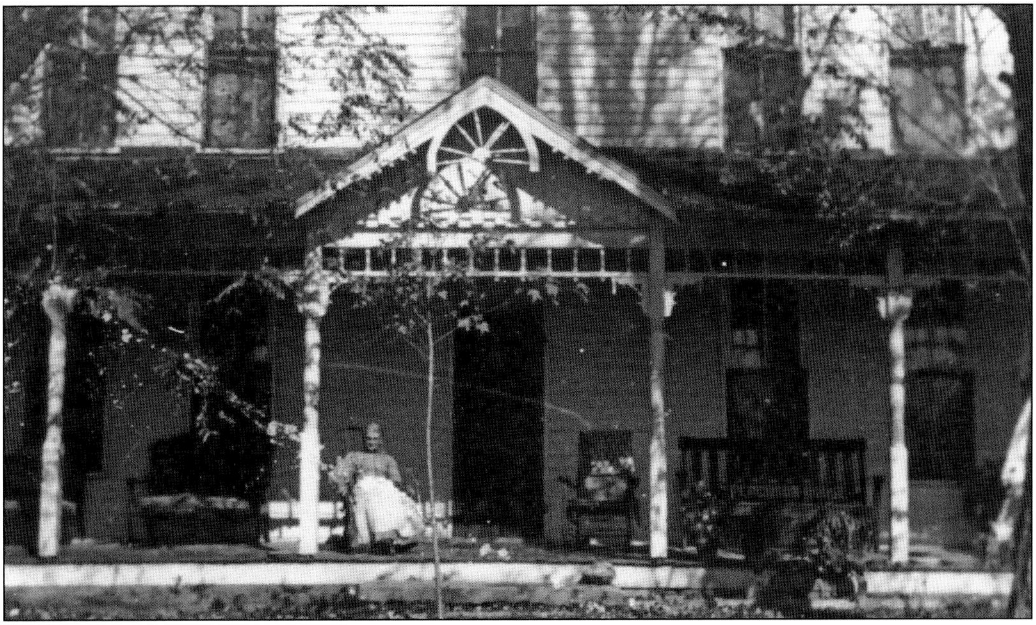

Photographer Frank Hohenberger stayed at Alli Ferguson's boardinghouse after first moving to Nashville, and even after he moved out was said to take his meals there. Alli and her sister Mollie Lucas, who lived down the street in what had been the Banner Brummit house, the oldest house in Nashville, were well known for their cooking. Their specialities included greens, flavored with salt pork, and corn bread. Here Alli sits in front of her house. (Brown County Historical Society.)

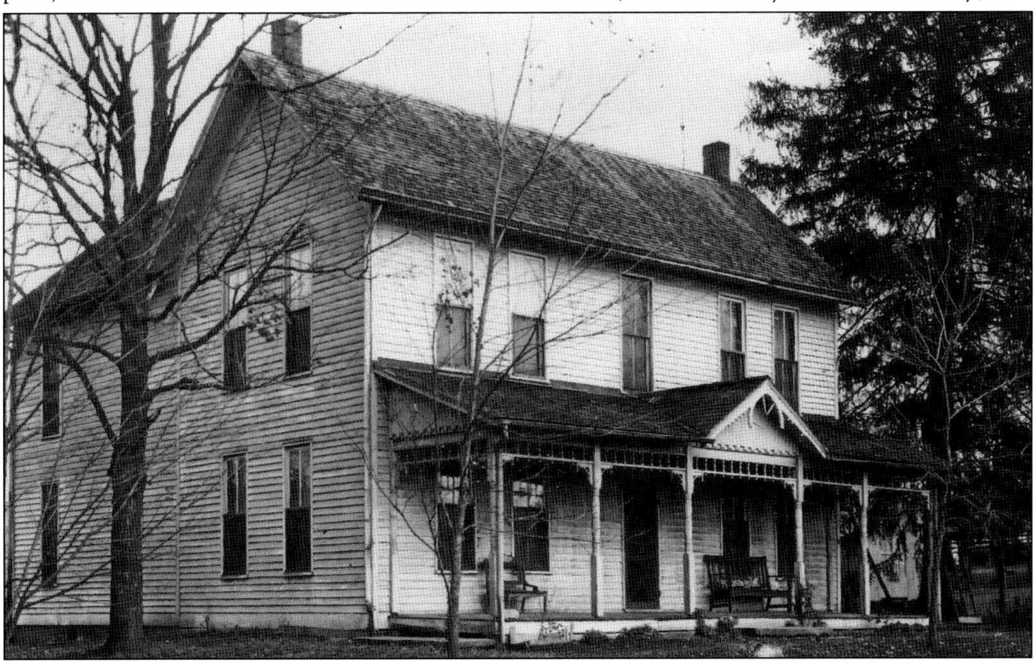

Around 1900, Bill and Alli Ferguson bought this two-story house and added rooms on the back. Bill was active in politics, and Alli was a caterer. After Bill's death in 1912, Alli's sister Molly moved in and operated a boardinghouse known for "good food and comfortable beds with feather ticks." (Brown County Historical Society.)

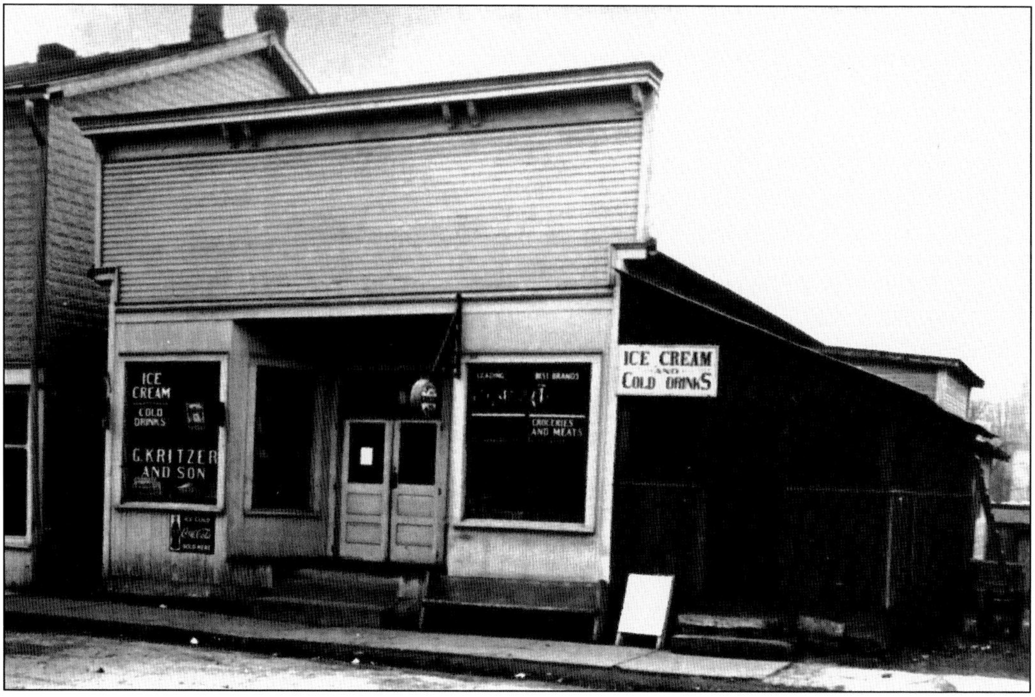

G. Kritzer and Son General Store is an example of the many small stores that were found in the towns and villages of Brown County. "It might help th' consumer t' take a more cheerful view o' life if th' butcher would let th' meat stay on th' scales long enough t' see what it weighed," wrote humorist Kin Hubbard in his book *Short Furrows*. Hubbard made Brown County famous through his characters that included Abe Martin. (Brown County Historical Society.)

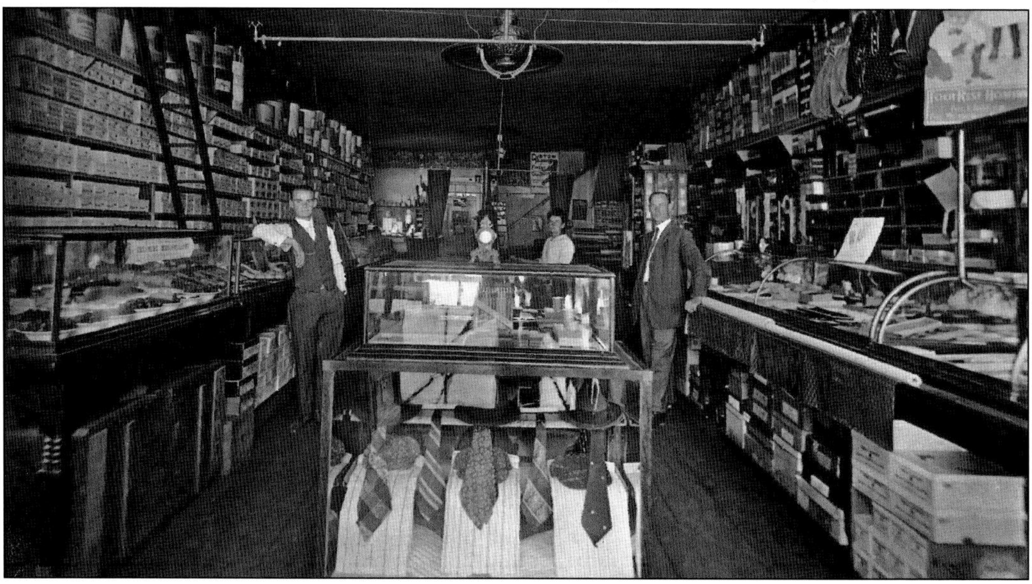

Ira Taggart's store is shown here when it was operated by the Hoppers. Rex Hopper, husband of Stella Taggart Hopper, is on the left and Mart Hopper on the right. The store, located on the southwest corner of Van Buren and Main Streets, later became the Miller's Drug Store and is now the Hob Nob Restaurant. (Brown County Historical Society.)

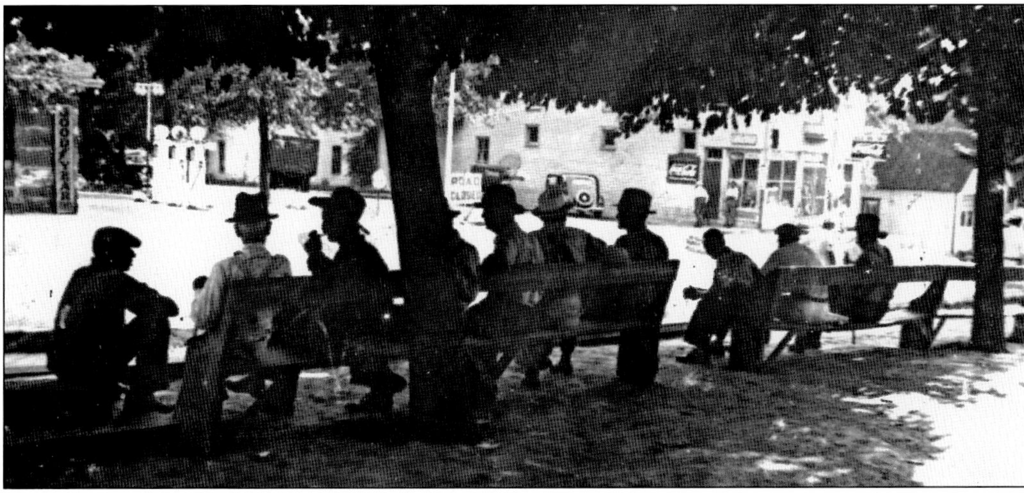

In his 1933 article about Frank Hohenberger, Webb Waldrun wrote, "Under the locust trees on the main street of the village, in front of the courthouse and the old log jail, stood a bench immemorially called the Liars' Bench. Here certain local characters lounged through the long afternoons . . . whittling and swapping tales. The one who told the biggest, it was said, went to the head of the bench." Hohenberger took a picture of the "Liar's Bench," and this picture became so popular that he sold over 500 copies at $2 to $5 a print. (Brown County Historical Society.)

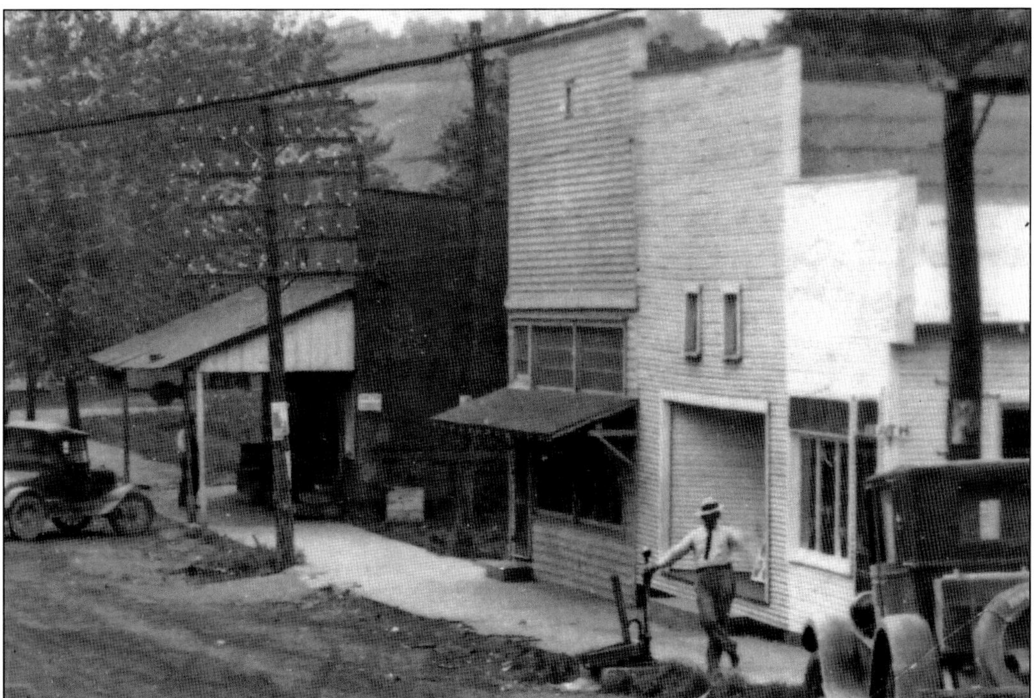

The Melodeon Hall Movie Theater was operated by Cecil and Leila David from 1923 to 1937. It was named after the theater in Kin Hubbard's famous cartoons of Brown County. "Ever'buddy stood up at Melodeon Hall last night when th' orchestry played 'My Country, What is it t' You?' " wrote Hubbard in his book *Short Furrows*. (Brown County Historical Society.)

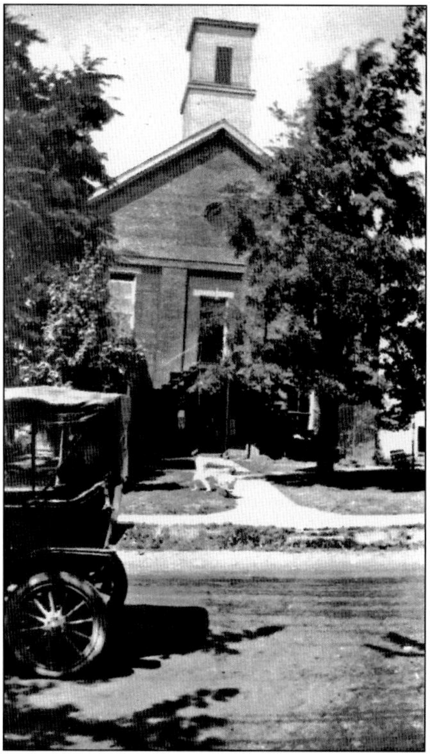

In 1837, Nashville was made the county seat and a log courthouse was built on a square in the center of the small city. At the time, about 75 people lived here, and bears, wolves, and panthers were so abundant that the county commissioner offered $1 per wolf scalp. The present courthouse, seen in this photograph, stands in the same spot. (Brown County Historical Society.)

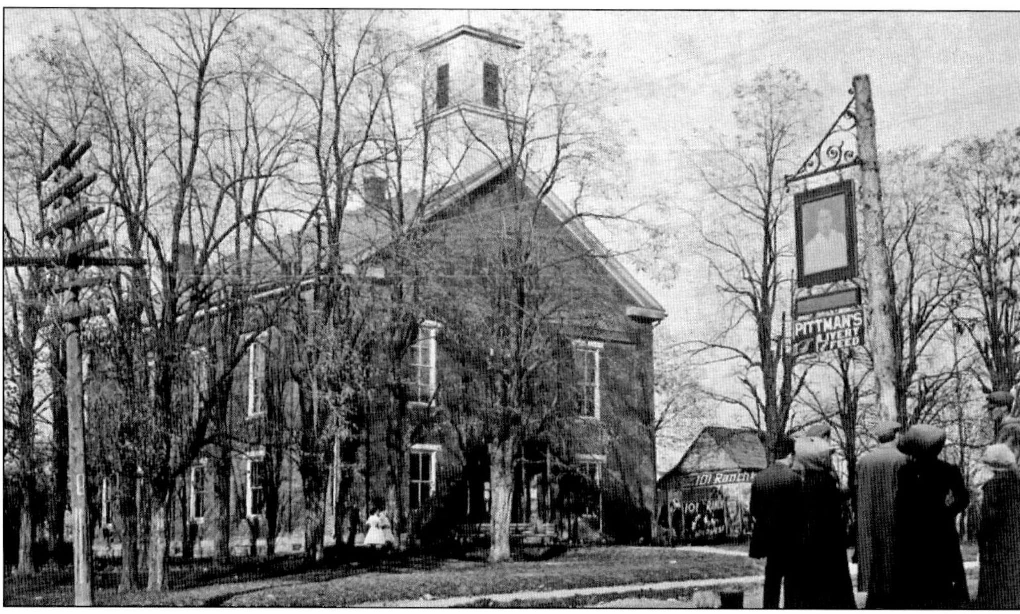

Another view of the present courthouse reveals the sign for the Pittman Inn in the right-hand section of the photograph. When T. C. Steele moved here in 1907, he said, "Many natives I suspect have never been out of the county. The people seem kindly, but not progressive, except in a small way. (Brown County) is a little corner that the rest of the great strenuous world has swept around and missed. Whether they are contented with their lot, I do not know." (Brown County Historical Society.)

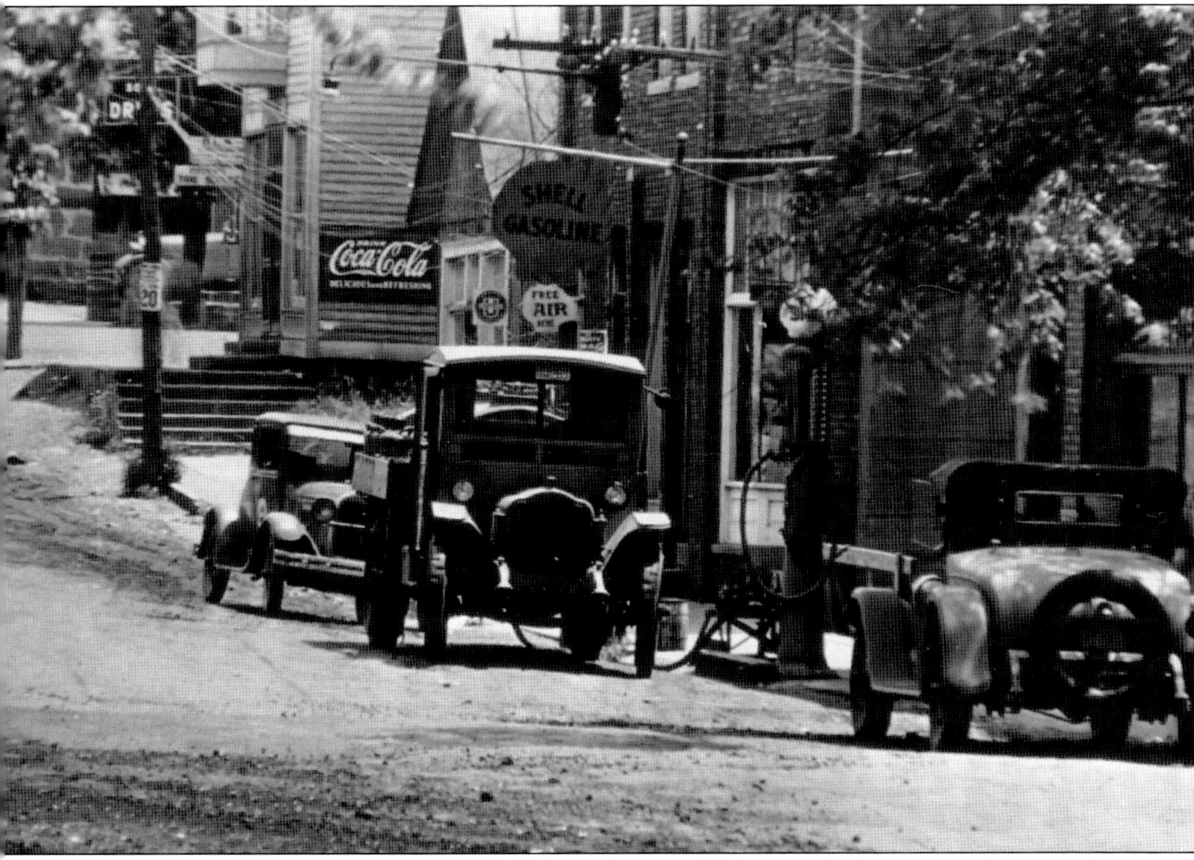

The population in Brown County declined from the late 1800s to mid-20th century because of poor land management and the Depression. The county had a population of 10,308 in 1890, in 1900 it was 9,727, in 1910 it was 7,975, in 1920 it was 7,019, and by 1930 it was down to 5,168. As roads improved, word got out about the beauty of the area, and tourism increased. In the background on the right is the building that now houses the Hob Nob Restaurant. (Brown County Historical Society.)

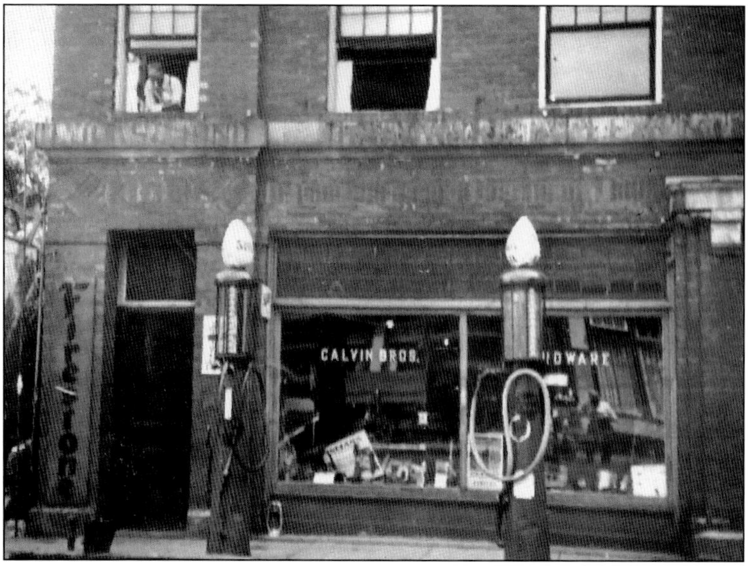

This is the Nashville Shell Station in front of Calvin Brothers Hardware. Kin Hubbard, creator of the widely syndicated *Abe Martin* feature in the *Indianapolis News*, drew heavily on Dennis Calvin for much of his material while sitting around the big potbellied stove in Calvin Brothers Hardware talking to Brown County residents. (Brown County Historical Society.)

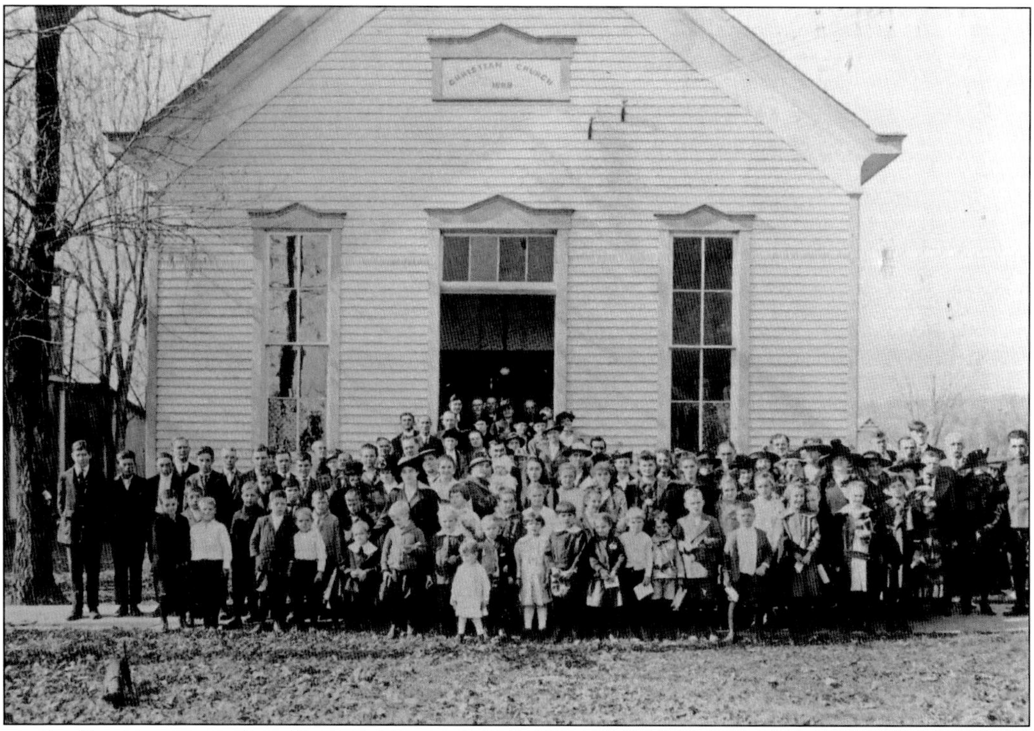

Nashville Christian Church was built in 1888 by James Gray, his son Ollie, and James Myers. According to information from *History of the Nashville Christian Church*, it was dedicated by Rev. Z. T. Sweeney of Columbus, a famous minister who lectured in the new church about his travels around the world. He sold a book on the subject called *Under Six Flags*. The church burned in 1931 after being remodeled at a cost of around $10,000 in 1926. A new Christian church stands on this spot in downtown Nashville. (Brown County Historical Society.)

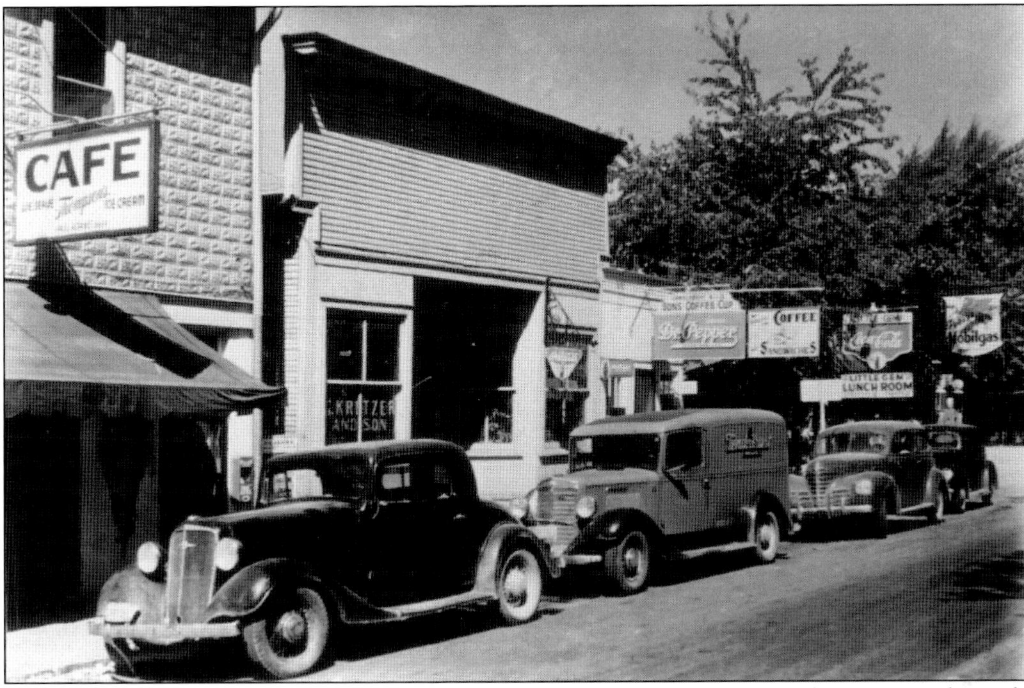

In this photograph of Nashville taken by Frank Hohenberger in 1939, the sign on the café, located on North Van Buren Street and owned by Paul Adams, reads, "Hamburgers 6 for 25 cents" and "We Serve Thompson's Ice Cream." (Brown County Historical Society.)

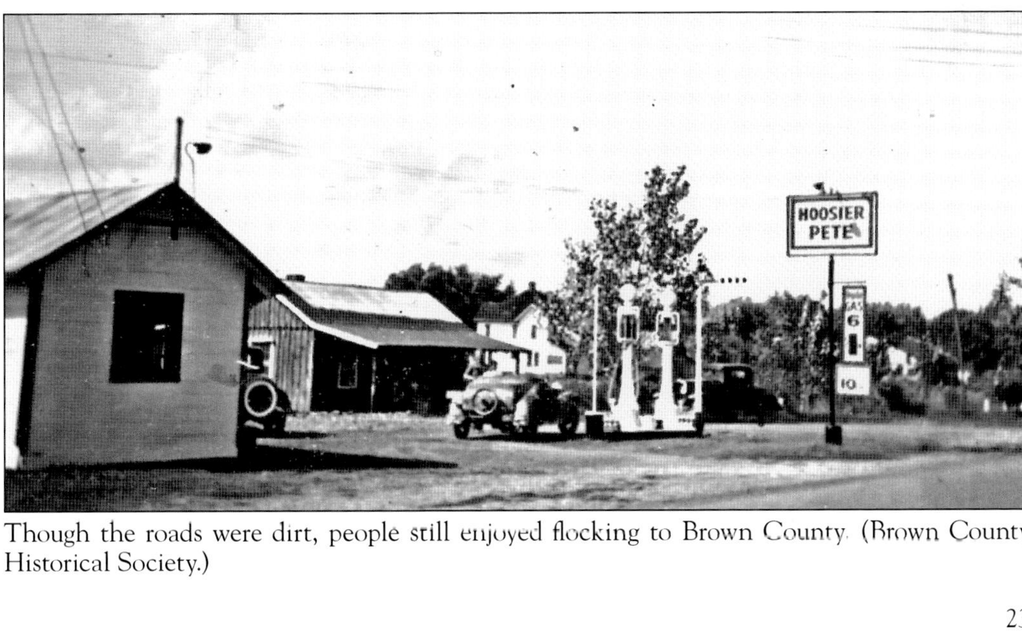

Though the roads were dirt, people still enjoyed flocking to Brown County. (Brown County Historical Society.)

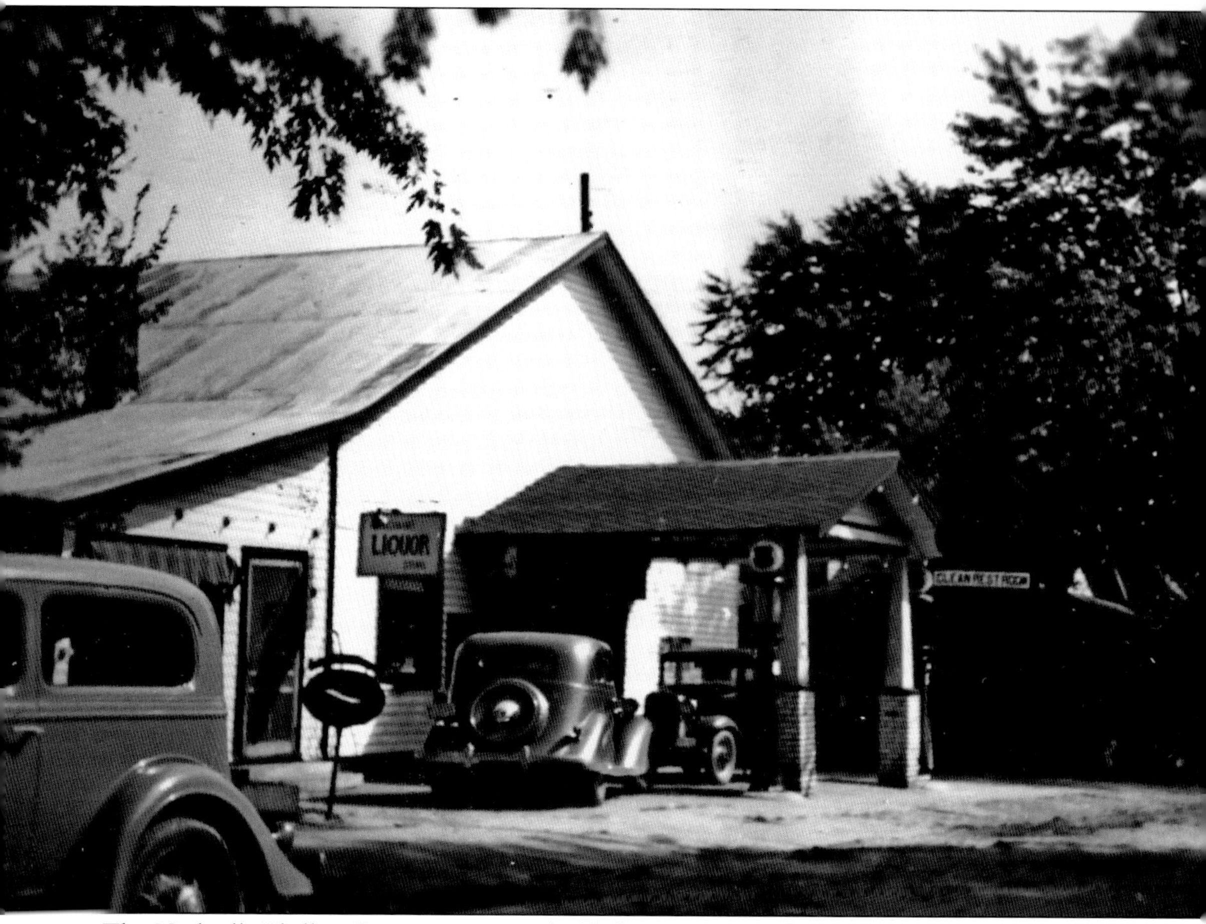

The Nashville Phillips Station is pictured. Gladys Mayne recalls in *Brown County Remembers* that motor oil was purchased in steel drums and transferred to quart glass containers with metal pouring spouts. She stated, "These were filled by hand with a pump. The oil bottles were placed in a rack something like the old-fashioned milk bottle racks. There were three kinds oil: twenty, thirty or forty weight. The oil bottle rack was set between the gas pumps and oil was put into cars from these bottles." (Brown County Historical Society.)

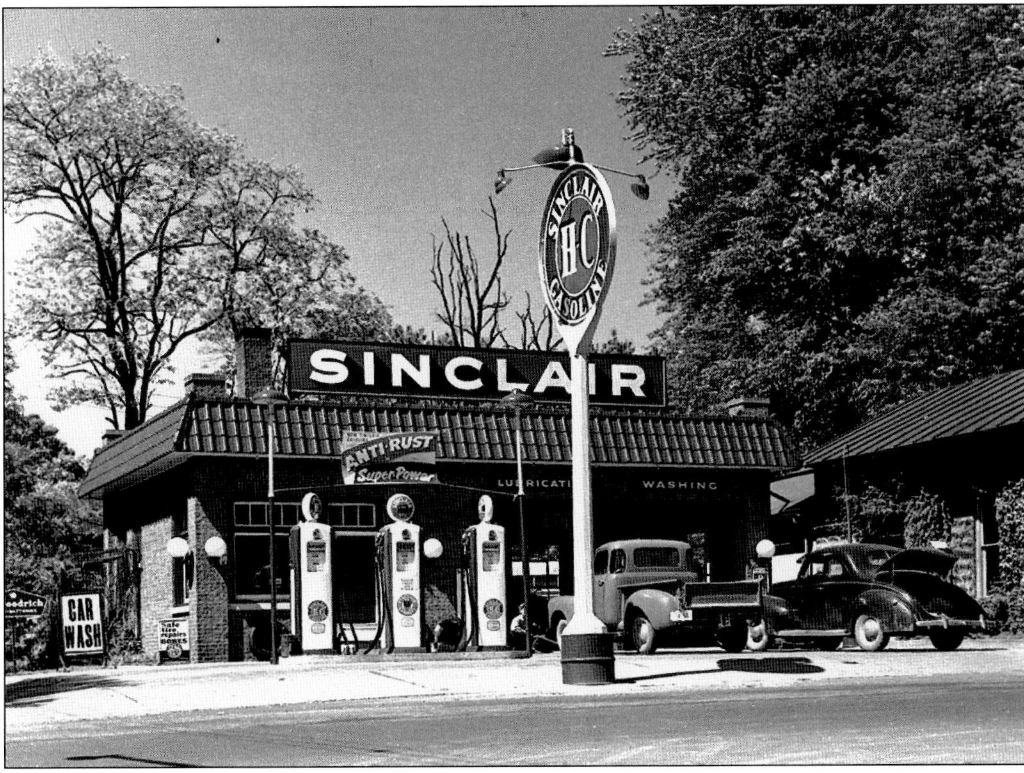

"A friend with an auto is a friend indeed," wrote humorist Kin Hubbard in his book *Short Furrows*. The Taggert Sinclair Station is pictured. (Brown County Historical Society.)

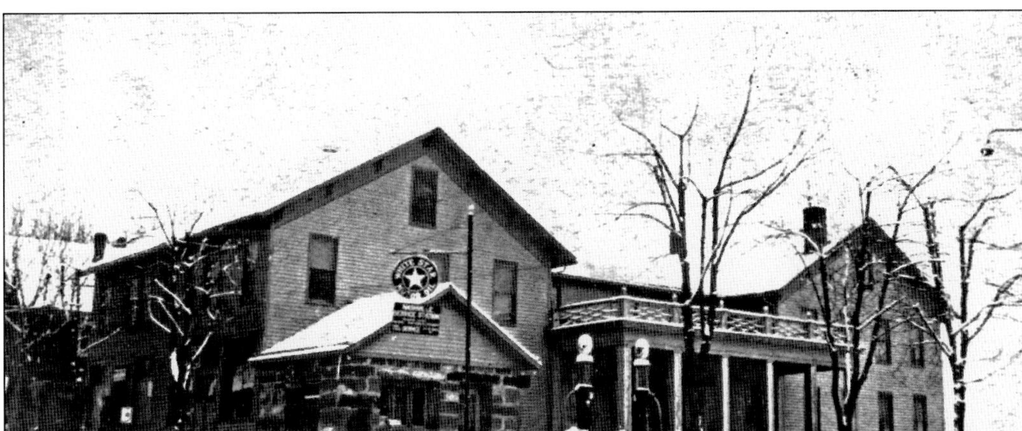

This photograph shows the Nashville House before it burned in 1943. The Jimmy Davis Service Station was located on the corner of East Main and Van Buren Streets. The original Nashville House was built in 1859 and was the county's first hostelry. Now rebuilt, the Nashville House still stands in the same location and is a popular place to eat, known for its country-style cookery including fried chicken, fried biscuits, and apple butter. (Brown County Historical Society.)

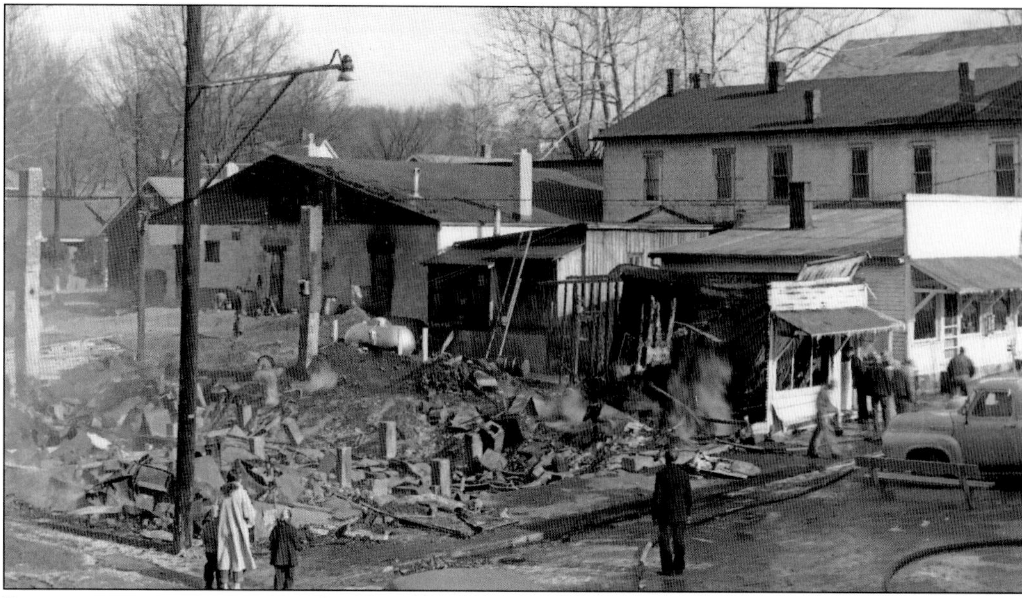

Fire was a constant enemy of towns and cities where the majority of buildings were made of wood. There seemed to be many things that could cause a fire, and one in nearby Helmsburg was started when a gasoline truck sprang a leak and the driver tried to stop the electric pump by pulling its plug. The resulting spark ignited the truck, driver, and station, and it caused an explosion, according to witnesses, that blew huge balls of fire into the sky. (Brown County Historical Society.)

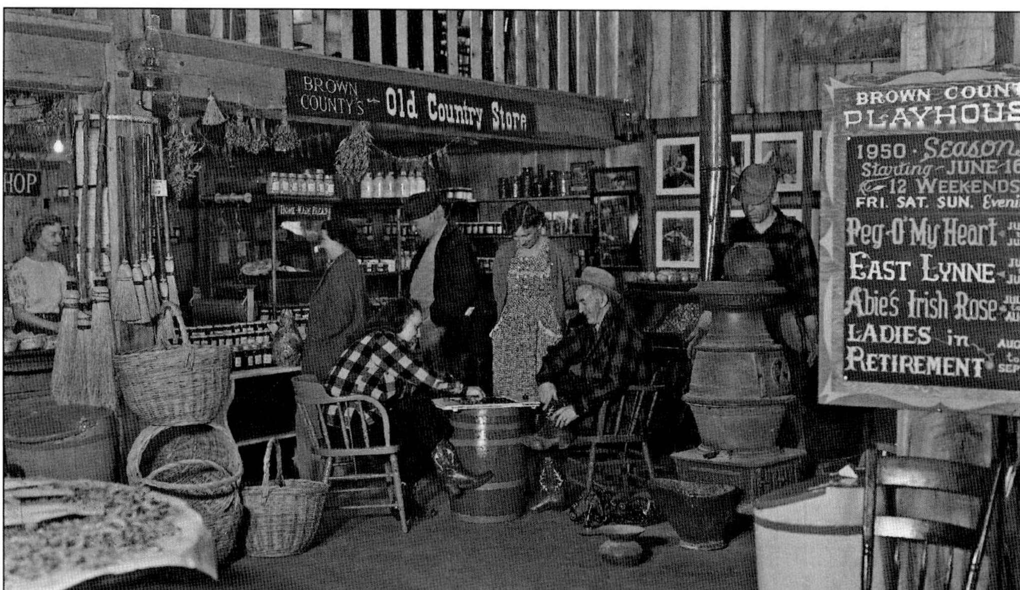

This interior shot of a Nashville general store, though taken in 1950, seems to hearken back to an earlier time. General stores not only provided townspeople with everyday items, ranging from food to clothing, they also were a place to gather and socialize. Gladys Mayne recalled in *Brown County Remembers* how groceries were on one side of the general store, dry goods on the other, and hardware was in the back. (Lilly Library, photograph by Frank Hohenberger.)

Two

A Village Named Story

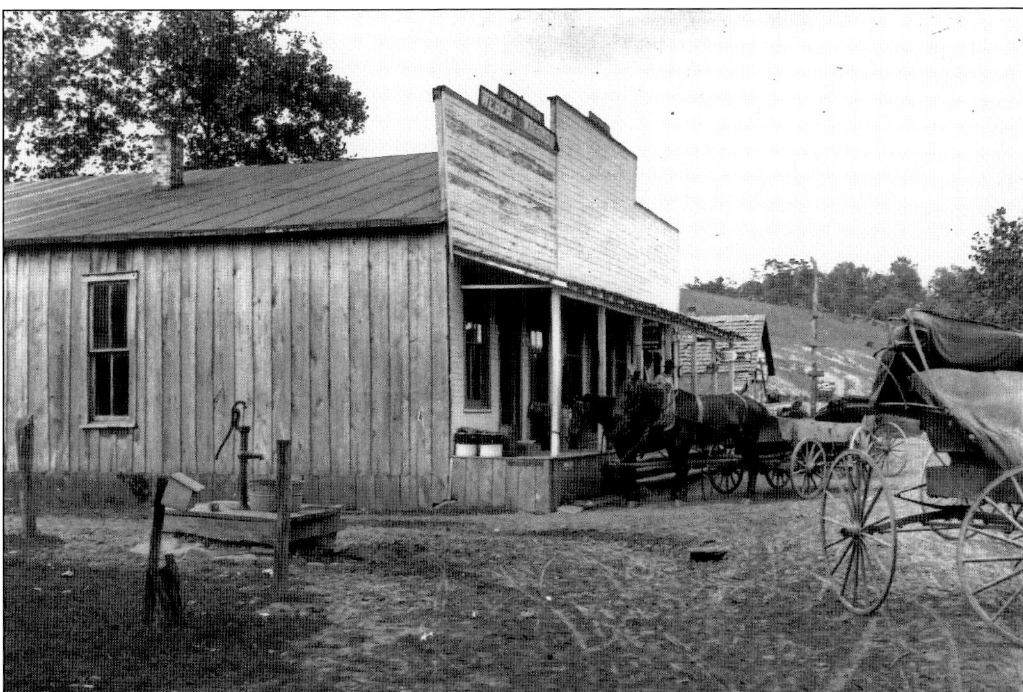

Alra Wheeler's old general store and wagon shop next to the village pump are visible in this photograph taken between 1914 and 1916. There likely was a general store in this location from the time the village of Story was founded in 1851 with the grant of a land patent from Pres. Millard Fillmore to Dr. George Story. This land patent is on display at the Story Inn. Author Rick Hofstetter, owner of the Story Inn, lives in Dr. Story's house. (Story Inn.)

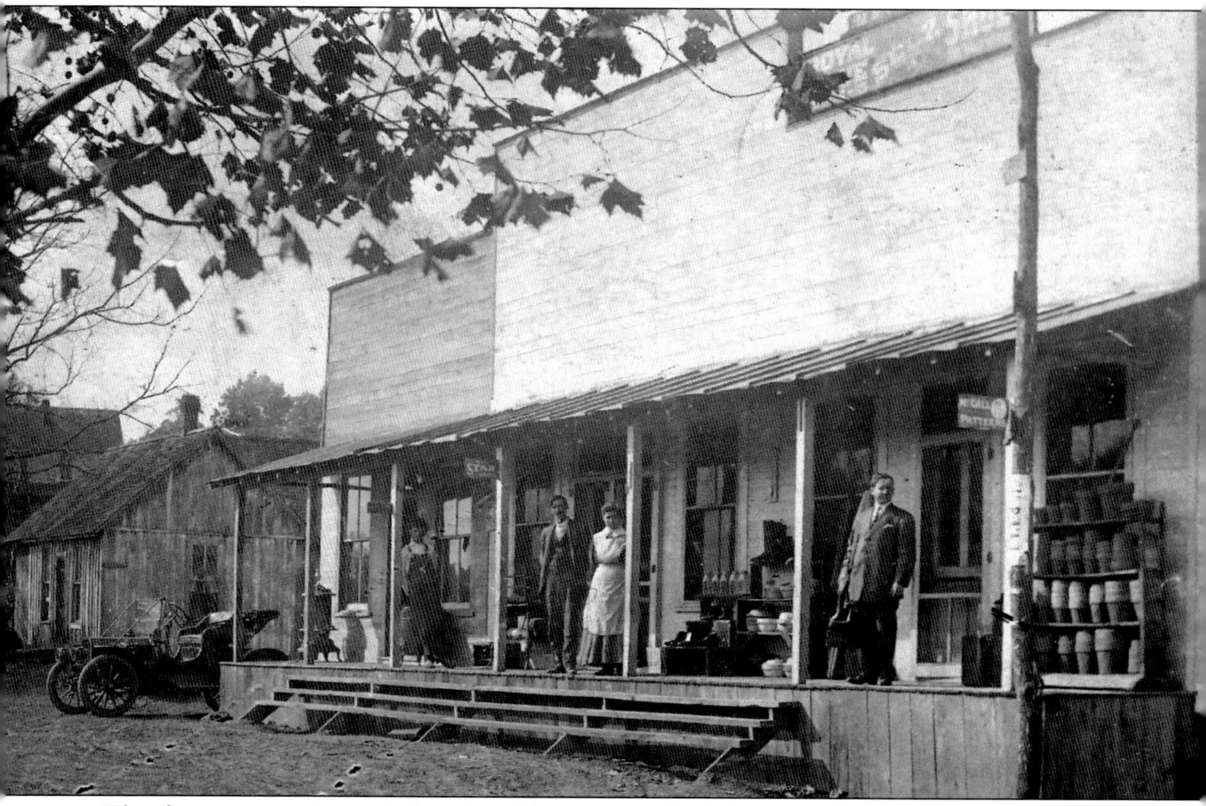

The first store at Story is shown in this postcard—or at least the first one captured in a photograph. This building burned at 6:30 a.m. on November 18, 1915. In the photograph are Alra and Mary Wheeler and Leonard and Fletcher Mock (a traveling salesman). The notation on this photograph states that the car parked to the side of the store is a red International Roadster, the second car in Brown County. Though it cannot be seen, the pump to the left side of the store remains to this day. Helen Ayers wrote about the pump and the general store, "City folks who were lost on our county's back roads occasionally found themselves in her (Clothie Hedrick Robertson) store quite by accident. . . . If they just wanted a drink of cold water, she would point them outside to the tall hand pump besides the store. It came equipped with an aluminum can which had held Vienna sausages in a previous life, but was used now to catch and hold drinking water when you pumped the handle." (Story Inn.)

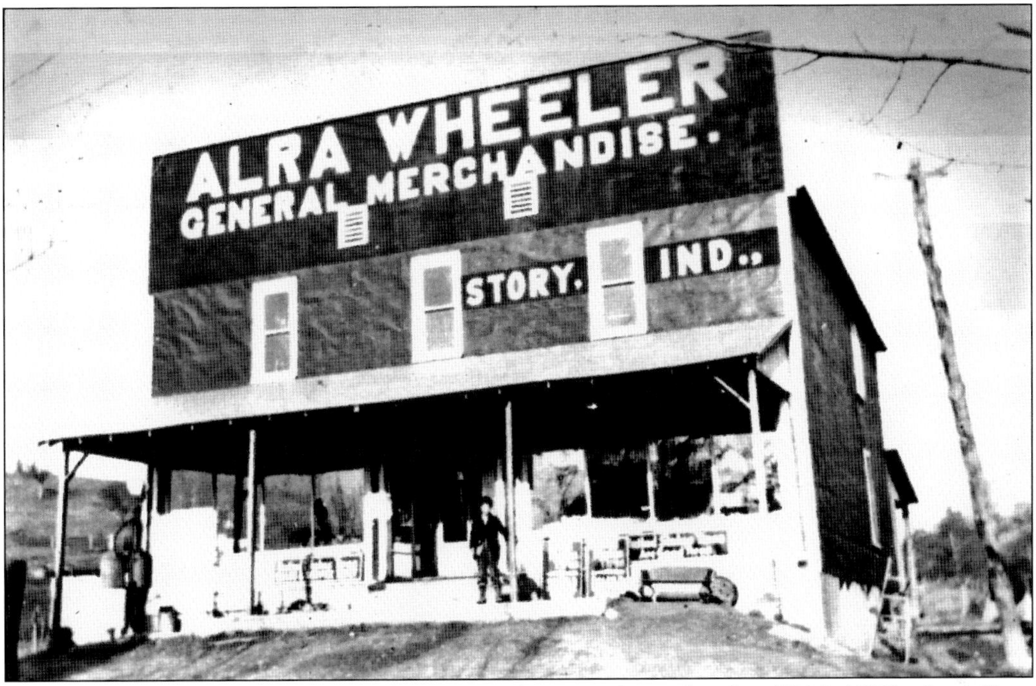

Story soon became the largest settlement in the area. In its heyday (1880–1929), the village supported two general stores, a nondenominational church, a one-room schoolhouse, a grain mill, a sawmill, a slaughterhouse, a blacksmith's forge, and a post office. Many of these buildings are gone, but the old grain mill still exists, located right next to the general store. The general store now houses the Story Inn's restaurant and tavern. (Story Inn.)

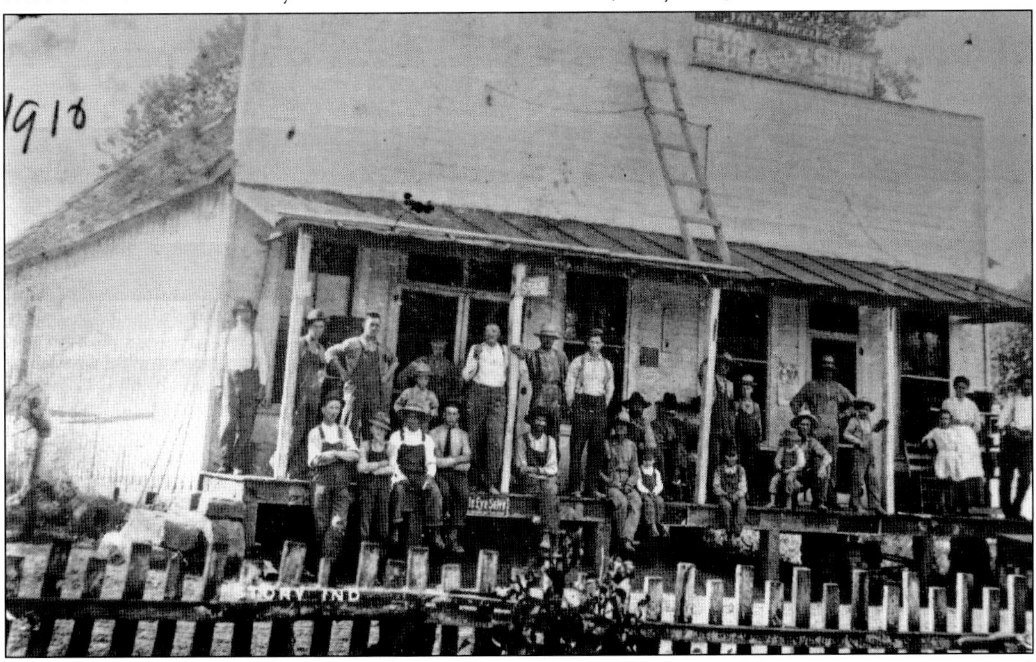

After being reconstructed in 1916, the building remained in use for the next 60 years or so until it finally closed. It was then reopened as an inn in the 1980s. (Story Inn.)

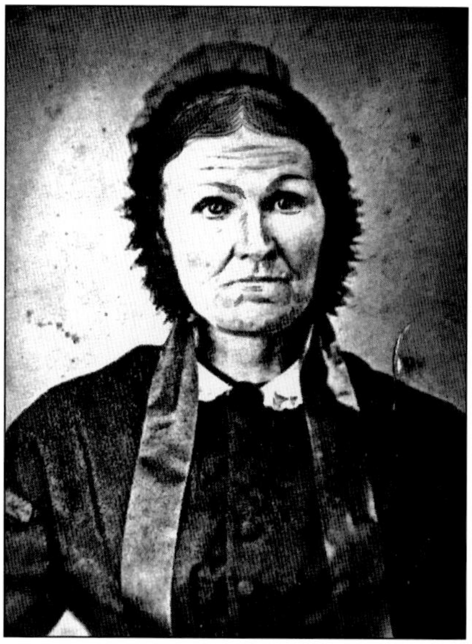

Every town should have its ghost, and the "Blue Lady," possibly shown here, is said to haunt the Story Inn. Not much is known about her except that she has a kindly disposition for those who see her (and there is a log at the inn where guests who stay in the appropriately named Blue Lady Room can write down their encounters with her). She wears Victorian-era clothing, so her sojourn on earth probably dates to Story's heyday. (Story Inn.)

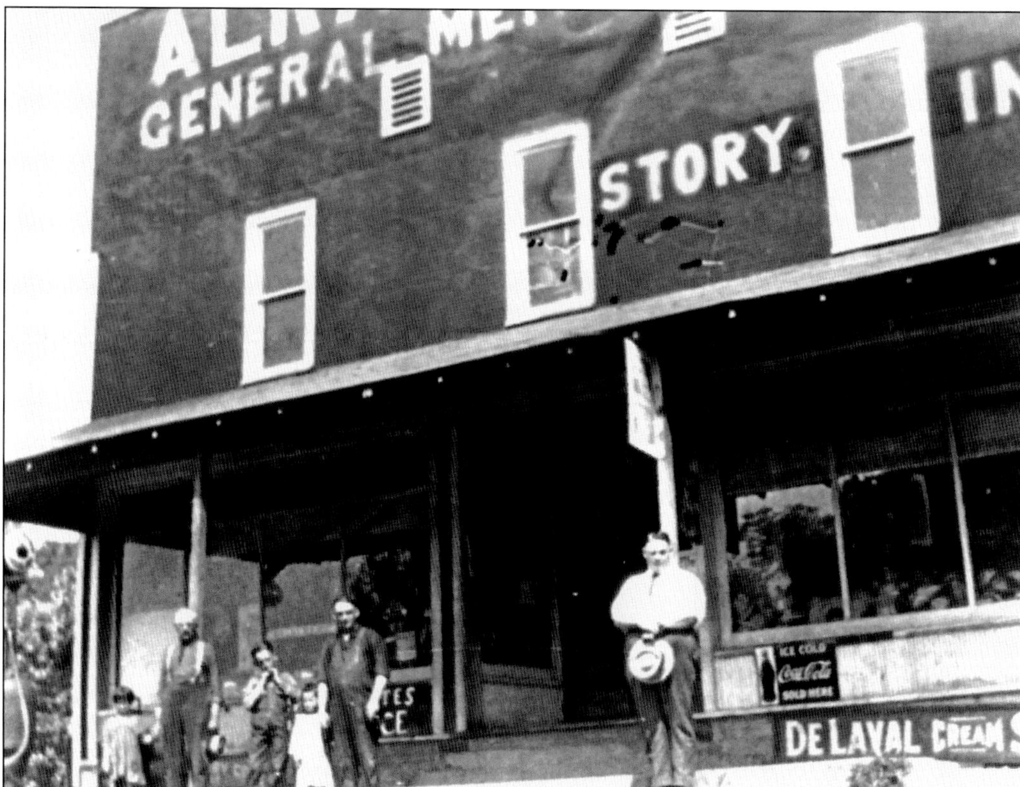

This postcard of the Story Inn was sent to Thomas Floyd on East Second Street on January 23, 1915, and reads, "Mary is pretty sick with lameback and cold. Had Ralphy Sunday and today. Hope she will be better soon. Mira has the measles also. Will let you know. A Wheeler." Dr. Ralphy Sunday was a physician in Brown County. Seen here are, from left to right, Dorothy (daughter of Omar and Grace Morrison), John Swaze Morrison, Dwight Kelley, Beulah Jean Kelley, Benjamin Richard Kelley, and Omar Morrison. (Brown County Historical Society.)

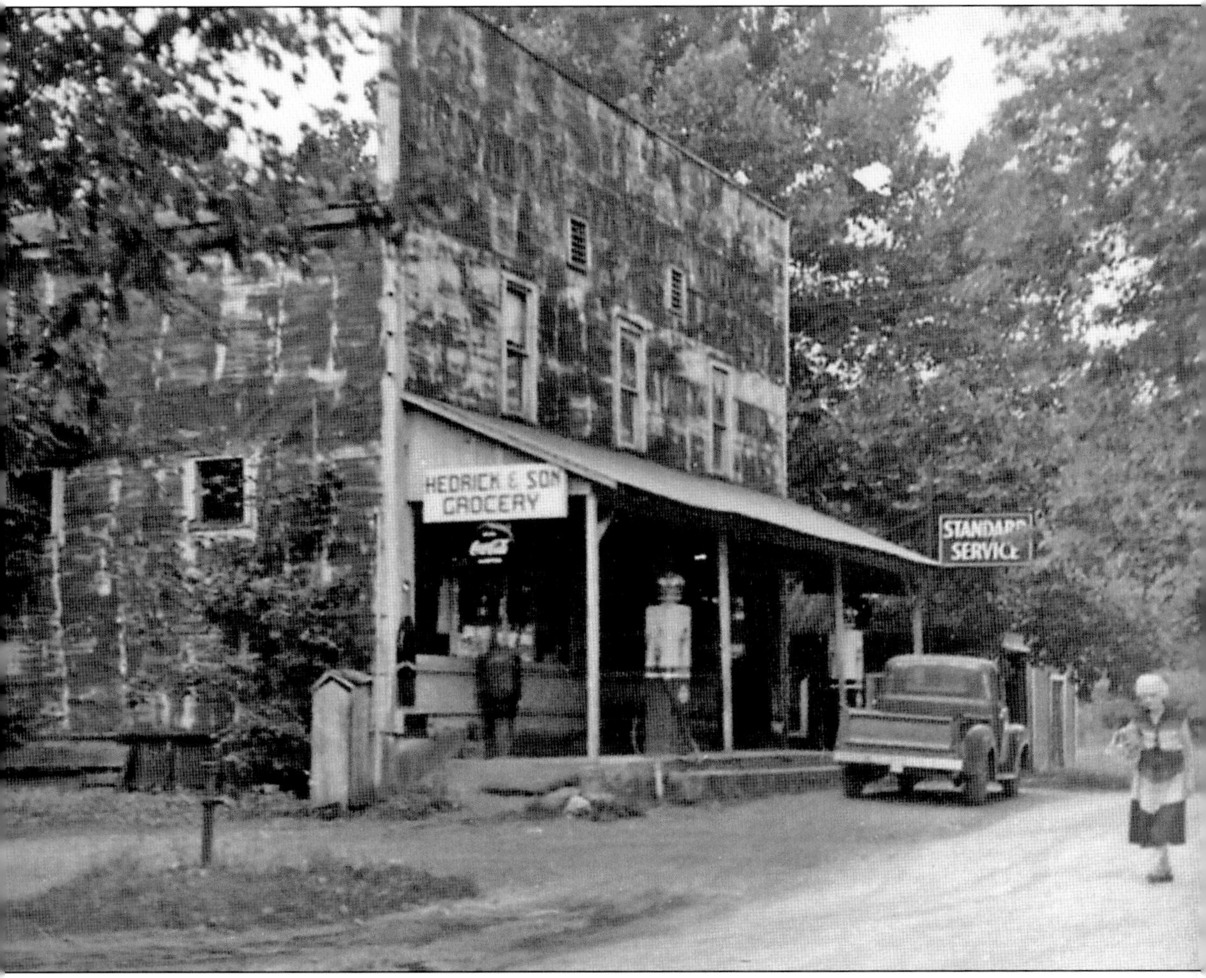

The Story Inn still looks much like the old Story general store did when this photograph was taken: it has the somewhat faded allure of years gone by, the tin metal front facade with its mottled colors accented by a hitching post, flowers cascading out of window boxes, an old wooden gate leading to the front porch, and best of all the red and gold hand-blown glass crowns on top of the gas pumps that are now set into recesses on the front porch. The inn is owned by author Rick Hofstetter, who bought the place in 1999. Rick, who has an undergraduate and graduate degree from Indiana University and a law degree from Duke University, is an avid preservationist. Rick also bought the entire town of Story in 1999. (Story Inn.)

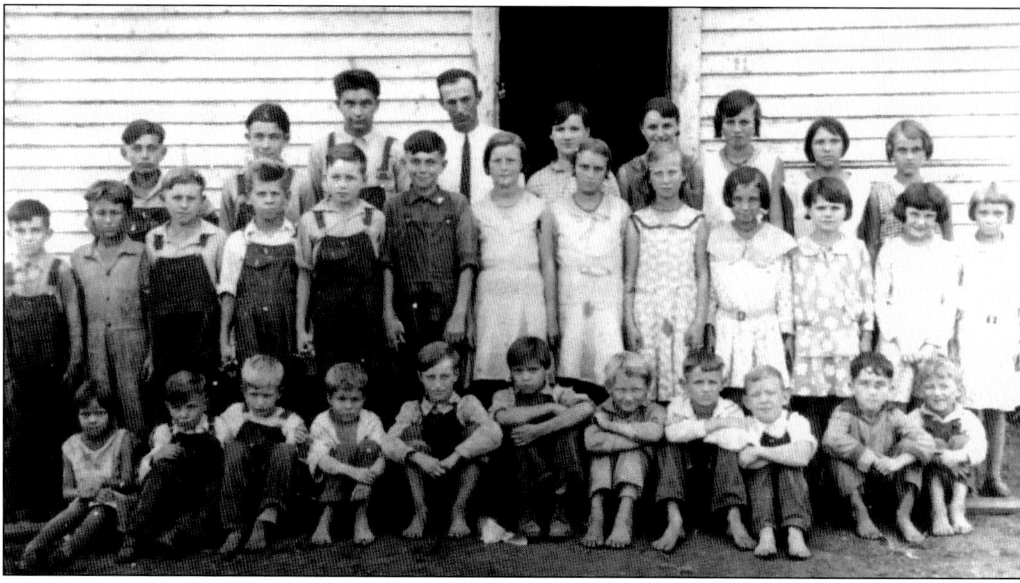

The schoolteacher, A. J. Ralphy, later returned to the small village after he became a physician. Pictured here from left to right are (first row) Arabella Ault, Winfer (Bud) Fleetwood, Plessie Hamblen, John Hamblen, Amos Wilkerson, Robert Ault, Virgil Hedrick, Estel Hashman, Russell Tabor, Garris Penrose, and Wendell Taylor; (second row) Gerald Penrose, Burnell Hedrick, Clifford Wilkerson, Fletcher Tabor (a relative owns the Manor at Tabor Hill), Glenn Noblitt, Chester Fleetwood, Geneva Ogle, Wilma Anthony, Thelma Tabor, Lucy Fleetwood, Esther Sinn, Maxine Carmichael, and Mabel Hashman; (third row, starting with man in tie) Lowell Ault (teacher), Beulah Mererillan, Lenore Wilkerson, Beatrice Hedrick, Lola Ault, and Edell Hedrick; among the three boys to the left of the teacher are Arthur Fleetwood and William Penrose. (Lilly Library.)

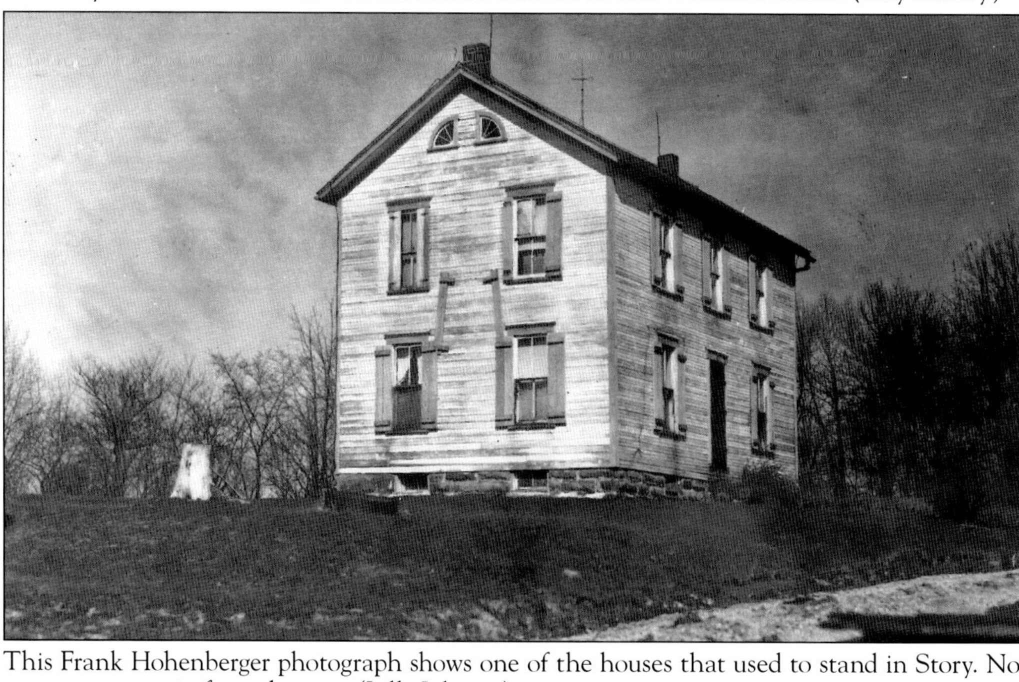

This Frank Hohenberger photograph shows one of the houses that used to stand in Story. Not very many remain from that era. (Lilly Library.)

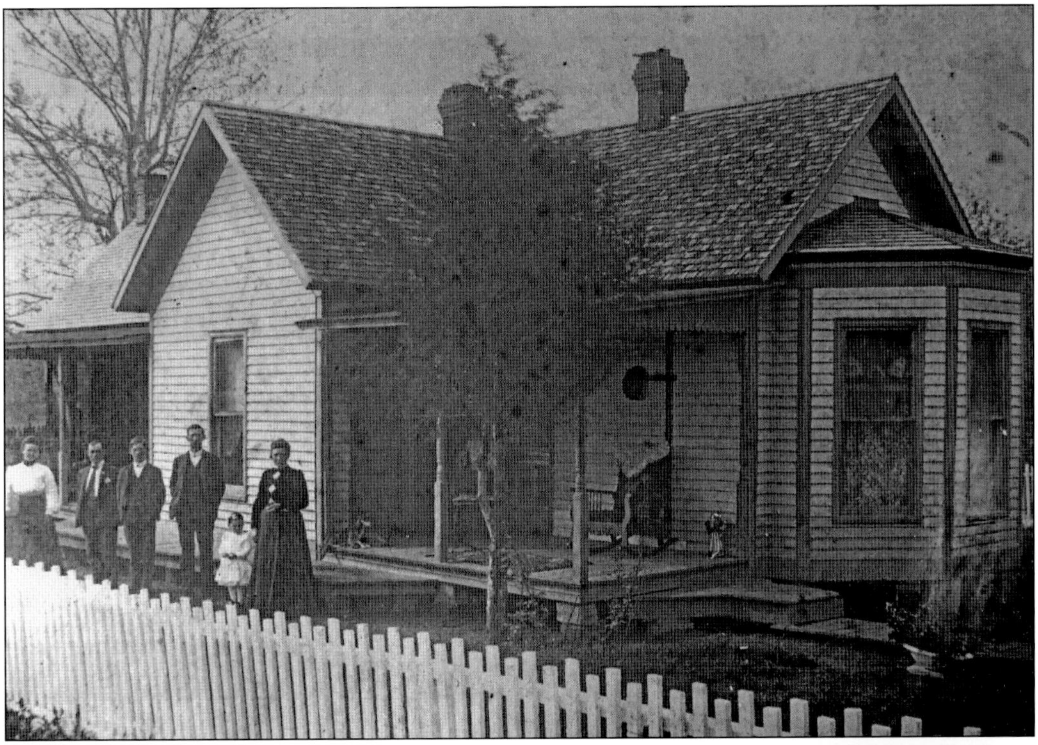

This historic tin-roofed, Vernacular-style house was constructed in the mid-19th century and occupied by Alra Wheeler, who successfully ran the general store during Story's heyday. This photograph shows the Wheeler homestead around 1905 with, from left to right, Mena Curtis, Van Sullivan, Leonard Wheeler, Alra Wheeler, Ruth Wheeler, and Mary Wheeler standing out front. The Wheeler home, just across the road from the old Story general store, is now a guest cottage for the Story Inn. (Story Inn.)

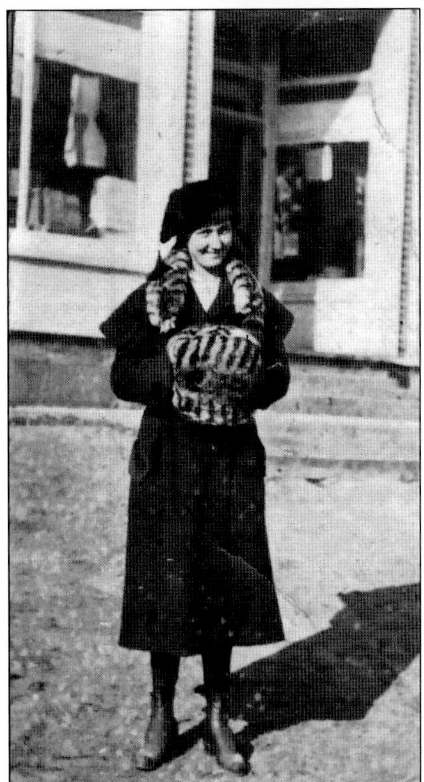

Alra and Mary Wheeler's daughter Ruth (1903–1984) is pictured in front of the general store in Story. Besides having a store in the village, peddlers and hucksters would come to town on a regular basis. According to Helen Ayers, "There were few vehicles in the area during the 1930s to mid-1950s, so residents depended upon huckster wagons for many of those years to bring groceries to them. There was a Monday peddler and a Thursday peddler who came every week to Story." (Story Inn.)

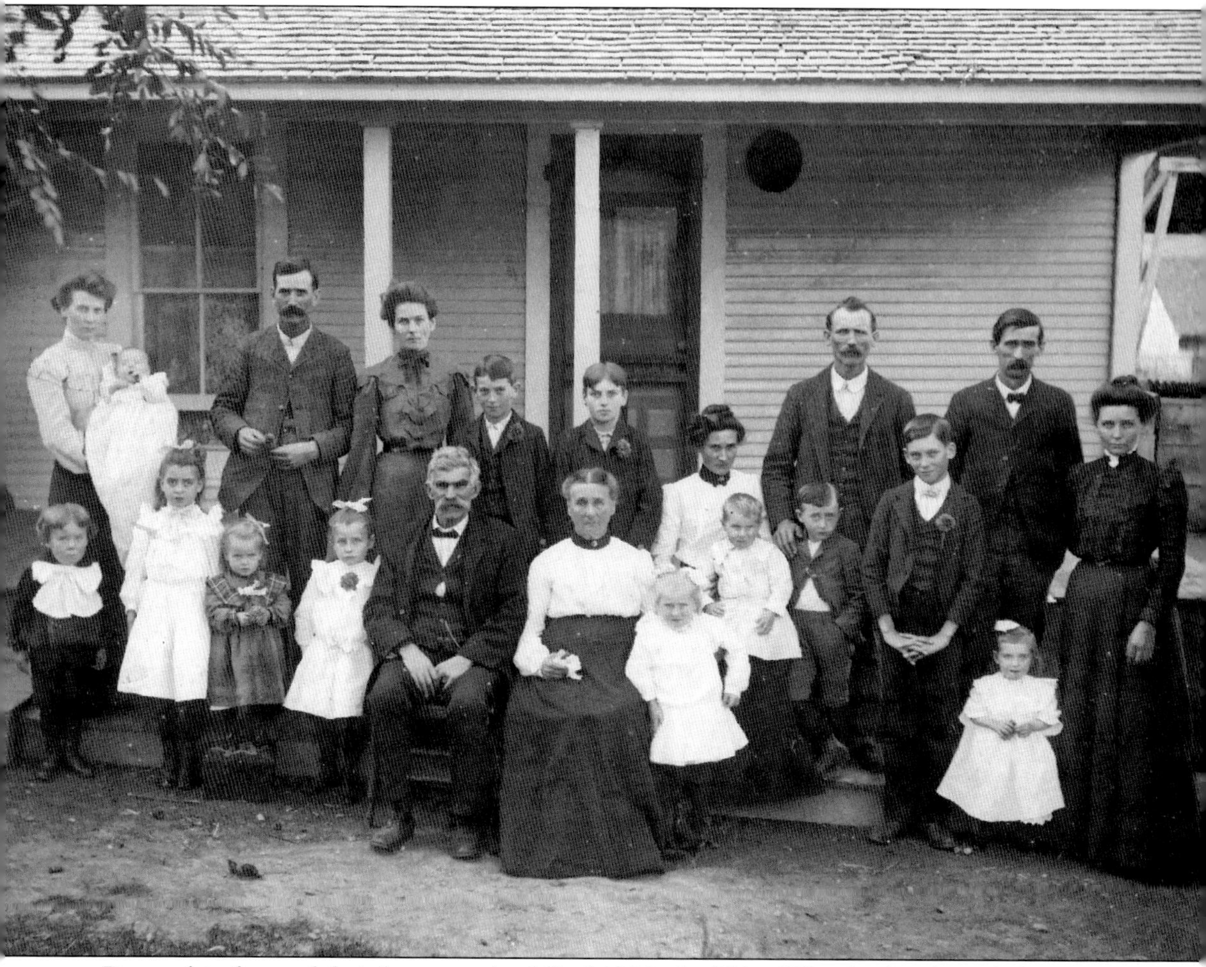

Pictured in front of their home in the fall of 1906, the Elihu Wheeler family includes Gladys Bond, Sallie Bond, Muriel Bond, Elihu Wheeler, Mary Wheeler, Eunice Lane, Bill Lane, Clarence Lane, Leonard Wheeler, Ruth Wheeler, Mary Wanda Allison Coleman baby, James Bond, Lonella Wheeler Bond, Elihu Bond, Claude Bond, Minnie Wheeler Lane, William Lane, Alra Wheeler, and Mary Wheeler. (Story Inn.)

A cousin of the Wheelers, holding a muff and in a remarkably familiar pose, stands in front of the store in Story. Electricity came late to many of the small villages in Brown County. According to Helen Ayers, "Electricity was strung from pole to pole through rural Van Buren (township) in 1947, though some residents still relied upon battery-operated radios to hear the news and weather report because, without a steady income, they couldn't afford a monthly electric bill." (Story Inn.)

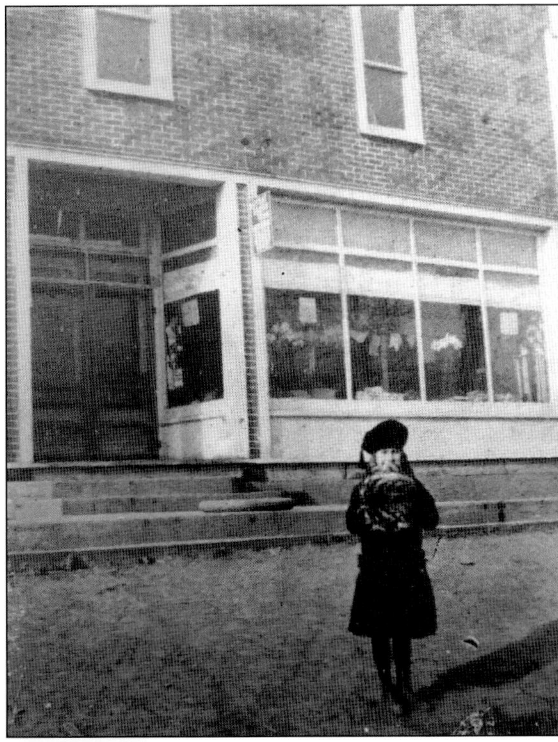

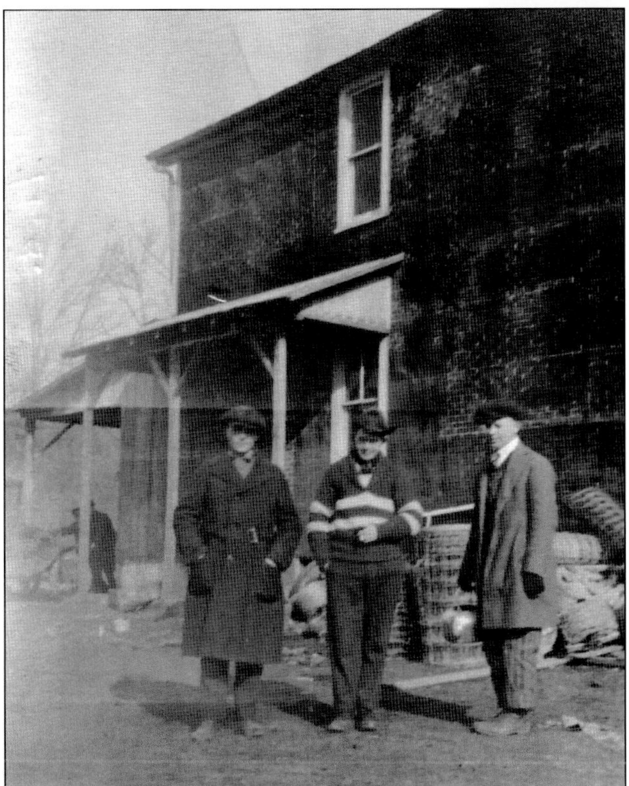

Men stand in back of the old general store in Story. They were lucky that no one attempted to modernize the venerable structures at Story when the rest of the nation embarked upon a campaign to eliminate unsightly wooden floors, stamped tin metal ceilings, and globe lighting and replace them with shiny asbestos floor tiles and dropped fiberboard ceilings sporting snazzy new recessed neon bulbs. (Story Inn.)

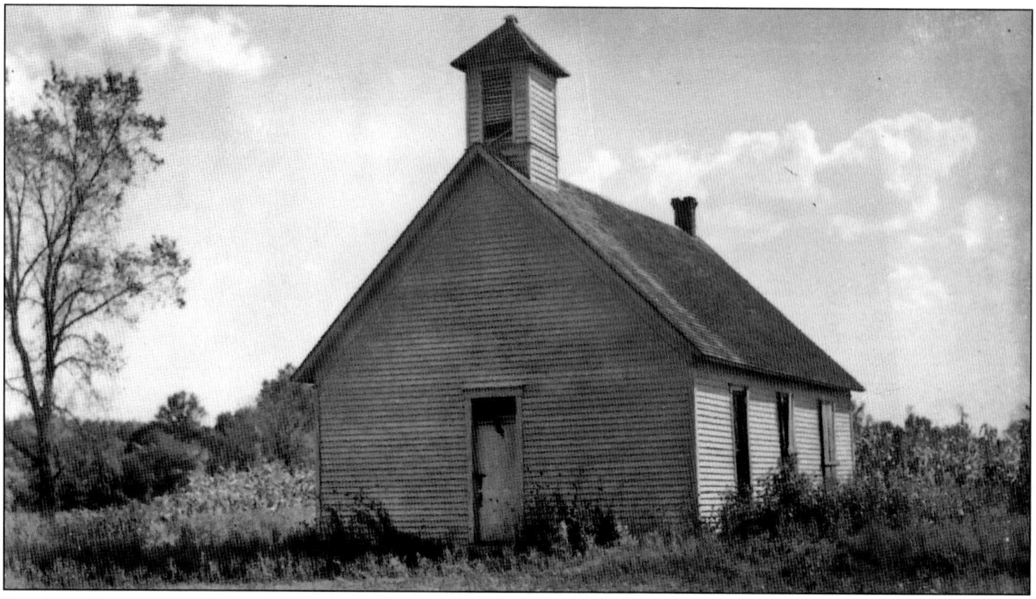

Each village, no matter how small, usually had a simple country church like this one that once stood in Story. During these times, country doctors were in short supply. According to Helen Ayers, "Well into the 1900s these early doctors would often attend a sick cow or horse in the farmer's barn, then go inside the home and assist at the birth of a baby or tend to a human illness without stopping along the way to wash and sterilize either his instruments or his hands." (Lilly Library.)

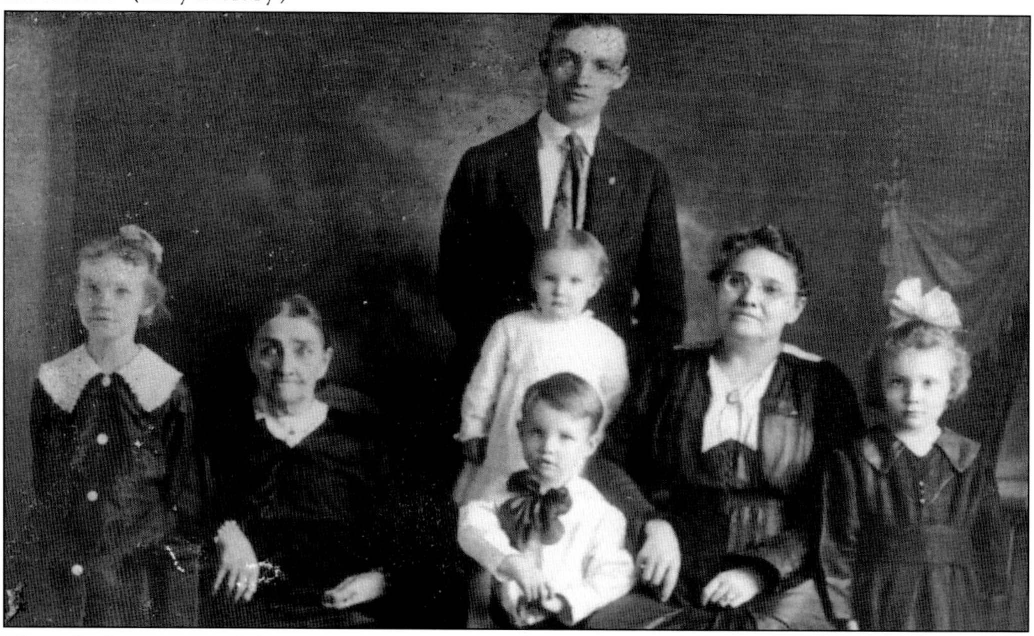

Though the names of this Story family are not known, their photograph, now hanging at the Story Inn, is another tie to the town's past. Once the town of Elkinsville 5 miles west of Story was flooded to create Lake Monroe in 1960, Story's access to Bloomington via Elkinsville Road was cut off. Elkinsville Road is Story's main street, which now dead-ends 4 miles to the west at a fallen iron bridge. (Story Inn.)

Enoch Sylvester Story was born in Story in 1862 and was the son of David and grandson of Dr. George P. Story, the founder of the town. Dr. Story was a medical doctor who hailed from a clan of timber harvesters in southern Ohio. He and his progeny built many of the structures that distinguish this town today from the then-ample supply of domestic hardwoods. Rick Hofstetter and his family now occupy Dr. Story's home. (Story Inn.)

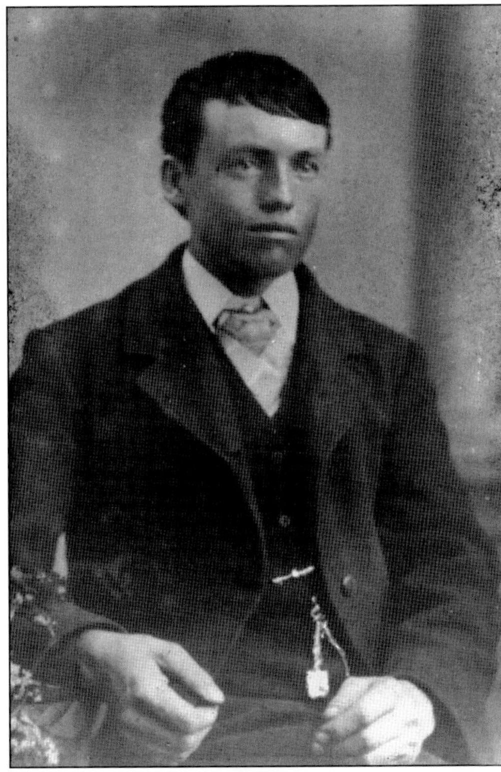

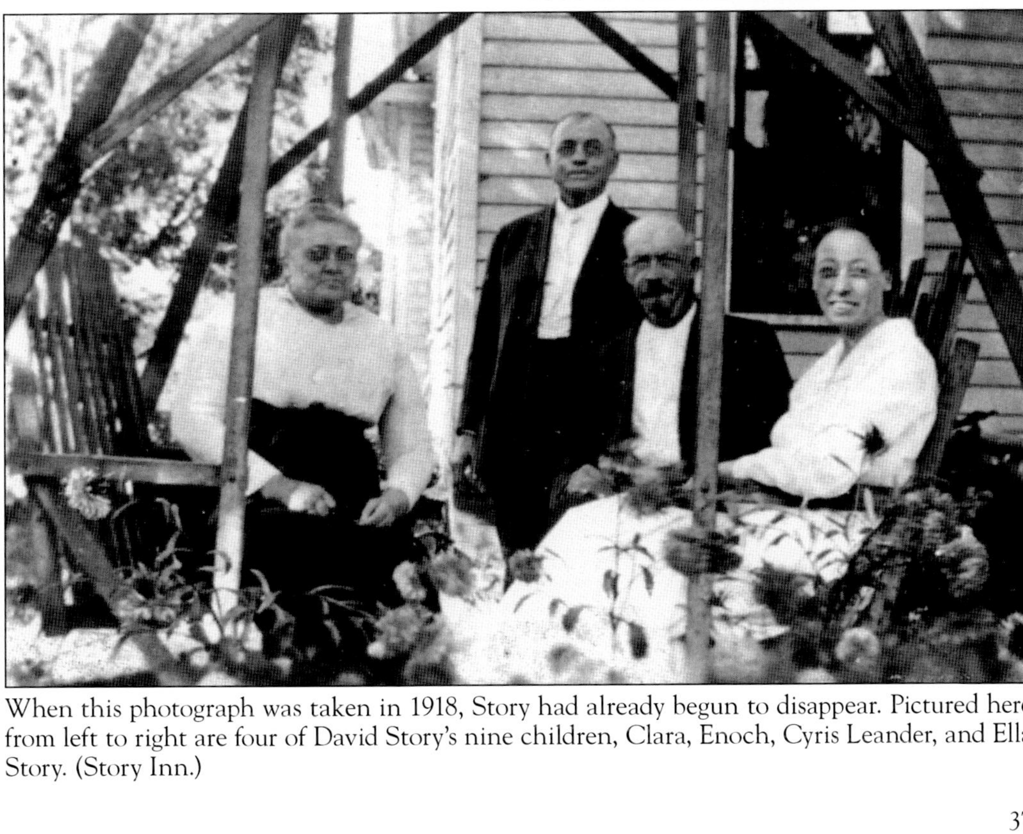

When this photograph was taken in 1918, Story had already begun to disappear. Pictured here from left to right are four of David Story's nine children, Clara, Enoch, Cyris Leander, and Ella Story. (Story Inn.)

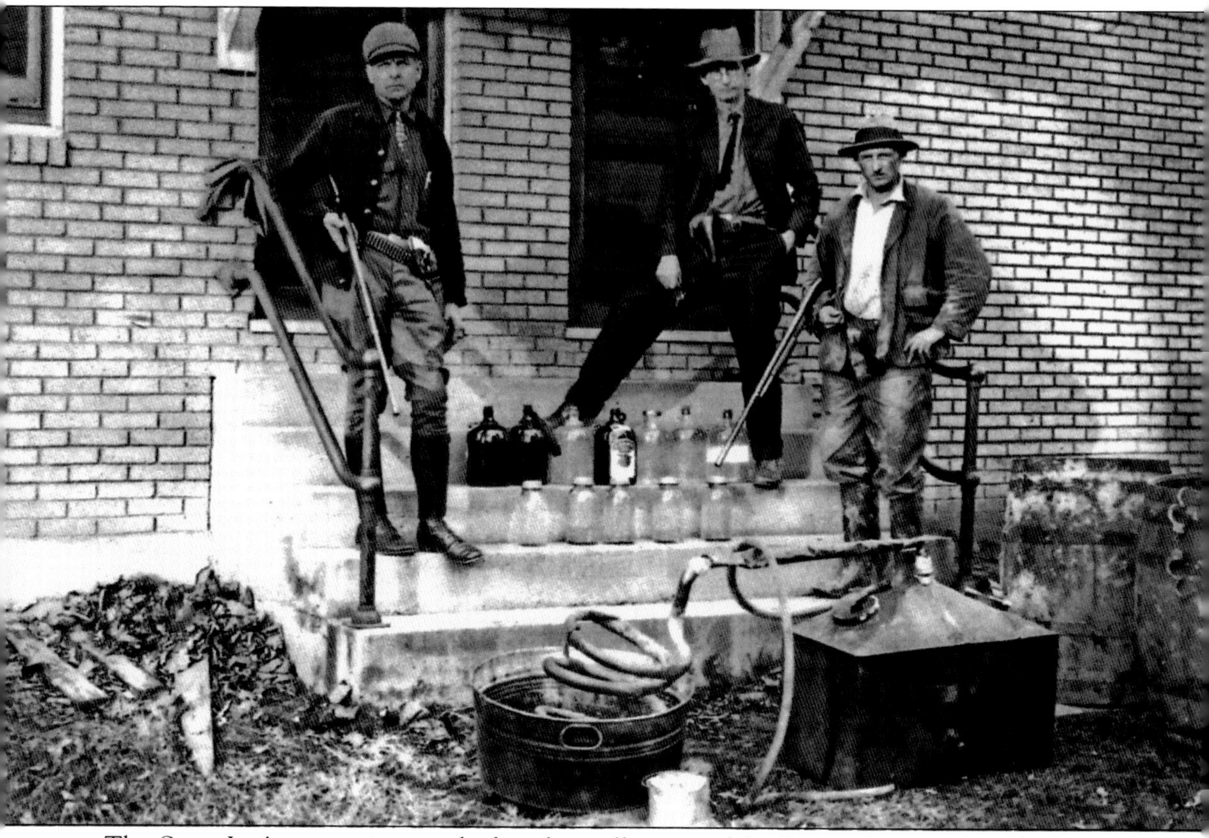

The Story Inn's tavern is named after this still captured by Brown County sheriff Clarence Moore (on right) and his deputies in 1932. Economic hardship also fostered a cottage industry producing bathtub gin of rather dubious quality, an activity that apparently kept the grain mill at Story occupied well into the 1930s. Curiously the grain mill that stands silently next door ceased operations not long after the enactment of the 21st Amendment, which repealed Prohibition. (Photograph by Frank Hohenberger.)

Benjamin and Cynthia Schultz purchased the general store building in the early 1980s. Benjamin employed his handyman skills and Cynthia her culinary skills, and they jointly pursued their vision of creating a bed and breakfast known as the Story Inn. Cynthia gave birth to their children in what is now known as the Morrison-Kelly Room upstairs. (Story Inn.)

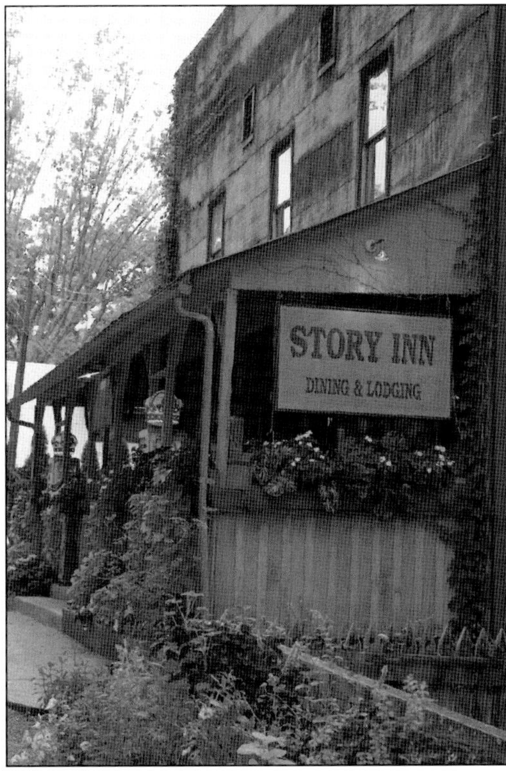

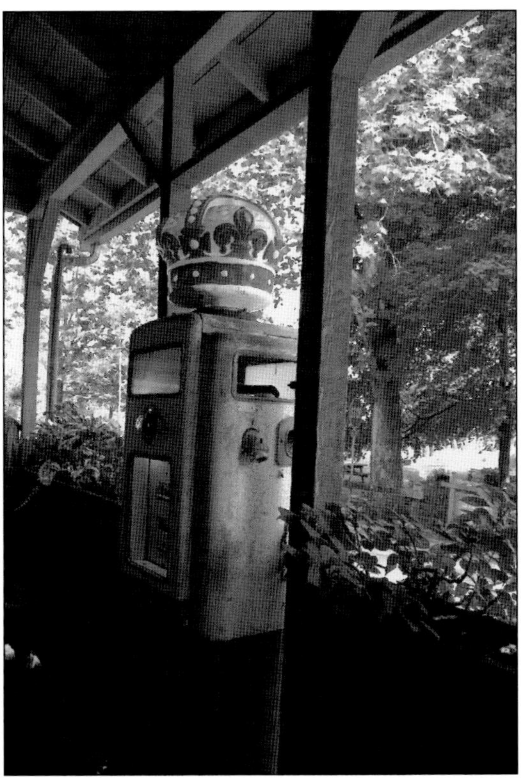

When Clothis Hedrick Robinson owned the general store in Story, she was famous for her pickled dogs, according to Helen Ayers. These rings of bologna, pickled in a vinegar solution, were so popular that people had Clothie, as she was known, send them by mail. She did not have a phone, so those wanting pickled dogs had to write her a letter. These old crowned gas pumps are now part of the Story Inn. (Story Inn.)

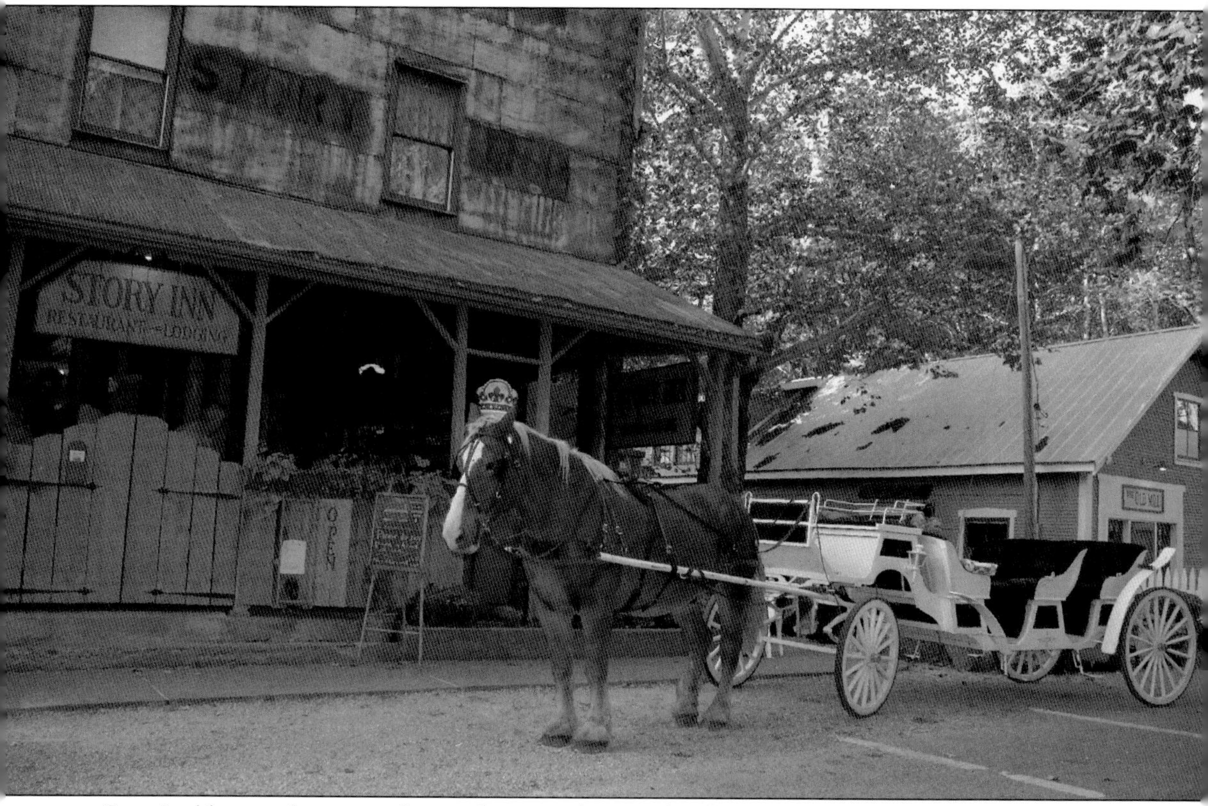

Story's old general store, replete with its creaky wooden floors, potbellied stove, and long-retired Standard Oil Crown gas pumps out front, is now a celebrated gourmet restaurant known as the Story Inn. Nature has reclaimed most of Brown County, and today the area surrounding Story is wild and natural. Story sits at the edge of Salt Creek, a labyrinthine 100-mile system of quiet, slow-moving tributaries that now form the backwaters of Lake Monroe. This moist bottomland, now under the protection of the Indiana Department of Natural Resources, is a spectacular spawning ground for fish and fowl alike, a place of serenity and raw beauty found nowhere else in Indiana. (Story Inn.)

Three

Stone Head

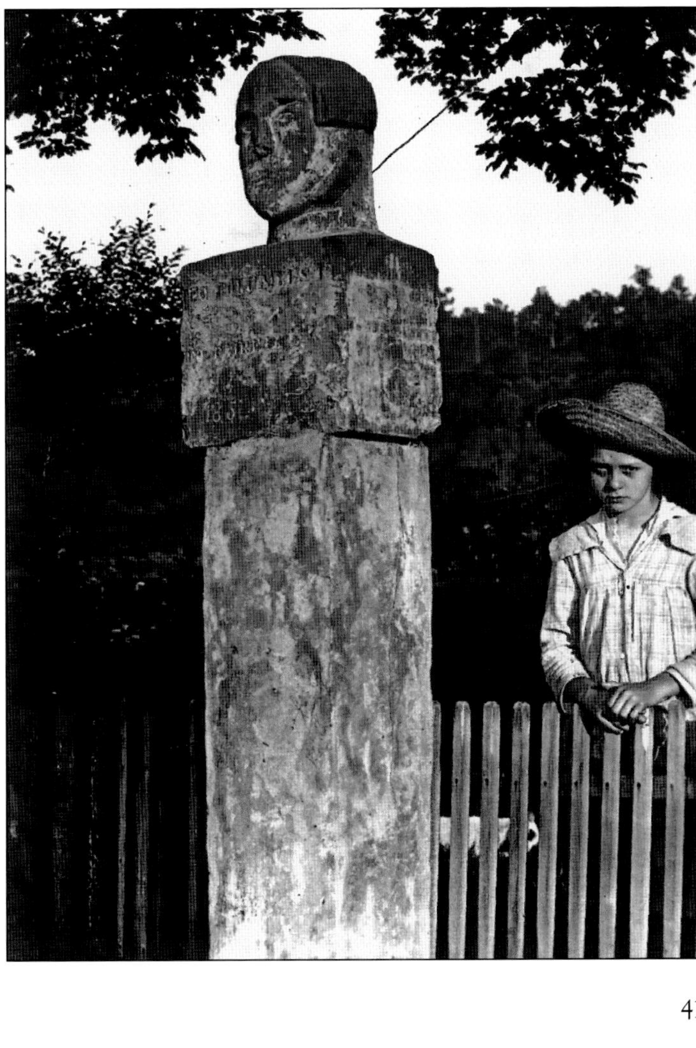

According to Mike Kelley, current owner of the House at Stone Head, "In the early days of Brown County, local residents had to comply with a decree that all able-bodied males work six days a year on public roads or waterways. Henry Cross, a farmer and part-time tombstone carver, was asked to carve three stone direction markers in 1851 in lieu of working the roads. Henry chiseled the figure out of a block of sandstone quarried from the streambed behind his house on Poplar Grove Road." (Brown County Historical Society.)

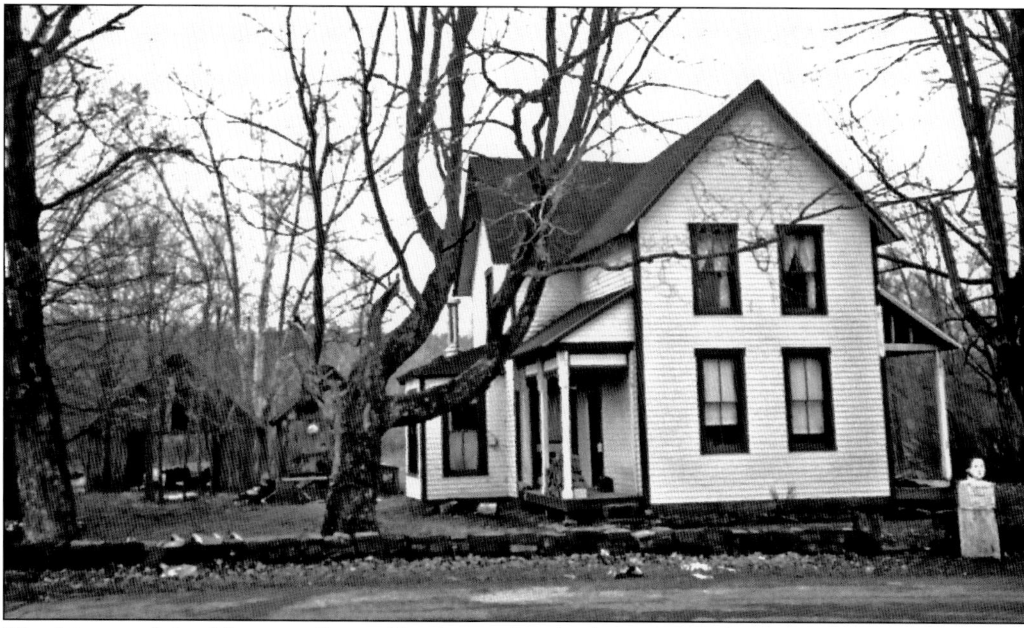

The history of the House at Stone Head stretches back to 1851, when the federal government issued a land grant to William and Margaret Hendricks, who had moved to Brown County from Ohio. The Hendricks family would own the land and its house until the early 1970s, when William and Margaret's son John Hendricks sold the home. The House at Stone Head was built in 1891 by William and Margaret's son Thomas. (Brown County Historical Society.)

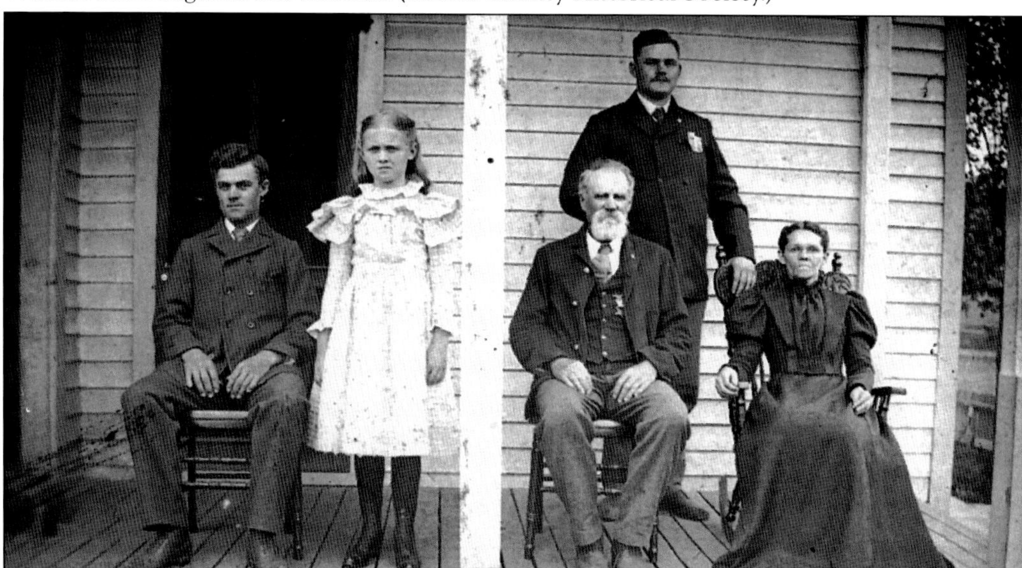

Thomas and his wife, Harriet Jane Mabe, who built the House at Stone Head, are shown in the family portrait on the porch of their home. The family had five children according to Suzannah Zody, the great-great granddaughter of Harriet and Thomas. Two of their children, Clara and Grace, died from diphtheria at ages 13 and 3 respectively. Shown in this photograph from left to right are John, Nellie, Thomas (with the long white beard), Harriet, and (standing behind) Will. (Sarah May.)

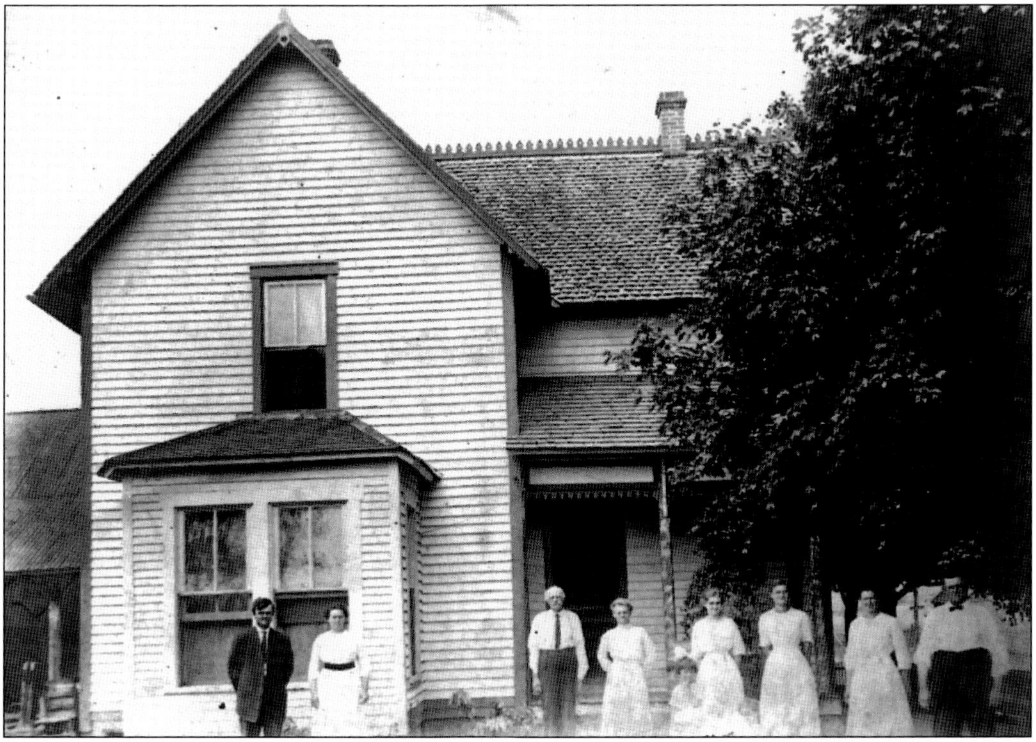

The Hendricks family stands in front of their house. A century after this house was built, Mike Kelley, an orthodontist from Indianapolis, fulfilled his lifelong dream of restoring a historic home in Brown County. In the process, he became intrigued with the Hendricks house and eventually bought the house and 27 acres. Turning it into a short-term vacation rental allows Kelley to rent the house to those who love its history and spend time there himself. (Mike Kelley.)

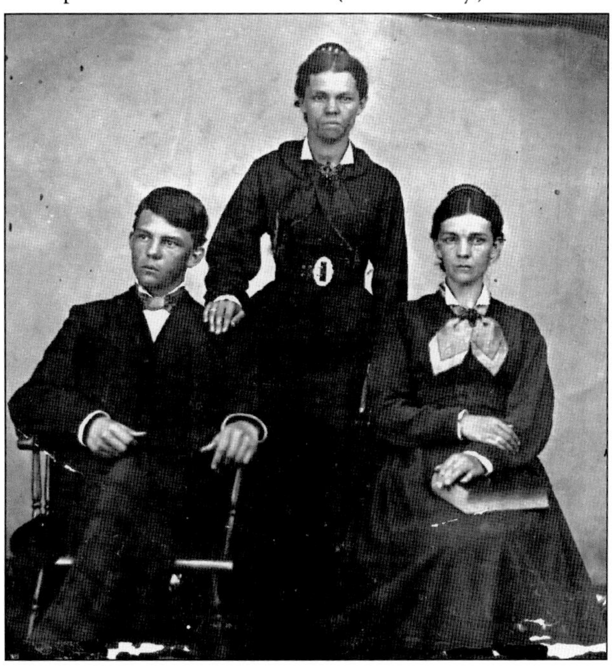

Mary Mabe Swain is pictured with her sister Harriet Mabe Hendricks (center) and brother Lemmon Mabe. One of the first families to settle in the Stone Head area was the family of Hiram (1794–1855) and Lucina (1793–1873) Mabe from North Carolina. Shortly after arriving, Hiram and his two sons acquired more land in the vicinity, eventually owning 72 acres. One son, William F. (Billy) Mabe (1825–1911), acquired the property where the house now sits. (Sarah May.)

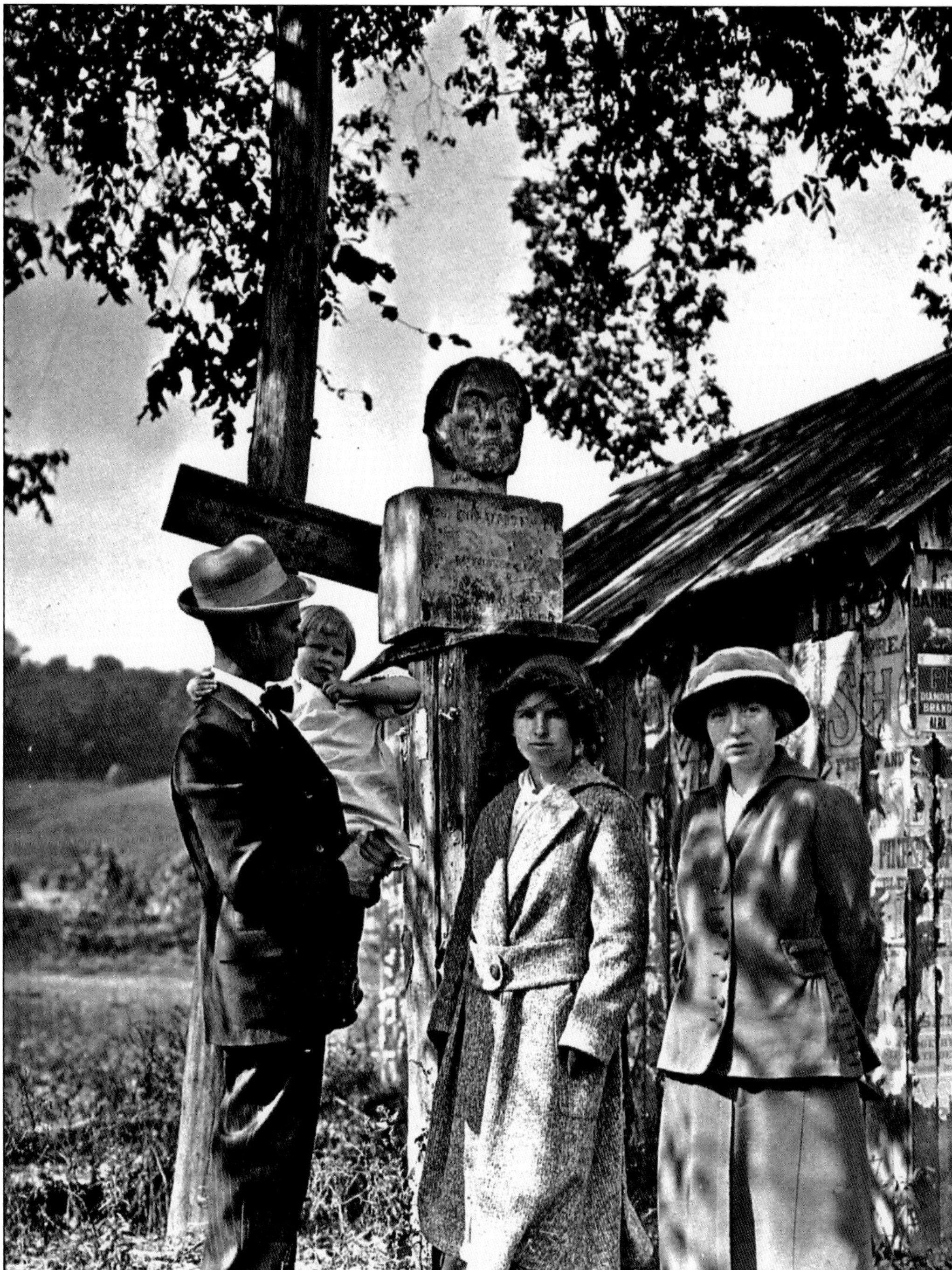

The Stone Head has always attracted visitors. This photograph shows, from left to right, Herman Burns, Marguerite Burns (daughter of Herman and Pamela), Pamela Wright Burns, and Anna Wright. The photograph was taken in 1915 by James Wright of Columbus, Indiana, the uncle of Anna and Pamela Wright, who were twin sisters. State Road 135, once a gravel road, is the main artery running north and south. (Brown County Historic Society.)

Thomas Hendricks is pictured. The home that he built for his family was entered with the National Register of Historical Places as the Thomas A. Hendricks House in 1984, about 90 years after it was built. This image was provided by Sarah May, one of Thomas's ancestors. (Sarah May.)

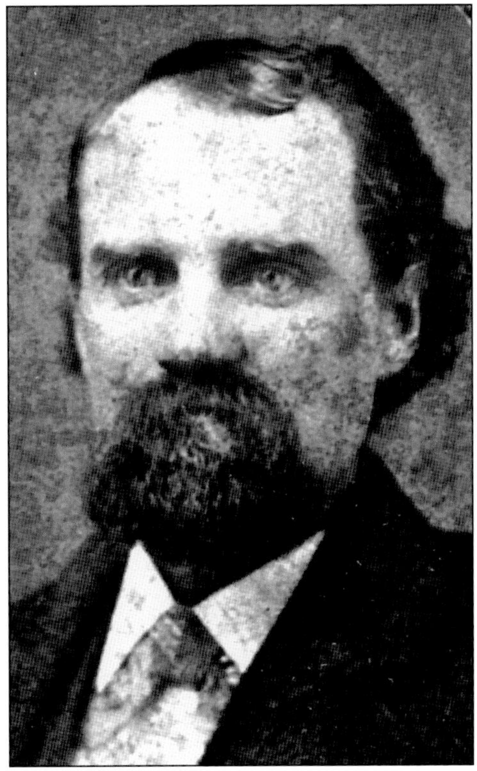

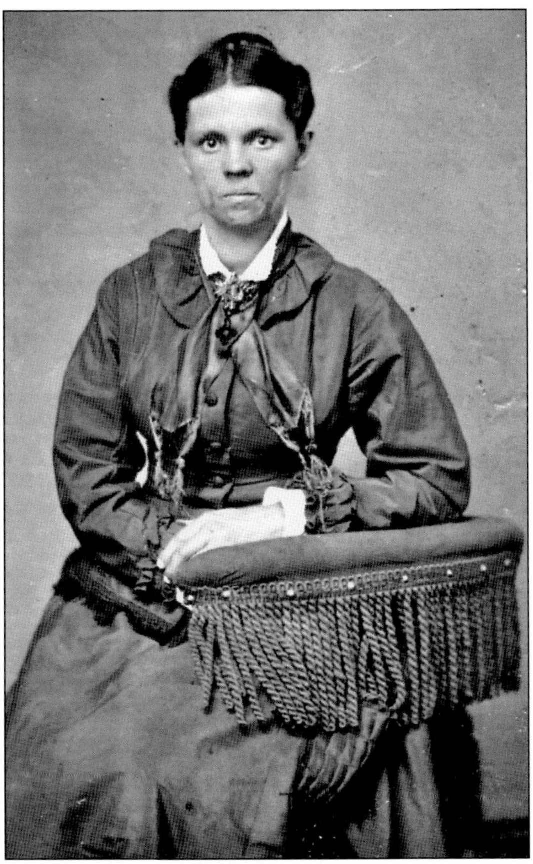

Harriet Mabe Hendricks (1852–1948), wife of Thomas Hendricks (1939–1920), was one of four children of Billy Mabe and Elizabeth Clark. P. King, a descendant of the Mabe family, forwarded William F. Mabe's 1911 obituary, which noted, "Mr. Mabe often spoke of seeing two bears in Brown County. . . . A few days later Mabe and his father were hunting deer and discovered another bear. They both shot at it but it ran over a hill where they soon found it, wounded. It was shot again and was attacked by the dogs but it whipped the dogs and made his escape." This photograph is dated July 29, 1911. (Sarah May.)

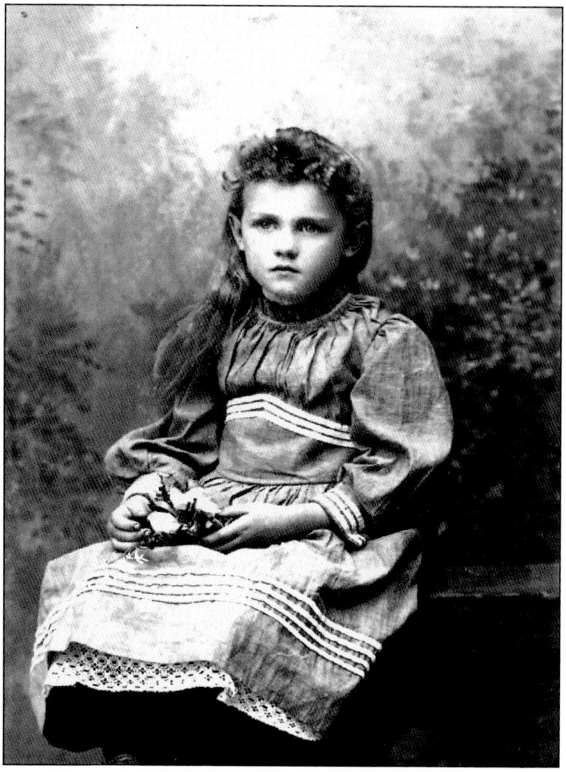

Of Thomas and Harriet Hendricks's three surviving children, only one married and had children in Brown County. That was Nellie Hendricks Wheeler Clark, whose grandchildren include Brenda Wheeler Zody, Annalee Wheeler May, Jennifer Wheeler Long Green, and Suzannah Zody. Nellie lived periodically in the Stone Head house until she married Lon Clark and moved to his farm in nearby Bellsville. (Sarah May.)

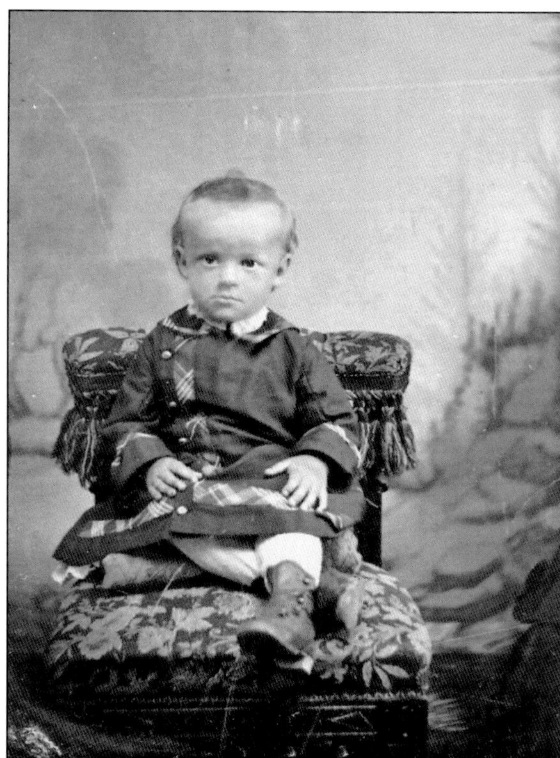

Thomas and Harriet's son John (shown here as a young boy) married Dollie Tipton, who was born and raised in the Tipton farmhouse near Pike's Peak, which is just a few miles from Stone Head. John and Dolly never had children. Dolly died in 1965, and when John was not able to care for himself, the house was sold out of the family, but it still remains part of the community. (Sarah May.)

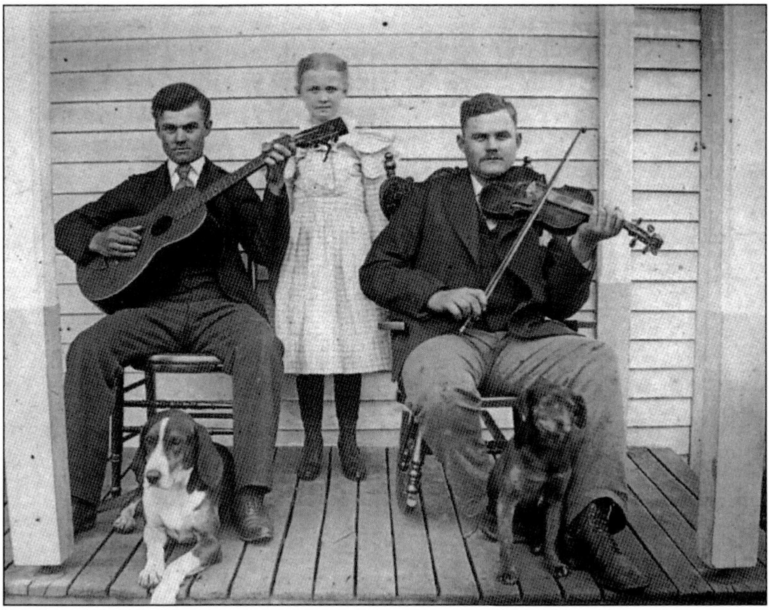

The three Hendricks children, (from left to right) John, Nellie, and Will, play music on the porch of their home at Stone Head. John would continue to live in the house for most of his life. Nellie would marry and raise a family in nearby communities. William, known as Will, married Bertha E. Moore and homesteaded in North Dakota where he raised his family, died, and was buried. (Sarah May.)

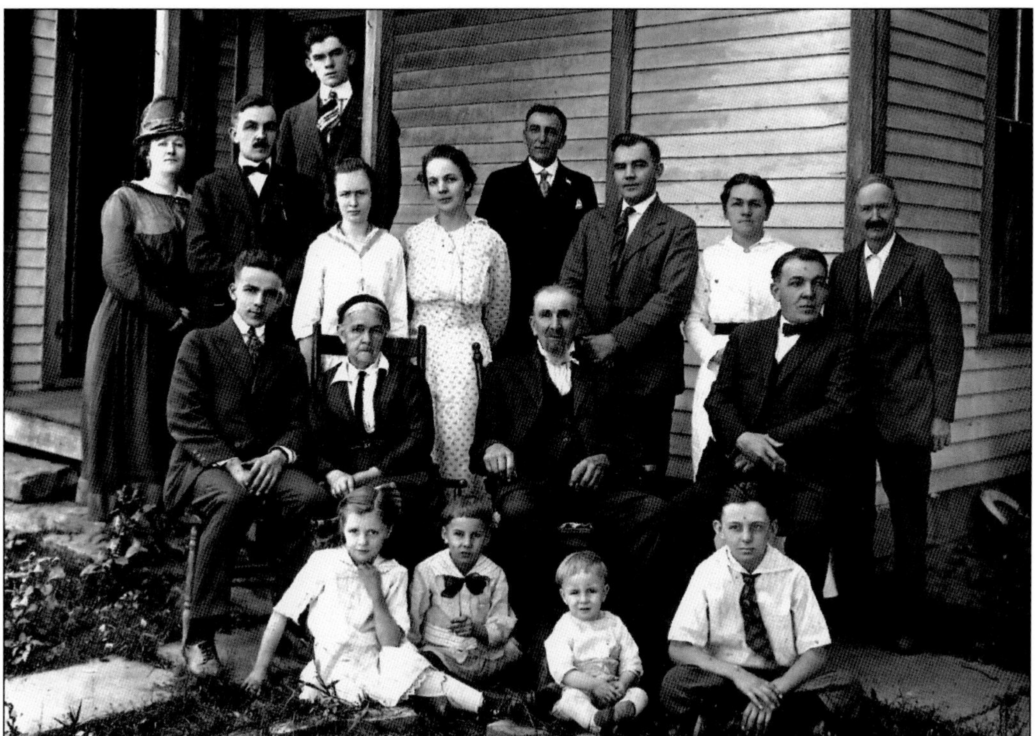

A gathering on the porch at the House at Stone Head includes, from left to right, (first row) Grace Lemley King, Eugene Horner, Charles Horner, and Franklin Swain, son of Joe; (second row) Edward Swain (died on USS *Mississippi* in 1919), Mary Mabe Swain, Thomas Eli Swain, and Joe Swain; (third row) Fidelia and Lee Swain, Stella Swain Horner, Mary Merritt, S. J. Horner, Jim Swain, Elva Swain Lemley Merritt, and Lafe Merritt; and (fourth row) Ray Lemley. (Sarah May.)

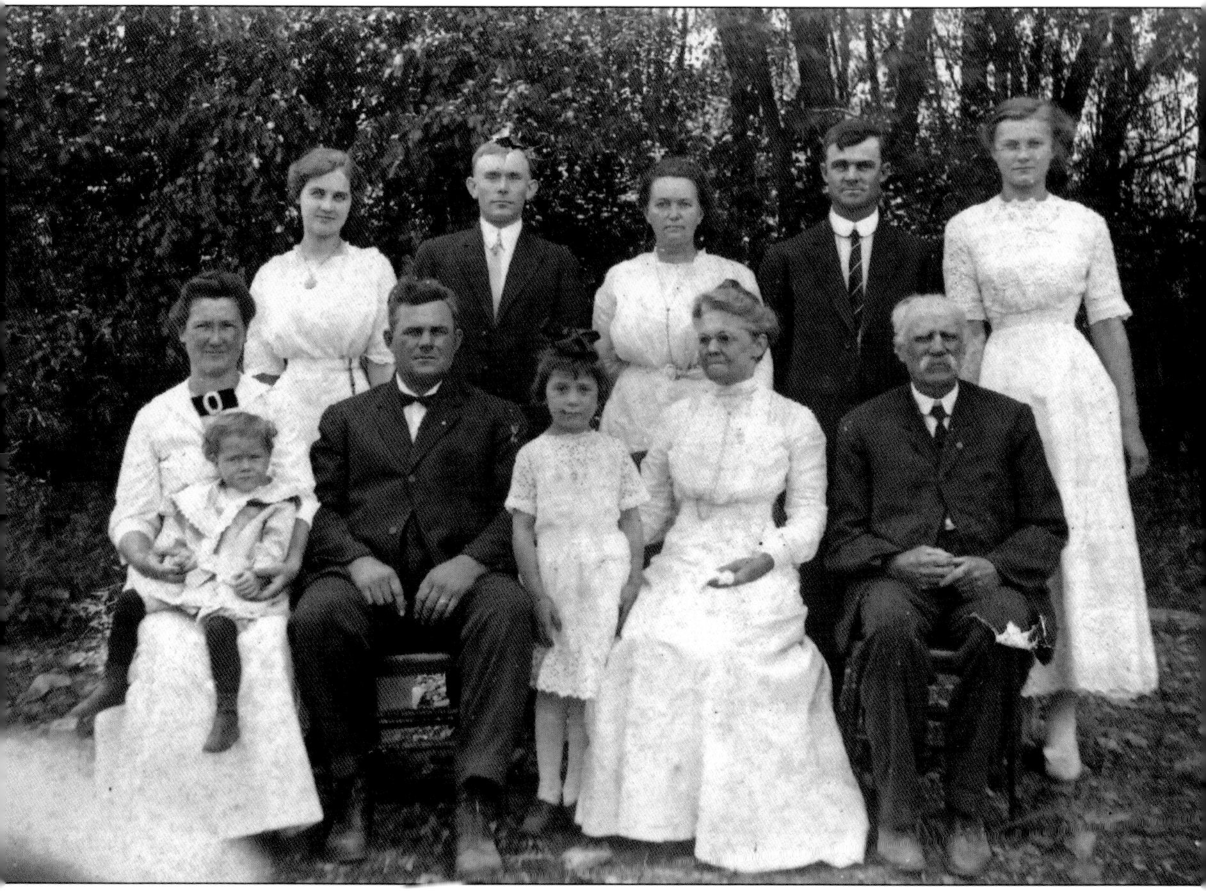

The Hendricks family, pictured in their garden in 1913, includes, from left to right, (first row) Bertha Moore Hendricks (wife of Will), Glen Hendricks (son of Will), William (Will) Hendricks, Grace (daughter of Will), and Harriet and Thomas Hendricks (parents of Will); (second row) Nellie Hendricks (daughter of Harriet and Thomas), Curtis Ray Wheeler (husband of Nellie, father of Emerson Wheeler), Juanita (daughter of Will and Bertha), John (son of Thomas and Harriet), and his wife Dolly Hendricks. (Sarah May.)

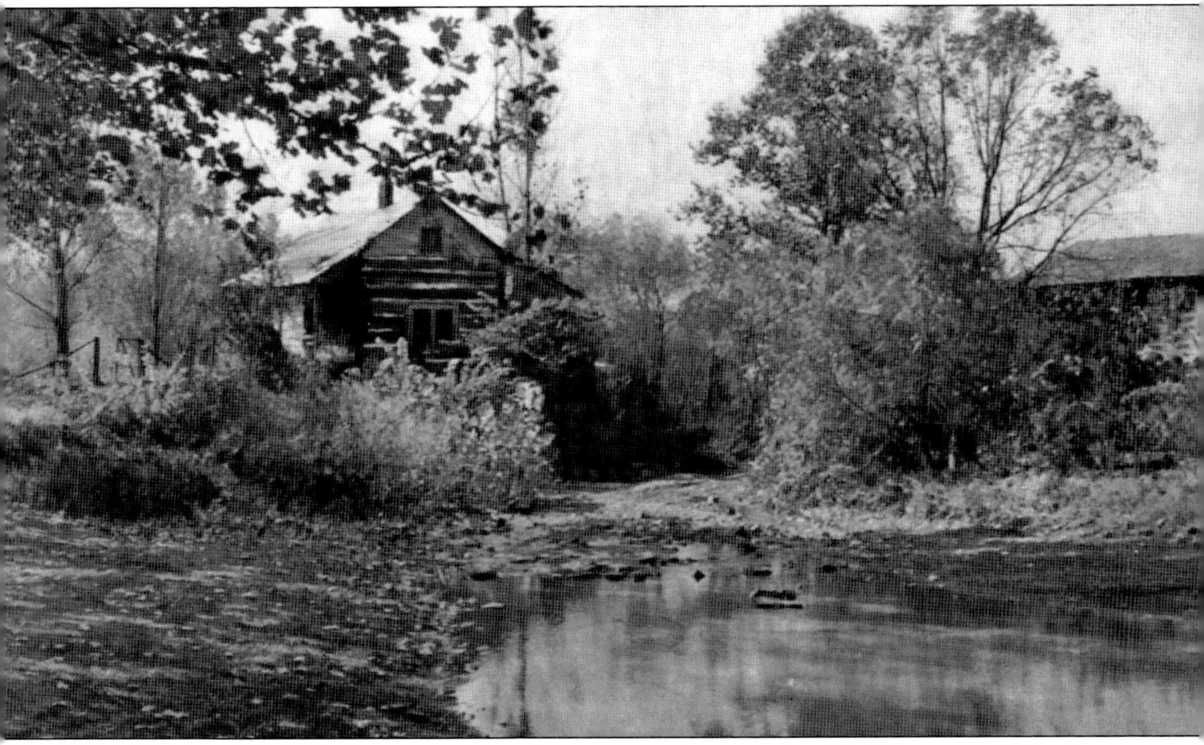

This scene at Stone Head was so pretty that a postcard was made of it. Thomas and Harriet Hendricks lived in this log cabin, similar to many in Brown County, while building their home located just out of view on the left side of the photograph. The cabin eventually fell into the creek, and all that is left today is an abandoned stone-lined well. The ford, where travelers could easily make their way across the creek, now has a concrete bridge. Current owner Mike Kelley notes that the location of the house was at the "confluence of two rivers, known now as the middle fork of Salt Creek and Pleasant Creek." (Sarah May.)

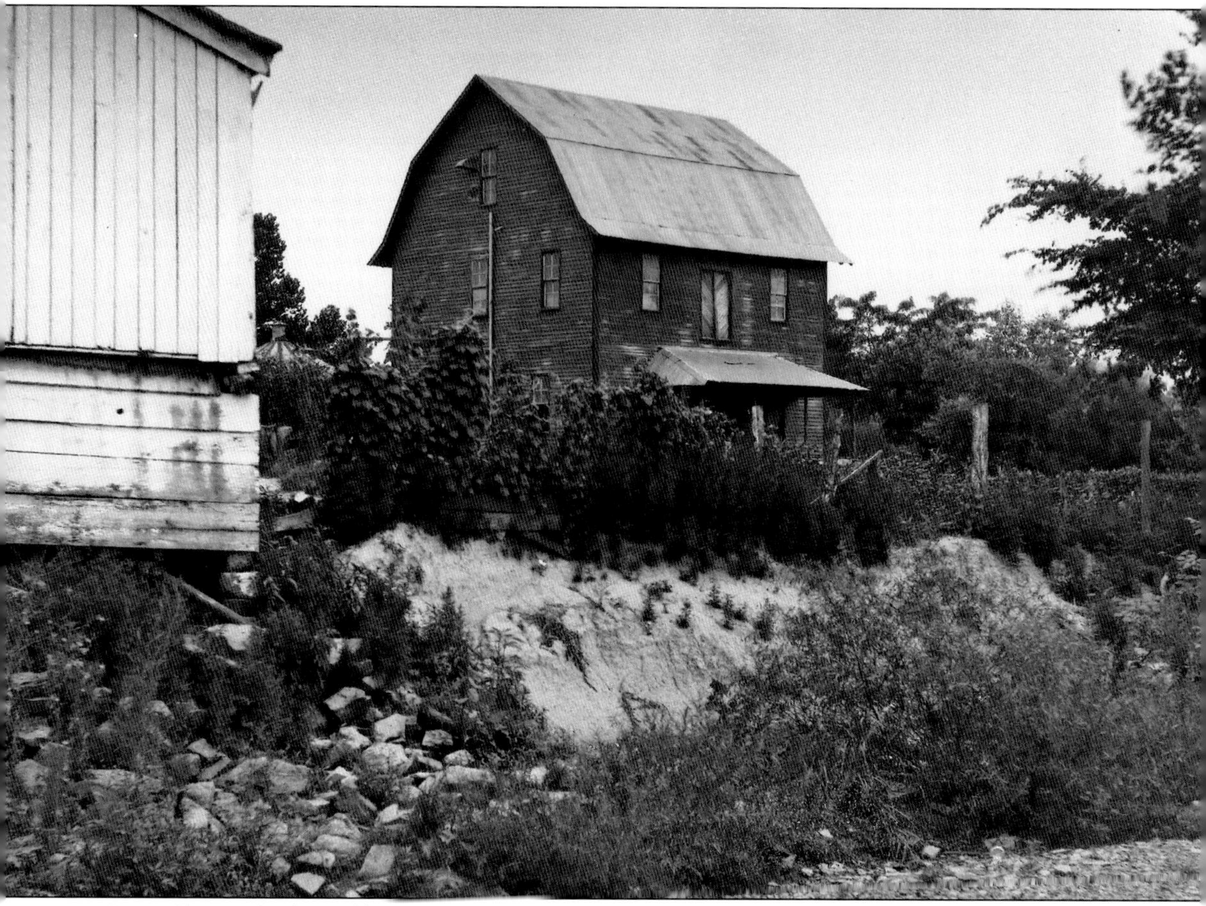

According to Mike Kelley, owner of the House at Stone Head, "The Van Buren Township census of 1870 lists Samuel Fulks as a millwright. The *Brown County Democrat*, issued December 17, 1914, stated that the flour, saw, and planning mill at Stone Head, owned by Willard Fulks (son of Samuel Fulks) and Joseph Gillaspy, was destroyed by a fire the night of December 14, 1914. The mill was rebuilt. In 1920, Willard Fulks sold his interest in the milling operation to Alra Wheeler." (Lilly Library, photograph by Frank Hohenberger.)

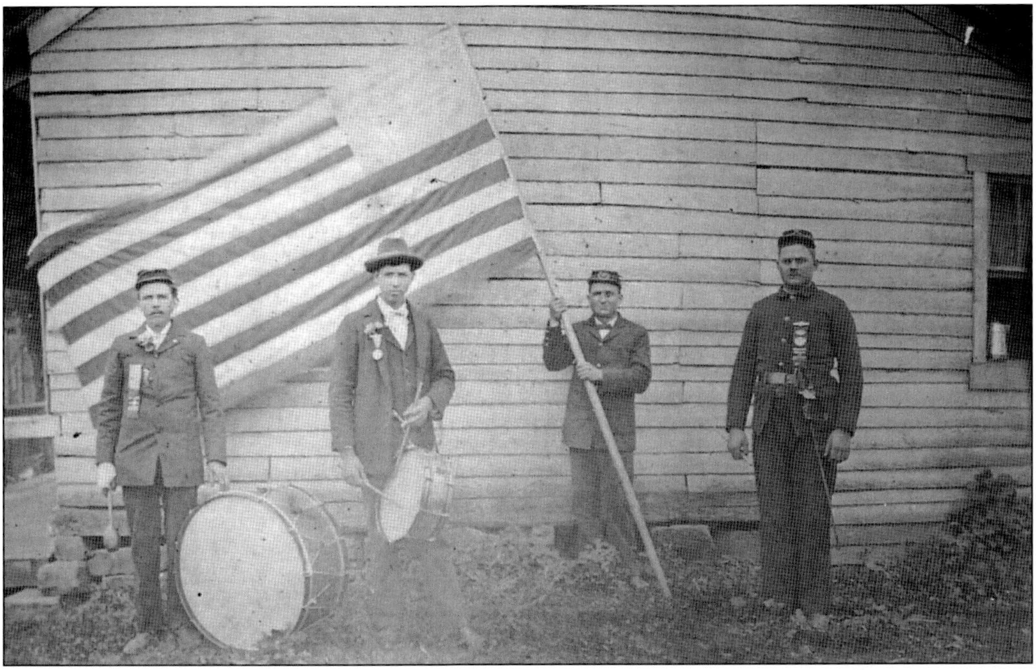

Will Hendricks (far right) is shown in uniform in this undated photograph. Many Brown County men went off to war. Cpl. Water Shulz, son of artists Adolph and Ada Shulz, fought at Cantigny, Marne, St. Michiel, and Argonne before dying of disease on December 12, 1918, in Traben, Germany. The well-educated Claude William Tipton, who studied at the Carnegie Institute of Pittsburgh, also died during World War I. His sister Dolly married Will's brother John. (Sarah May.)

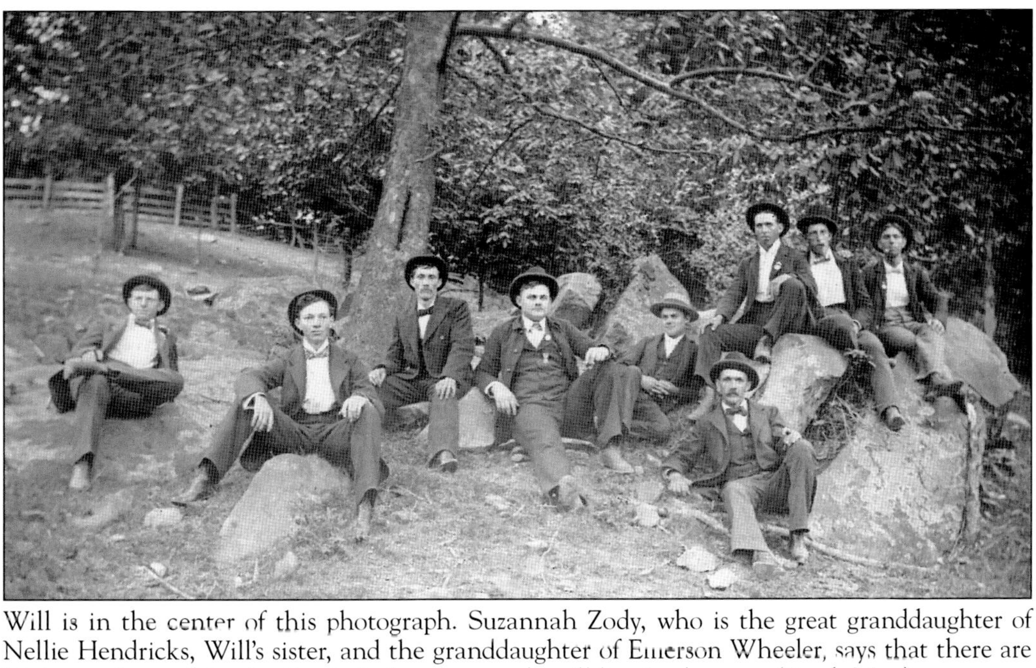

Will is in the center of this photograph. Suzannah Zody, who is the great granddaughter of Nellie Hendricks, Will's sister, and the granddaughter of Emerson Wheeler, says that there are 14 descendants of the family, 6 of whom currently still live in the area. (Sarah May.)

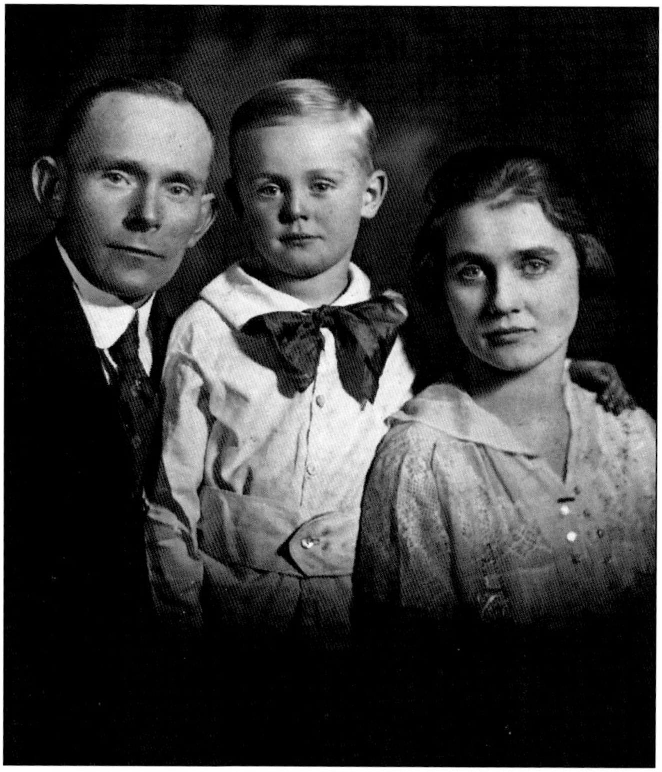

Curtis Wheeler is seen here with his wife, Nellie Hendricks (daughter of Thomas and Harriet), and their son Emerson. Emerson's family remembers him saying that he gave the Stone Head its first coat of white paint. Though over 100 years old, the House at Stone Head, built on property owned by the Mabry family since 1851, still looks much the same. (Sarah May.)

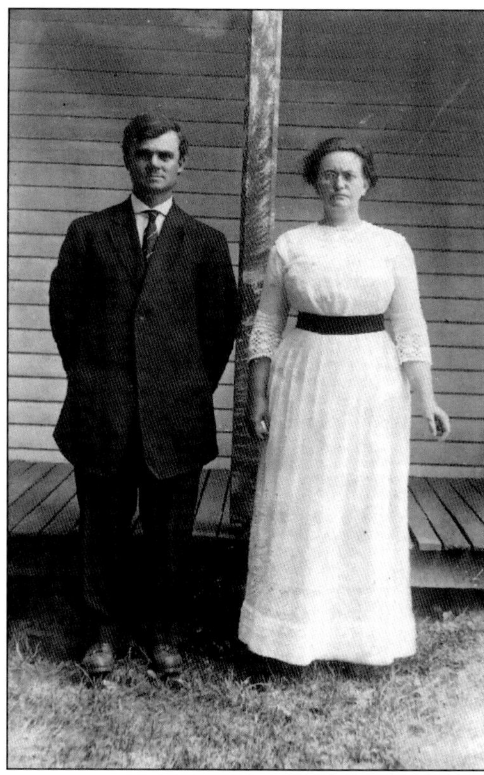

John and Dolly Hendricks are shown here in a 1913 postcard sent to Mr. and Mrs. G. R. Wheeler in Evansville. Dolly was the daughter of Joshua and Emma Tipton, who owned a farm with a two-story, wood-frame house built in the late 1860s that still stands. The Tipton farm grew to include 22 buildings, and the family also operated a button factory that used mussel shells from the creek. John and Dolly lived in the House at Stone Head for most of their lives. (Sarah May.)

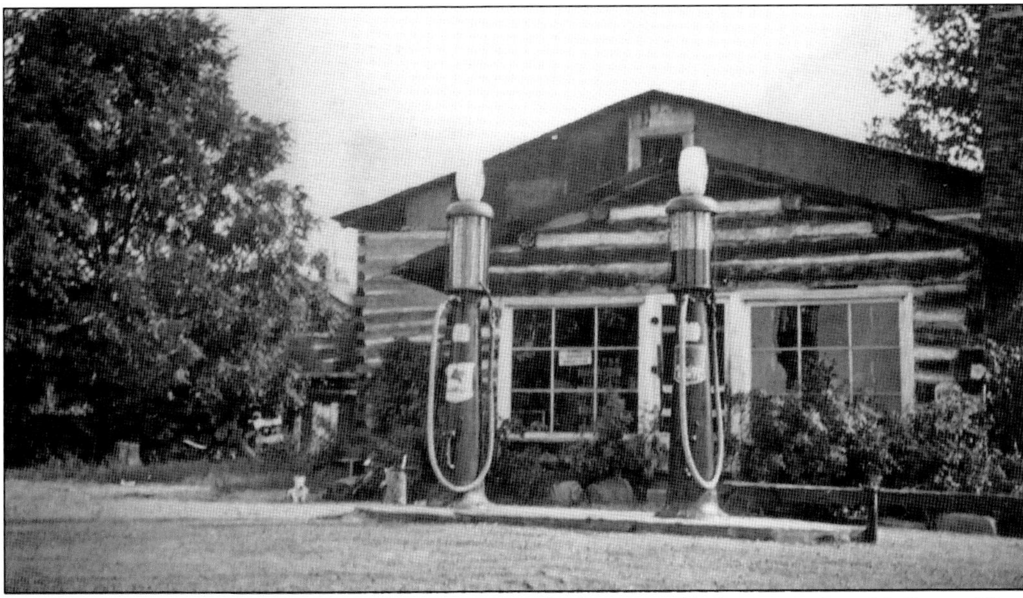

According to Brown County resident Jim Greedy, his grandfather ran the old Stone Head grocery store from the 1920s until about 1962. Stone Head was never a town but rather a small community. The roads were dirt and gravel back then, and when enough cars went by it formed a haze of dust that could be seen for miles. The Stone Head Flour Mill was one of the last mills to remain open in Brown County. Its remains can be found on the grounds of the House at Stone Head near the hiking trailhead. (Brown County Historical Society.)

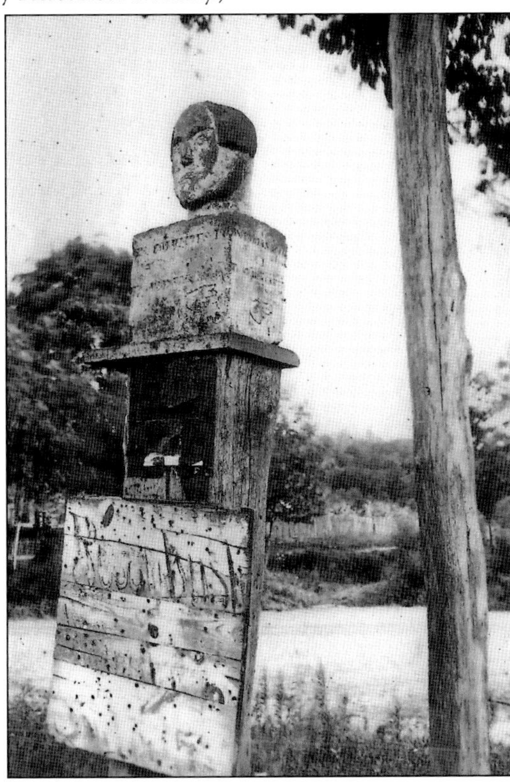

This is one of the earliest known photographs of the Stone Head; note the wooden sign. According to information from the Brown County Historical Society's 2007 Historic Home Tour, "In 1851, the stone head was designed by tombstone carver Henry Cross in the likeness of the then county road superintendent George Summa. In lieu of paying a road tax or working to build roads as all residents were asked to do each year, Henry Cross decided to provide several stone directional markers. Thus the neighborhood was known as Stone Head. When Thomas Hendricks built the home in 1891, it was said that he competed with his neighbor to see who could build the finest home. The house was carefully restored in 2005 by owner Dr. Michael Kelley." (Brown County Historical Society.)

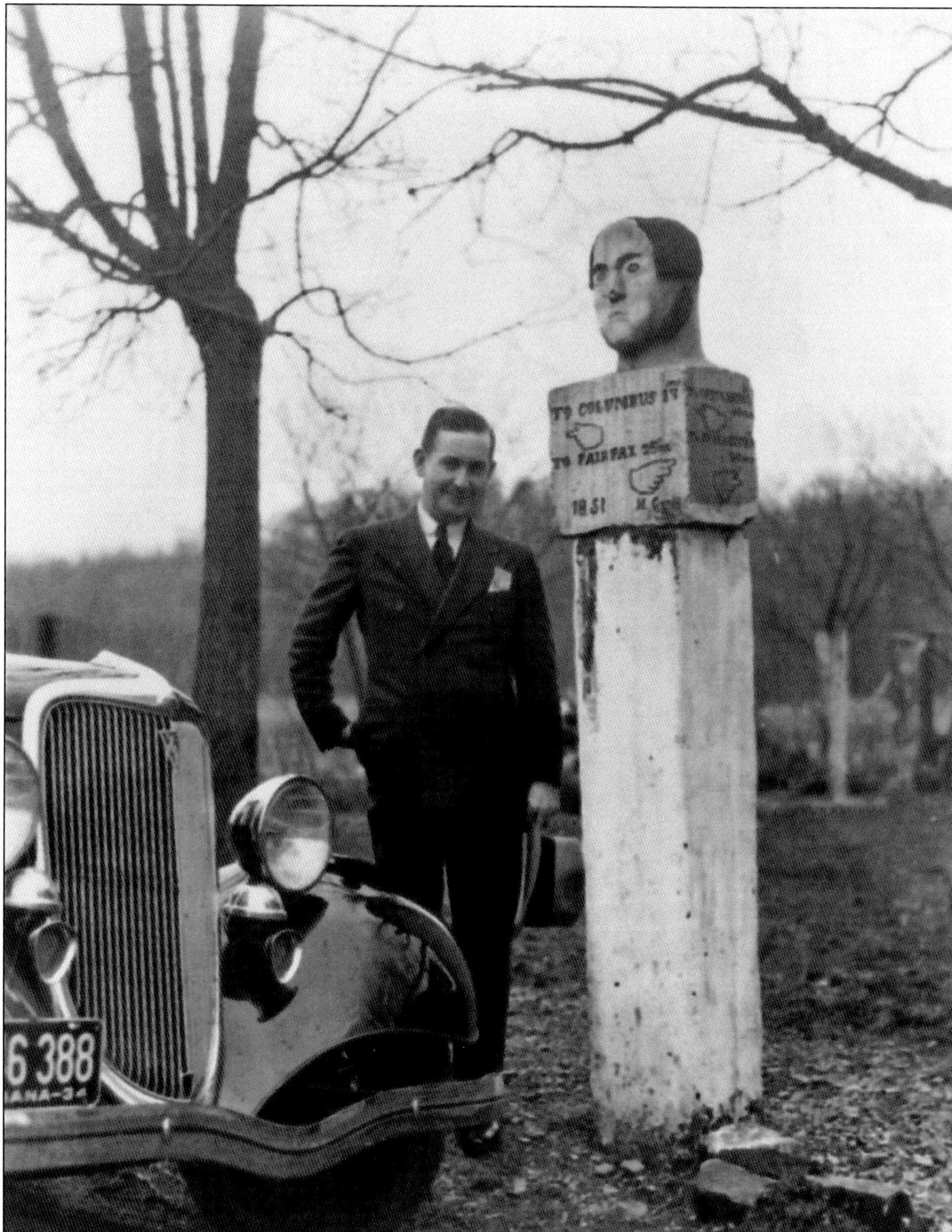

A dapper-looking man poses between his car and the Stone Head. The marker sits at the juncture where State Route 135 curves west towards Story and Pikes Peak Road branches east towards the small town just a mile or so away. A replica of Stone Head, which was stolen and remained missing for several years before being found in a dormitory at nearby Indiana University, is on display at the Brown County Historical Society. (Lilly Library, photograph by Frank Hohenberger.)

Four

Brown County Personalities

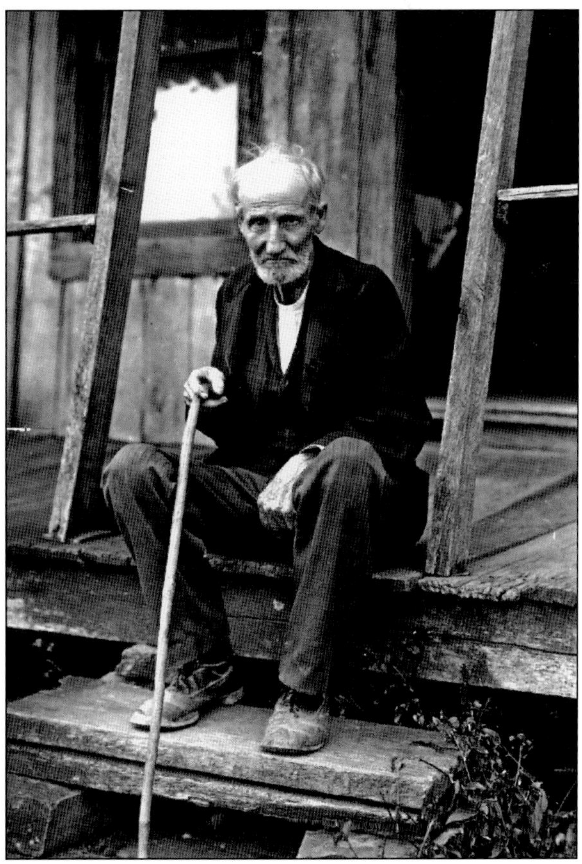

The back of this photograph reads, "Ransom Sturgeon, who was taken by the Indians." The photograph was taken by Frank Hohenberger, presumably after Ransom had been returned. Though Native Americans were a big part of the area, by the 1820s almost all had either left or been driven from Brown County. (Brown County Historical Society.)

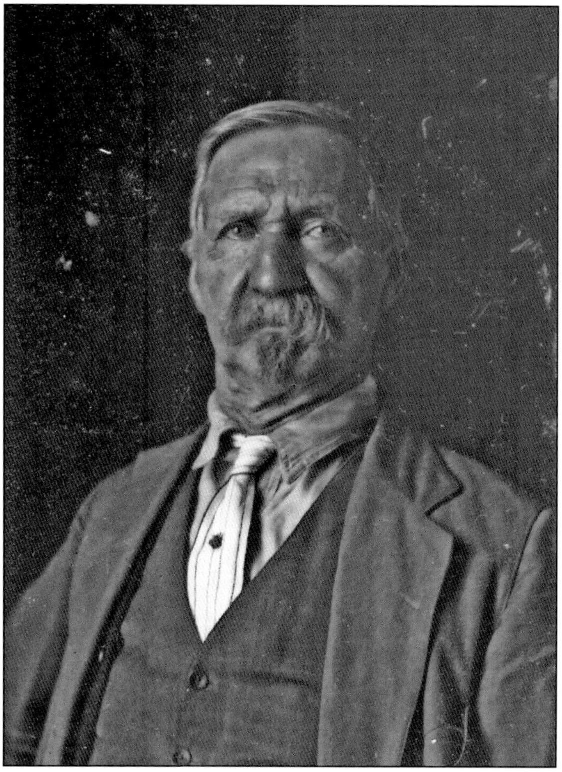

Rufus Reddick was at one time the sheriff of Brown County. His father-in-law, James Wise, owned the Wayside Inn, also called the Schooner Valley Tavern, which was built in 1830. The tavern was used as a stagecoach inn and a freighting station for those traveling between Indianapolis and Louisville, Kentucky. "Schooner" is thought to be the first white settler in the county limits, settling on the creek that bore his name around 1820. (Brown County Historical Society.)

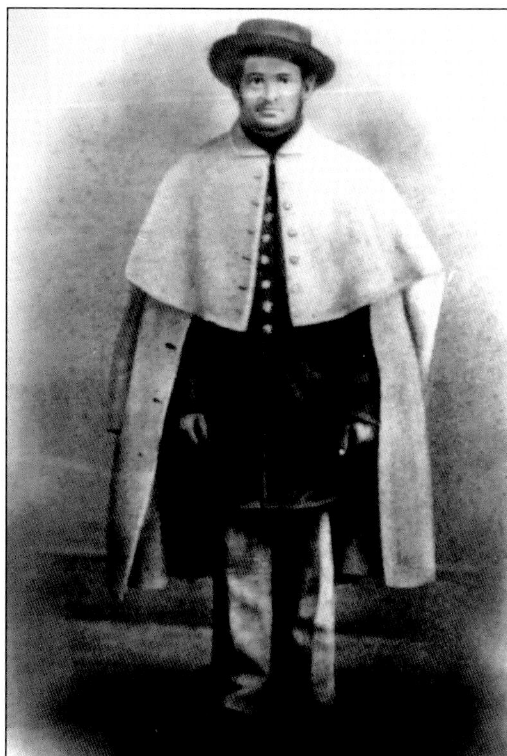

John Weyrich moved here from Germany and changed his last name to Wirey (though it was sometimes misspelled as Weirich). He was born January 10, 1827, and died on January 28, 1889. He is buried in a cemetery off of Mount Morich Road where there are two tombstones commemorating him, including one for his service in the Civil War. (Brown County Historical Society.)

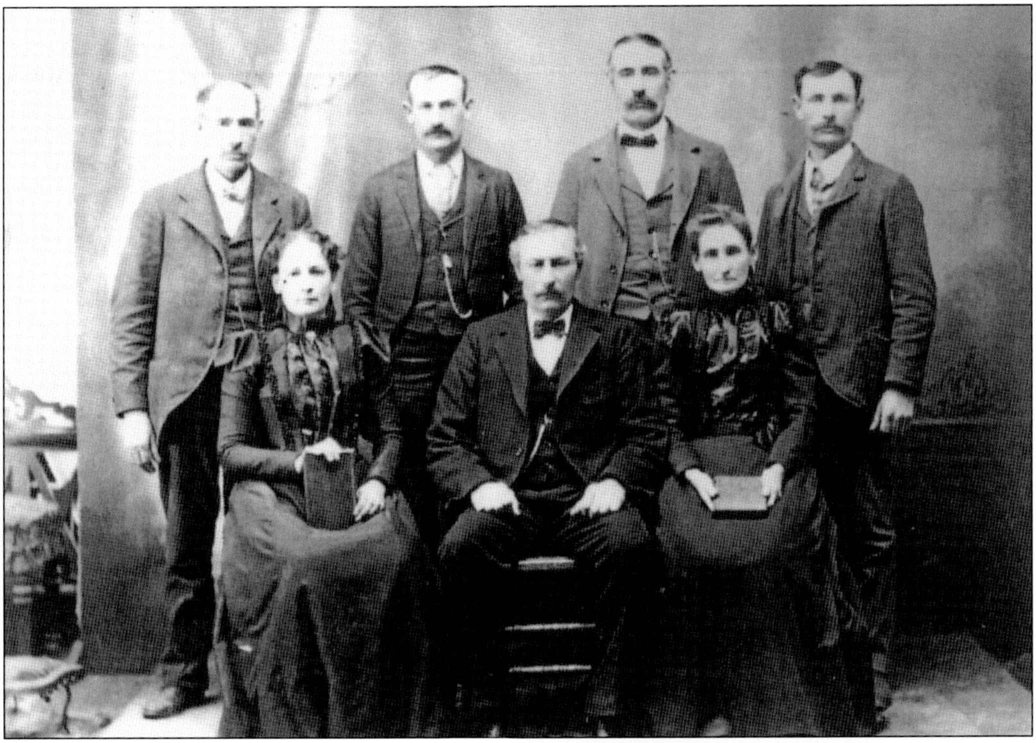

This photograph, taken in 1890 several years after the death of John Sr., shows the children of John and Elizabeth Wirey. The couple had 13 children, 7 of whom lived to adulthood. Seen here from left to right are (seated) Barbara, John Jr., and Elizabeth; (standing) Jacob, William (Will), Michael, and Charles. (Brown County Historical Society.)

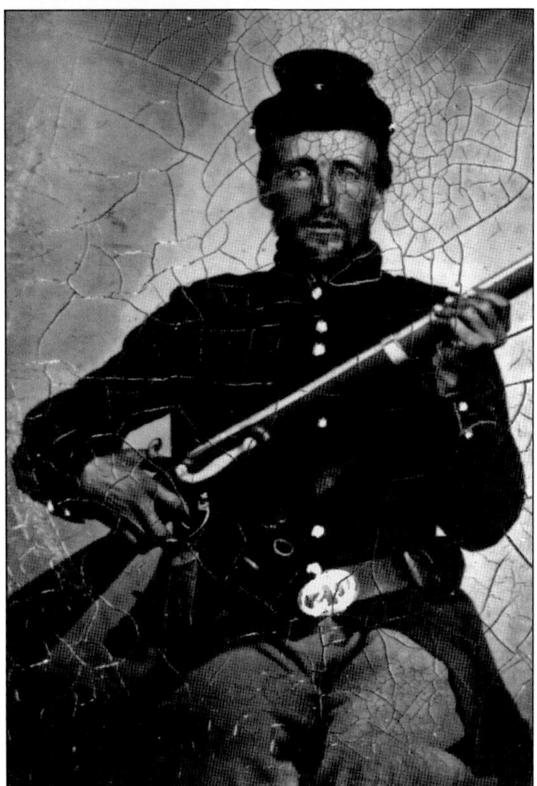

John Wirey poses with his rifle, wearing his Civil War uniform. In the late 1800s, the Wirey farm was located southeast of Sweetwater Dam and north of Mount Morich Road in Brown County. (Brown County Historical Society.)

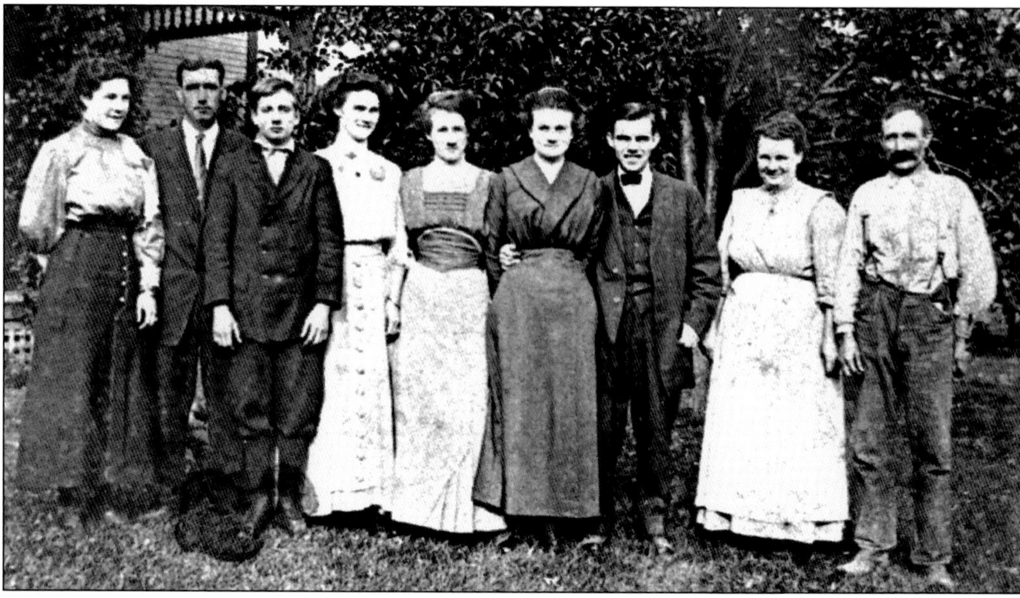

The caption on this photograph identifies the Long family at their home. There was an Elijah Long listed on the Jackson Township, Brown County poll-tax payers roll of 1848, stating that he was one the heaviest payers with a tax of $8.95 (the highest was A. G. Bergen at $11.64). (Brown County Historical Society.)

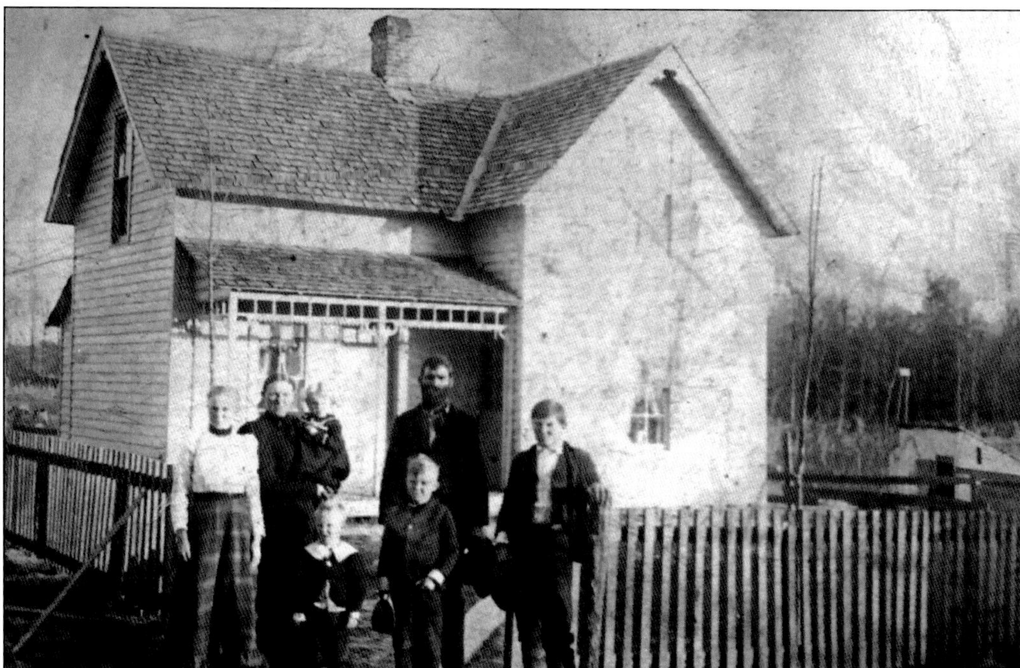

This photograph shows the Fleener family in front of their house in 1900. William and Sarah Stout Fleener are in the back; Sarah is holding Minnie; their son Fred, who was the principal at Helmsburg for 12 years, is on the right; George Fleener is in the middle; Leo Fleener is the small boy on the left; and Jamie Fleener is the girl on the left. The notation on the back of this photograph states that the house was built by William Fleener. (Brown County Historical Society.)

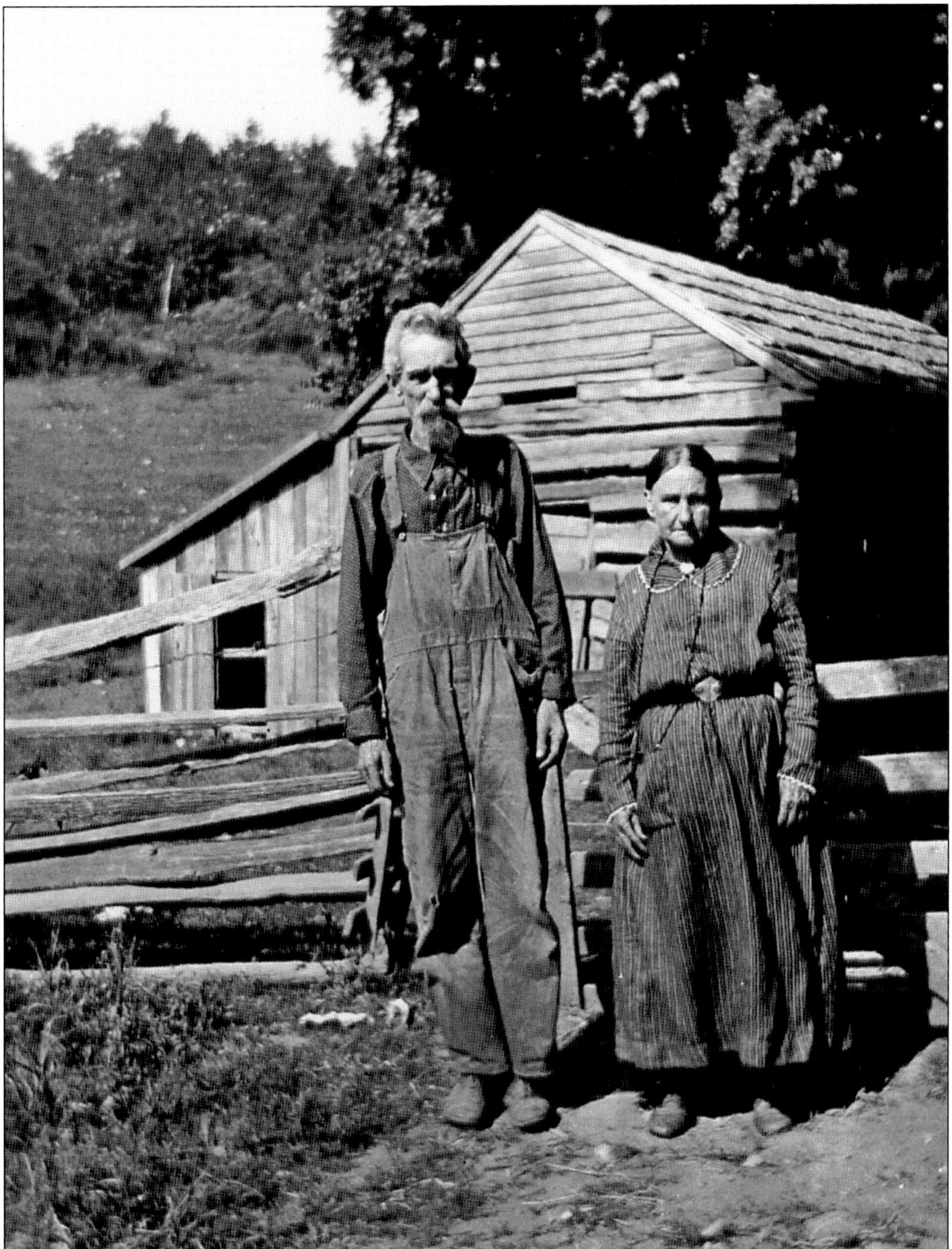

"I was interested in characters and types," said Frank Hohenberger, who moved to Brown County after seeing photographs of a log cabin, an old water mill, and some people who looked to him like Southern mountain folk. Indeed, the ancestors of some Brown County residents had migrated from the hills of Kentucky and Tennessee as well as Virginia and the Carolinas. (Brown County Historical Society.)

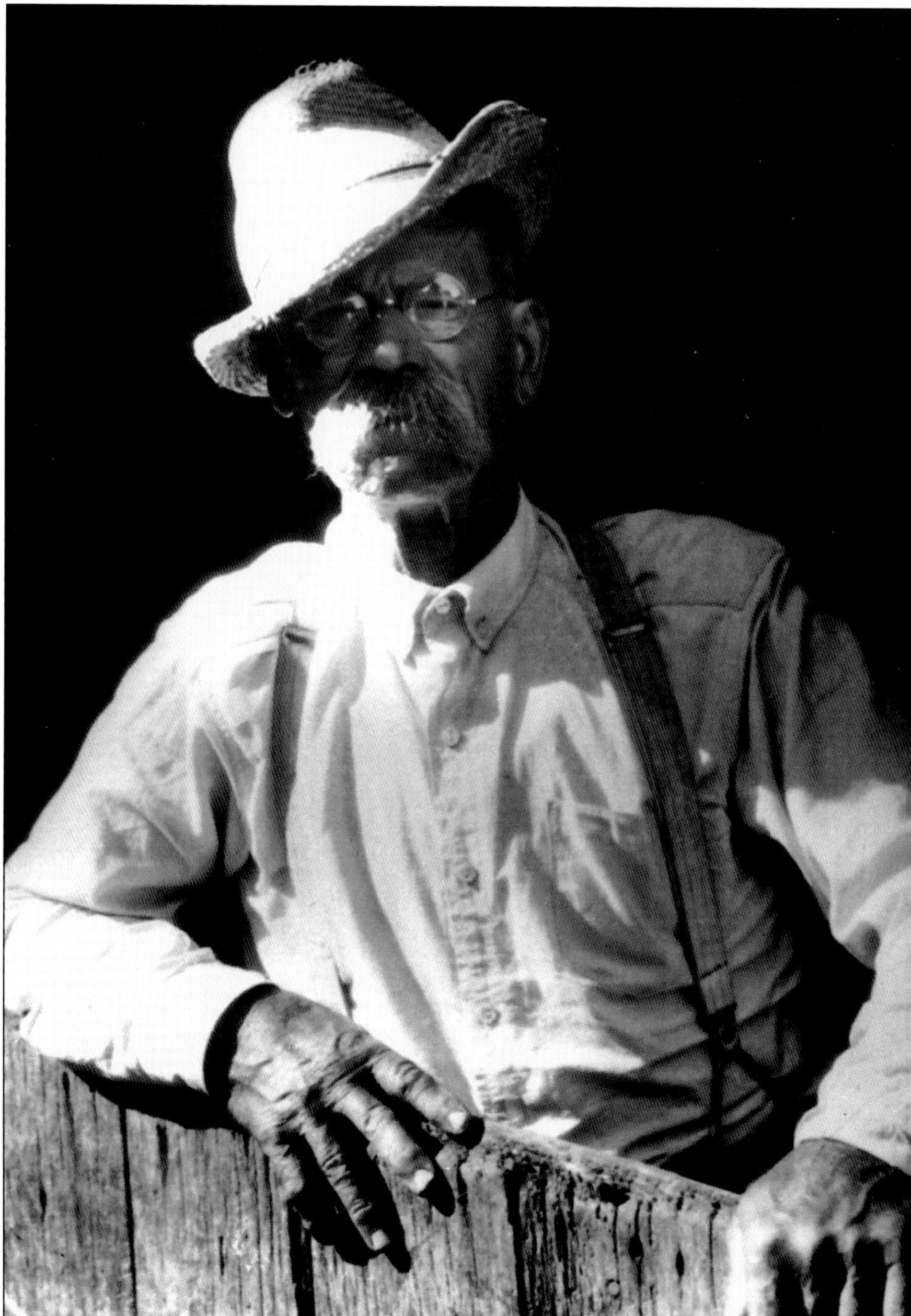

Seralvo McGuire (1849–1944) was named after Servale, a little village in Mexico where his father was during the Mexican War. When McGuire was about 87, he recounted his early pioneer days to Ray Mathis. Besides seeing two black bears near his cabin, one morning around 9:00 a.m. the sky was so dense with pigeons that it "seemed to be almost dark for over an hour during one of their flights." (Brown County Historical Society.)

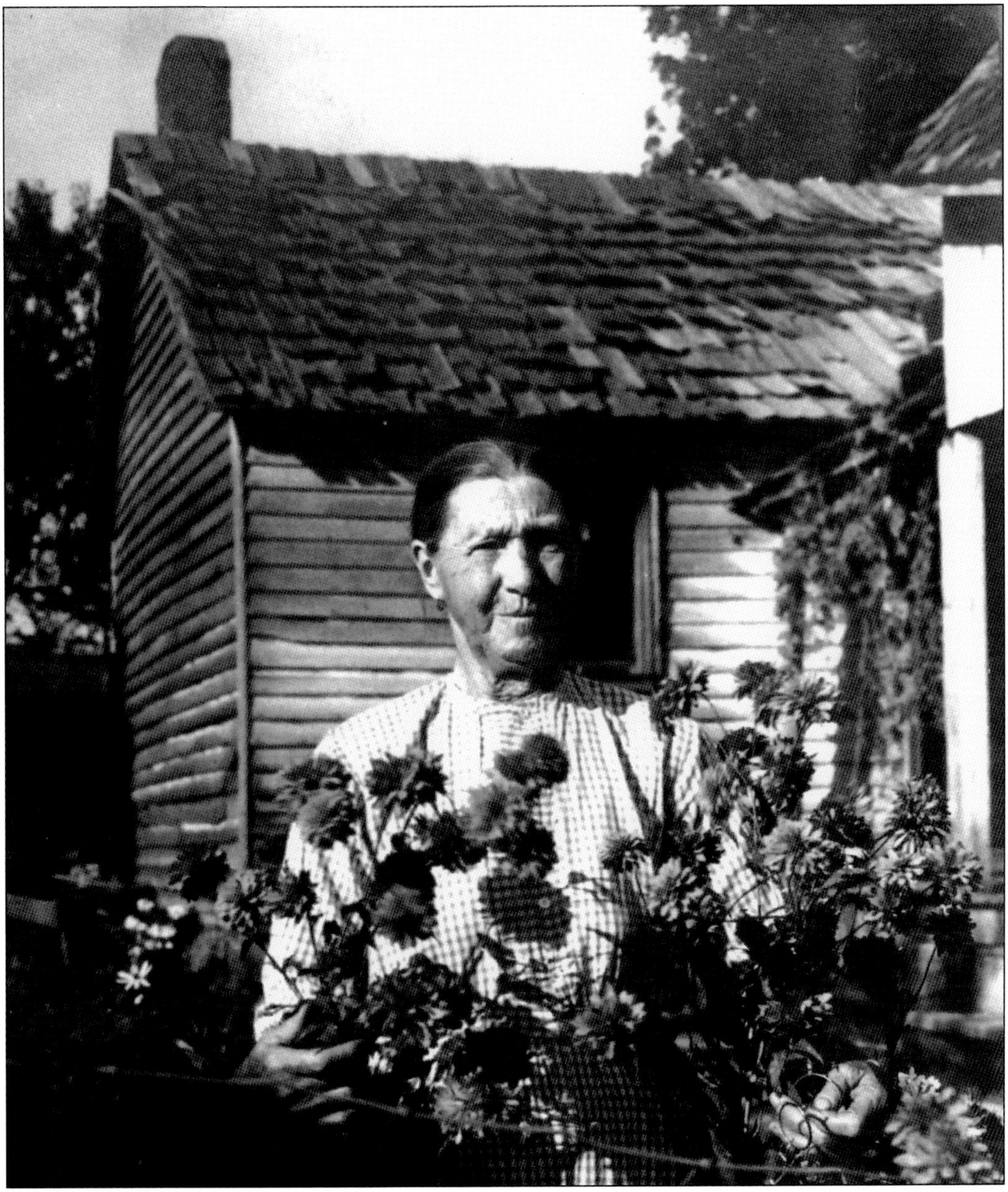

Lucy Jane Hatchett McGuire (1850–1936), the wife of Seralvo, also had stories about the mid-1850s including one about a Native American woman who lived on a hilltop in a one-room cabin with an old stick chimney. McGuire described her as being a "sort of yarb doctor," though there is no explanation for what that means, and said that her name was Yarrick and that she made her living selling medicine. (Brown County Historical Society.)

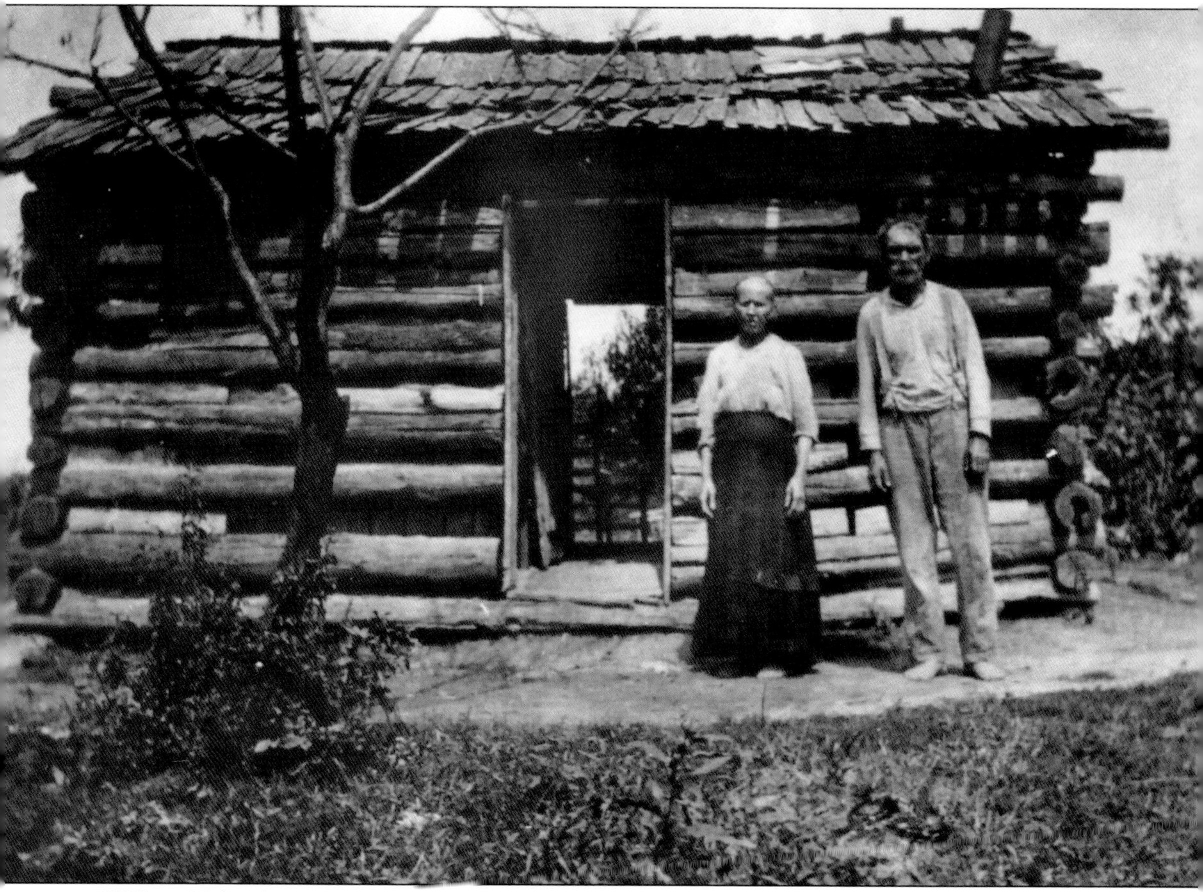

"When Hohenberger got out into the hills the people hid from him, in fear that his camera was an infernal machine or, if they knew what it was, because they didn't want their 'pitchers took,' " writes Webb Waldron in his 1933 article on Frank Hohenberger. "If you got your 'pitcher took' it meant that you left something behind you when you died, and your soul couldn't sleep peaceful. But gradually Hohenberger made friends with the hill-people and persuaded them that there was no harm in letting him point a camera at them and press the bulb." Bill Harden and his wife are pictured. (Brown County Historical Society.)

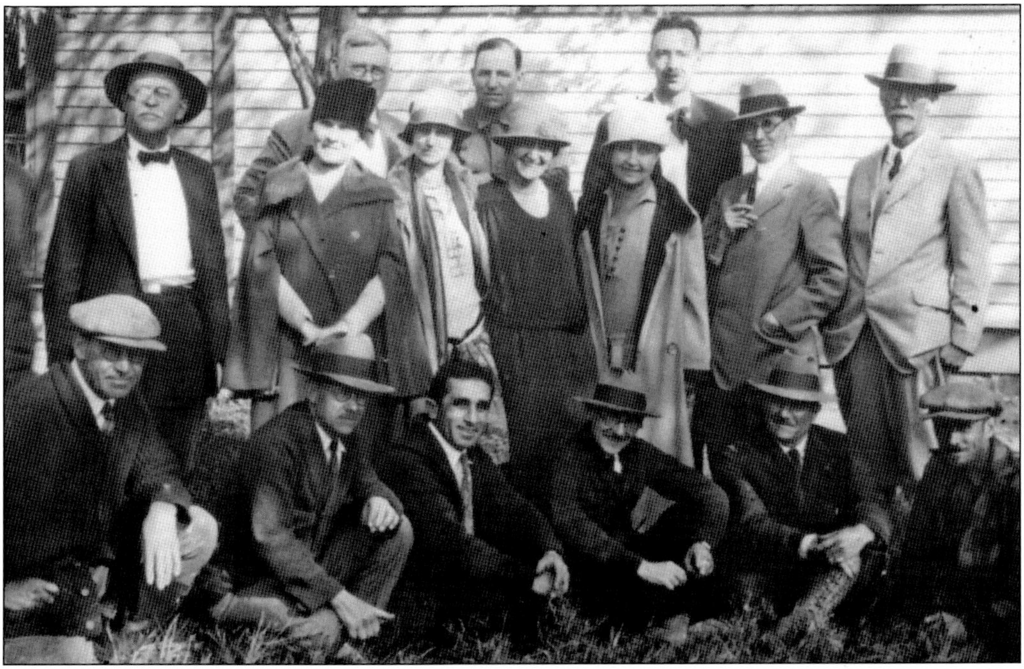

This October 16, 1927, photograph shows local and visiting artists. The Brown County Art Colony was formed in the early 1900s. Adolph Shulz is considered to be the founder of colony. He began visiting Brown County in 1908 and in 1917 became a permanent resident. (Brown County Historical Society.)

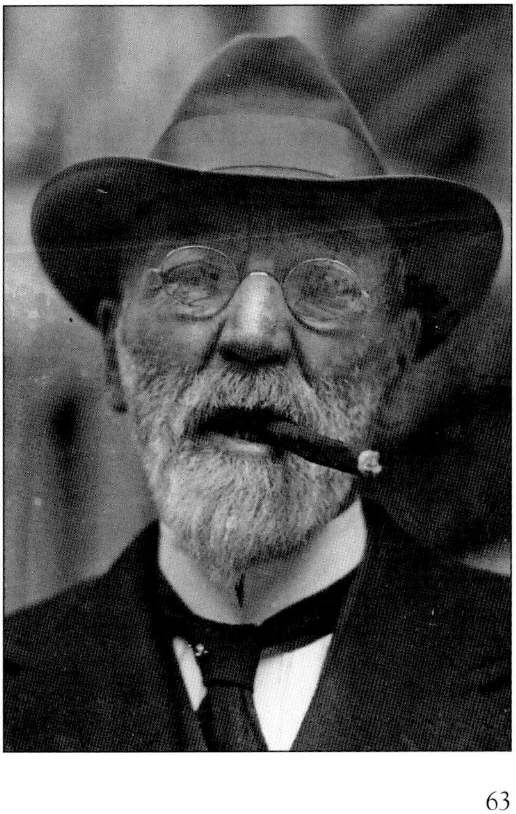

Shulz (seen here) and T. C. Steele influenced other artists and many began building cabins and moving to the area. Will Vawter and Gustave Baumann were among the first to make Brown County their home. Other artists such as Charles Dahlgreen, Lucie Hartrath, and L. O. Griffith came from Chicago, and by the early 1930s there were at least 18 artists with permanent homes in Brown County. (Brown County Historical Society.)

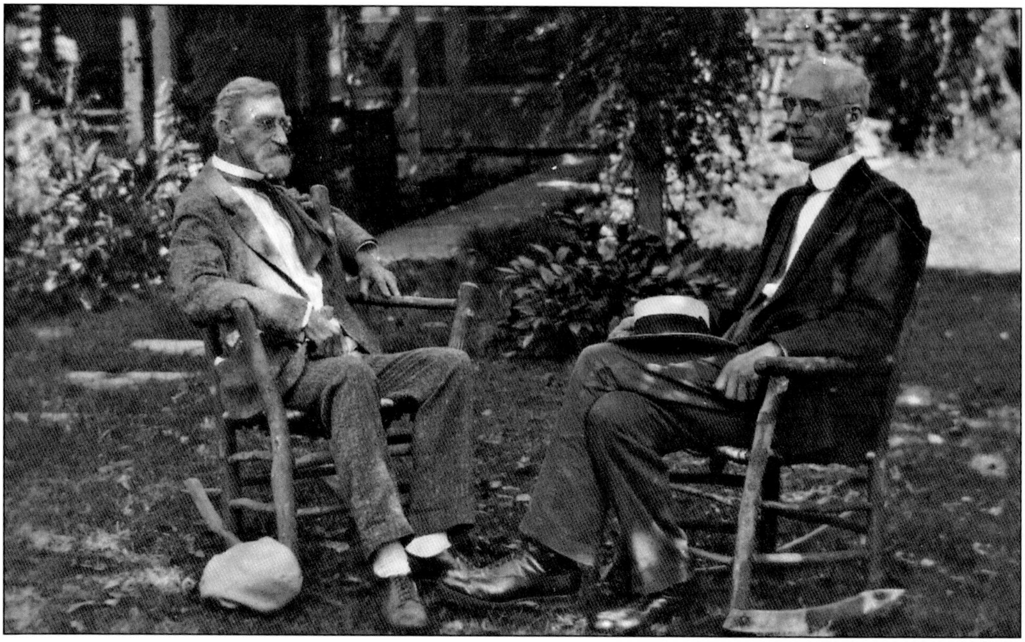

T. C. Steele (left) and Marcus Dickey sit in the garden at Steele's home. Both men had lived in Indianapolis but chose the rural charms of Brown County. The delicate, softly colored landscapes of T. C. Steele reflect the land surrounding him visible from the abandoned farmhouse he bought in 1907 and turned into the home where he and his wife, Selma, would remain for the rest of their lives. (Lilly Library.)

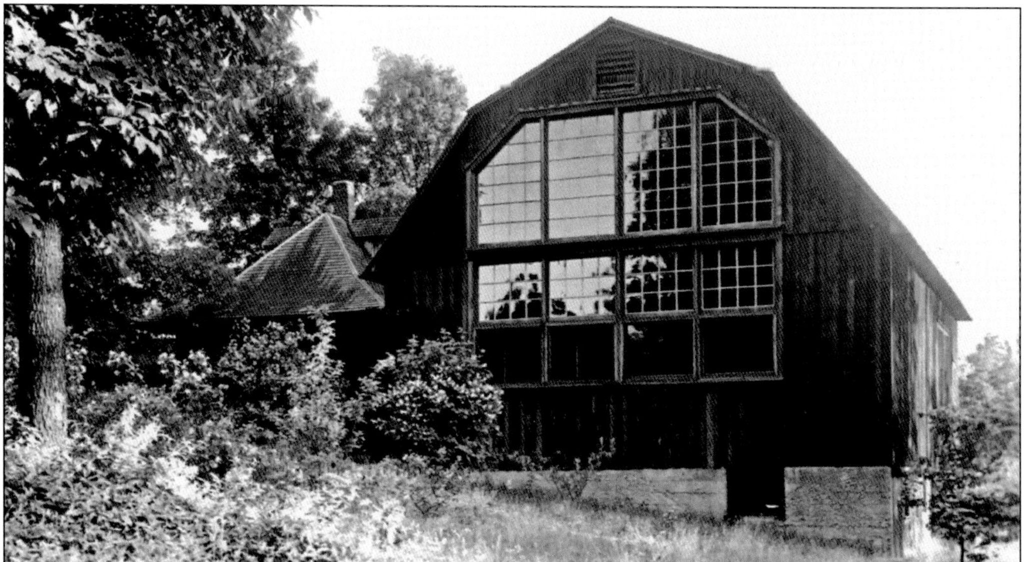

T. C. and Selma were entranced by the views that stretched for 15 to 20 miles from their home, and even Selma, a successful businesswoman from Indianapolis, agreed to spend time there. They originally thought of their place in Brown County as a seasonal home but soon made it their full-time residence. This photograph shows Steele's studio at the House of the Singing Winds, now a historical site. Selma remained at the home and is buried there. (Brown County Historical Society.)

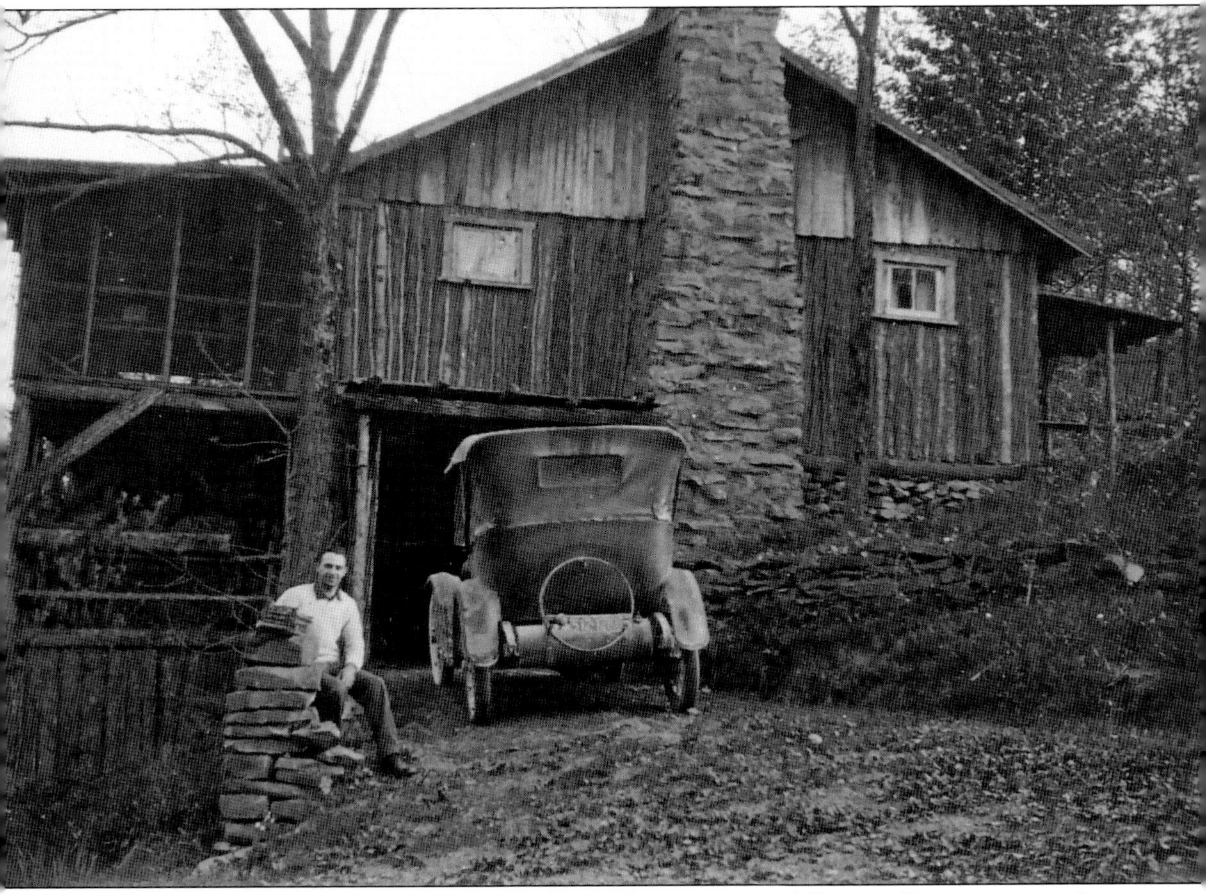

Both Frank and Art Humpal, originally from Chicago, painted Brown County scenes. In this 1934 photograph, one of the brothers sits in front of a Humpal cottage. (Brown County Historical Society.)

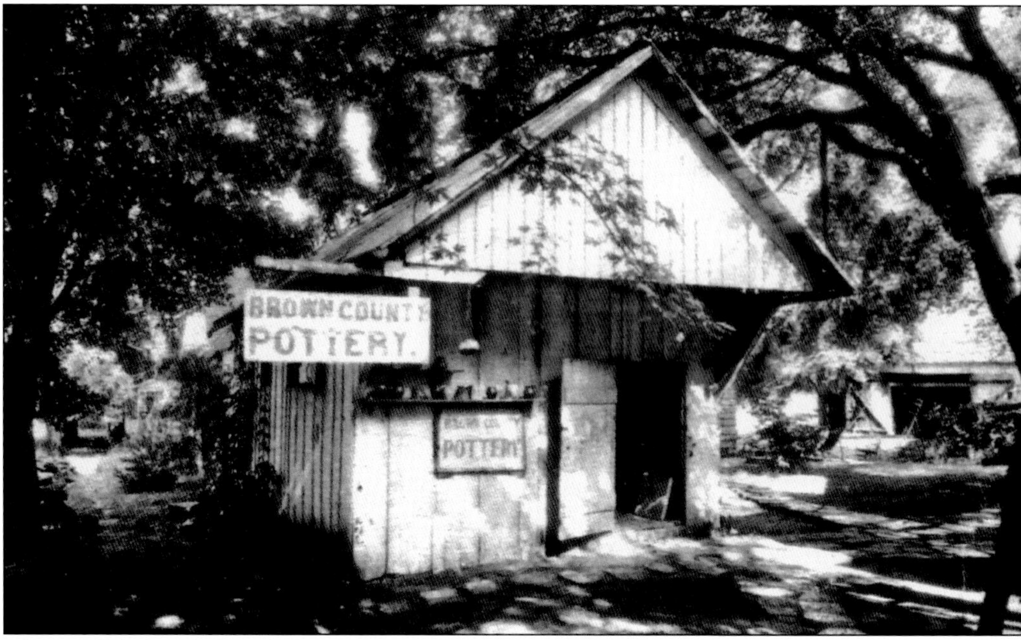

The Griffith family founded Brown County Pottery Works in the early 1930s with potter Claude Graham. Brown County Pottery Works pieces featured decorative motifs inspired by the local landscape. (Brown County Historical Society.)

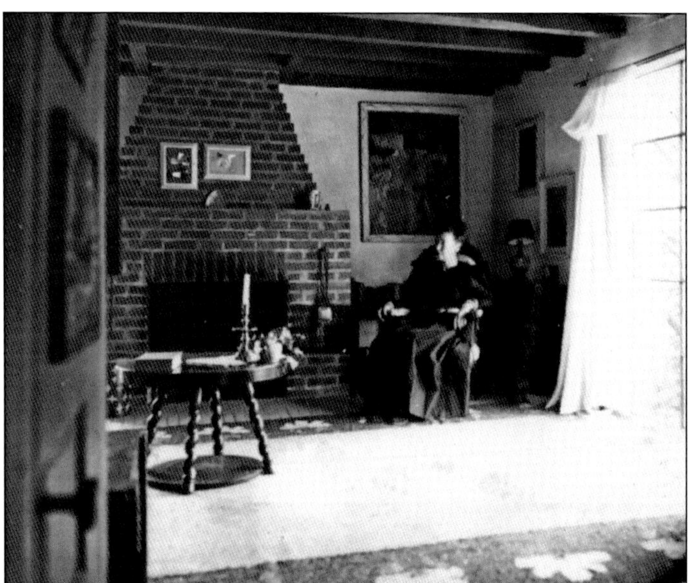

According to Brown County resident Henry Swain, it was an honor to be invited to the home of Onya LaTour, a patron of the arts, atop "a hill overlooking the Salt Creek valley at the north entrance of Brown County State Park. Near sunset guests would begin arriving. They would park their cars at the foot of the hill and walk the winding driveway up the hill. Statues lined the driveway and two tall cathedral candlesticks with their flickering tapers marked the approach to her patio." (Brown County Historical Society.)

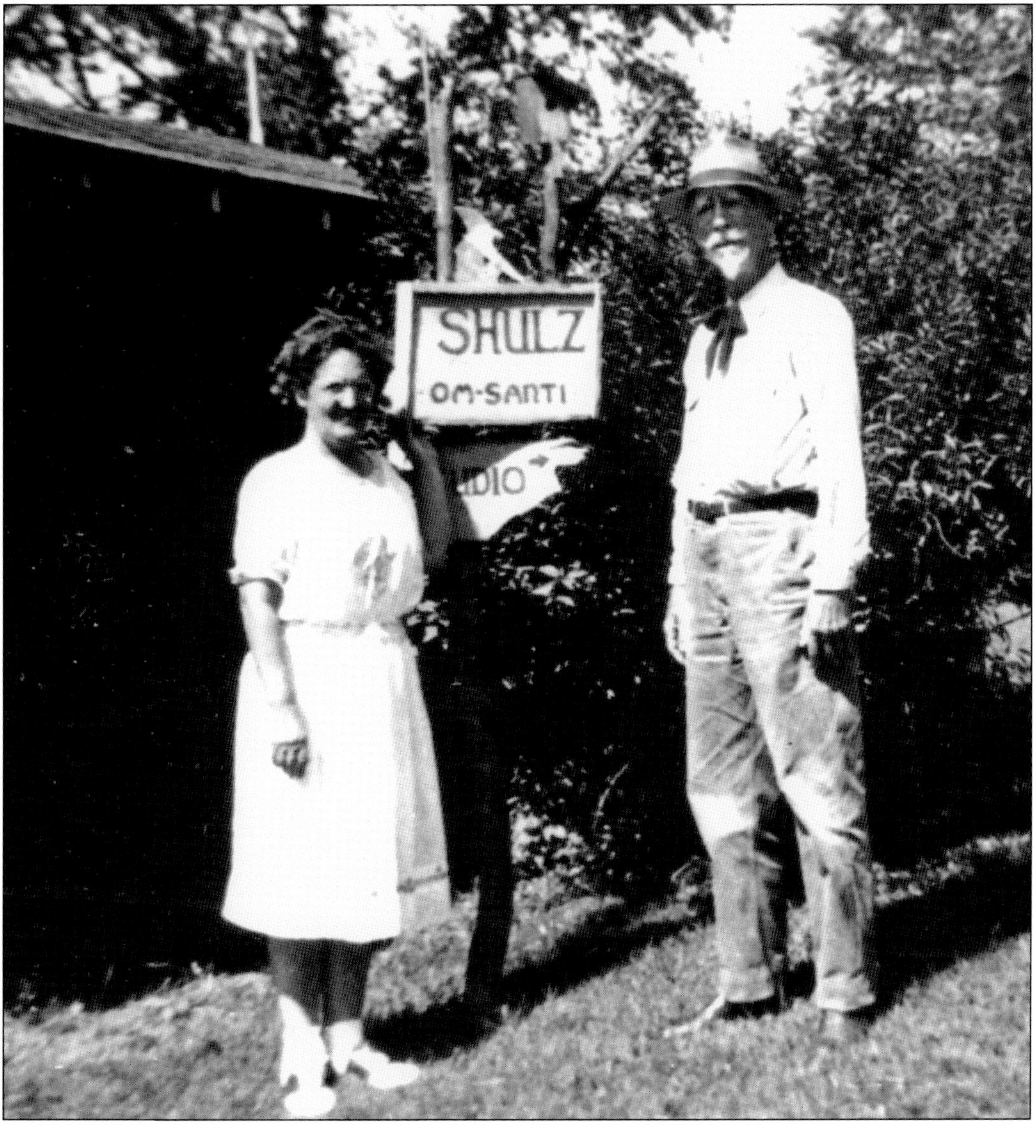

Adolph Shulz read about Brown County in the early 1900s and began visiting frequently. Finally, in 1917, the family moved permanently. He and Ada became charter members of the Brown County Art Association (though he would later leave Ada for Alberta, a young single mother the couple helped who is pictured here with Adolph). ,Adolph's work was exhibited in many places, including Nashville, Chicago, and Indianapolis. He also won many awards and prizes for his paintings. (Brown County Historical Society.)

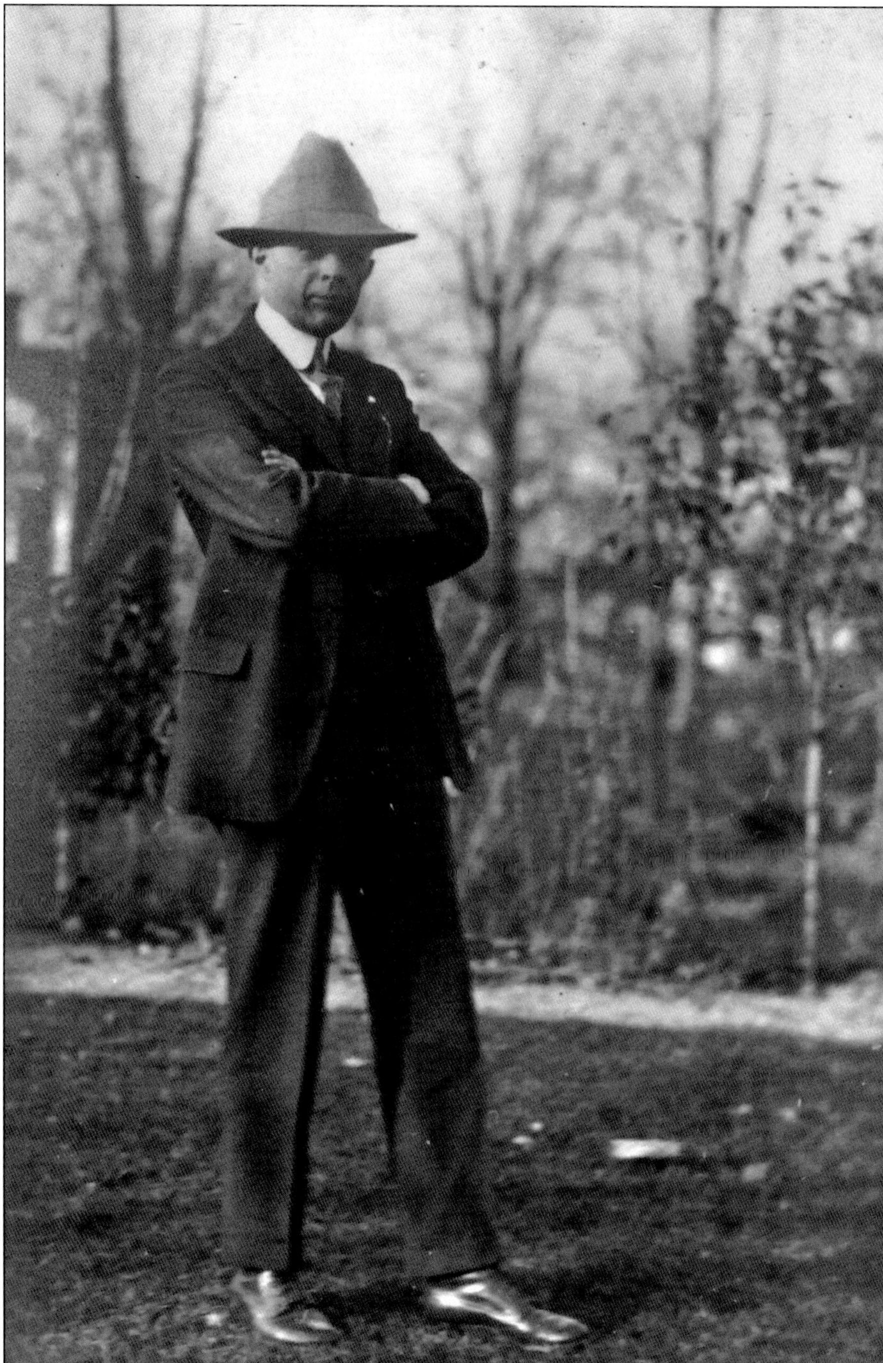

This is Frank Hohenberger, the famed photographer who captured early 20th-century Brown County in his compelling black-and-white photographs. Born in Ohio and raised by an uncle after being orphaned, Hohenberger worked in Indianapolis but migrated to Brown County after seeing photographs that showcased its rural beauty. He lived here until his death in 1962. He was often photographed wearing hats. (Brown County Historical Society.)

Five

Small Towns and Country Life

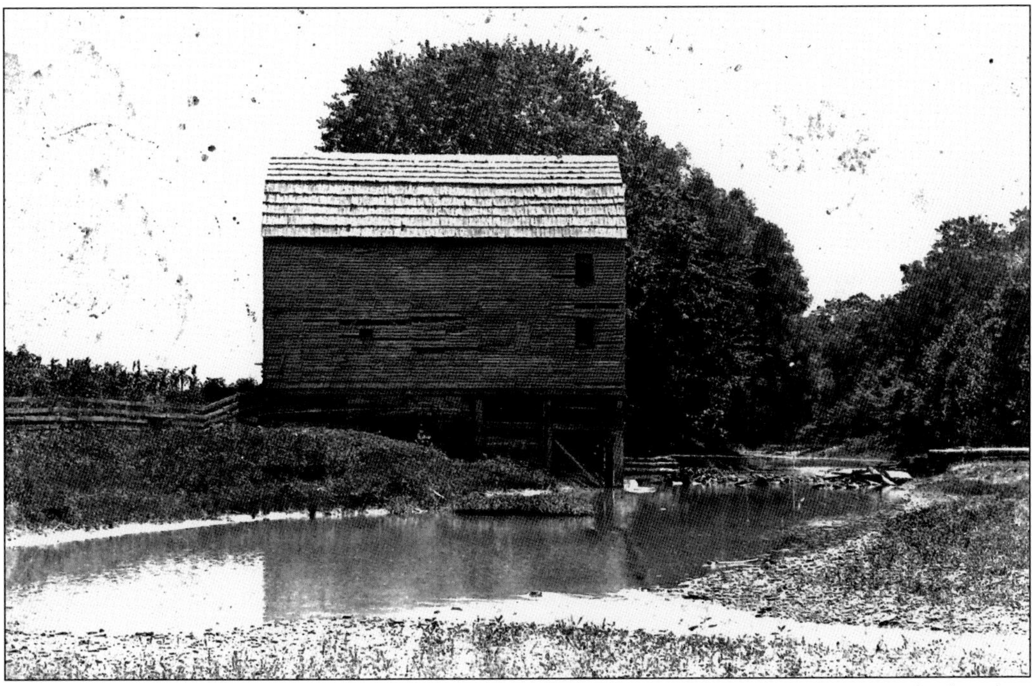

At one time, there were many mills in Brown County. The last one, at Stone Head, closed in 1920. According to Ray Mathis in his 1936 book *A Brown County History*, the first one was built on Salt Creek around 1827. Mills were plentiful as the power of water turned wheels that ground grain into flour and meal and timber into lumber. Traveling to the mill was a treat for farm folk, as it gave them a break from their hard work and provided an opportunity to visit with others at the mill. The mill shown here is probably the Petro mill. (Brown County Historical Society.)

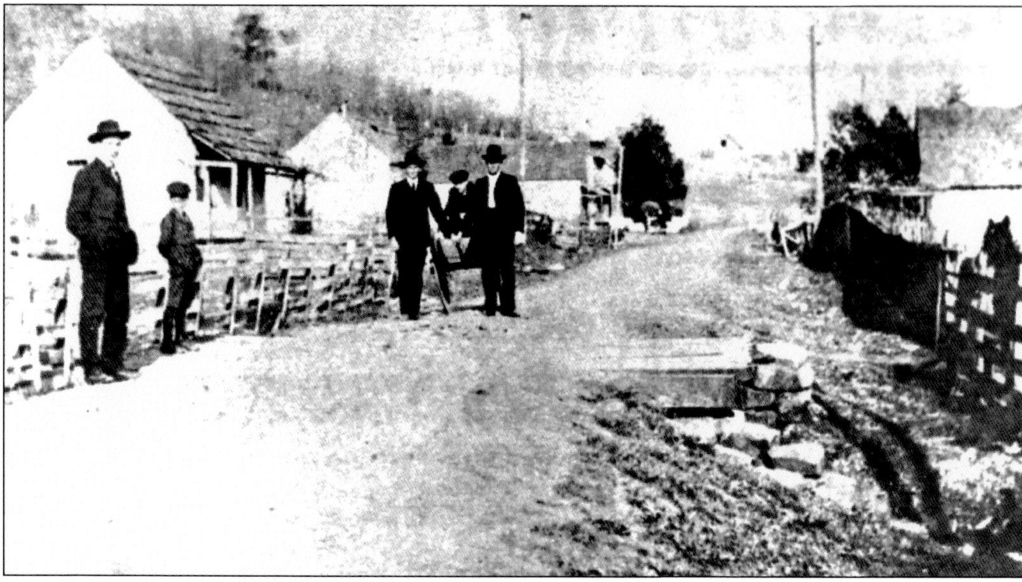

Otto Ping took this 1900 photograph of Pike's Peak, where at one time he ran a canning factory. Ping bought his first camera—a Monarch available through the mail from Sears and Roebuck—in 1900 at the age of 17. Though he earned money selling his photographs for $1 a piece, which included developing, printing, and delivery, he never was as successful as Frank Hohenberger. But Ping's photographs show what Brown County was like a century ago. In the left foreground are George Foreman and Lon Clark. (Brown County Historical Society.)

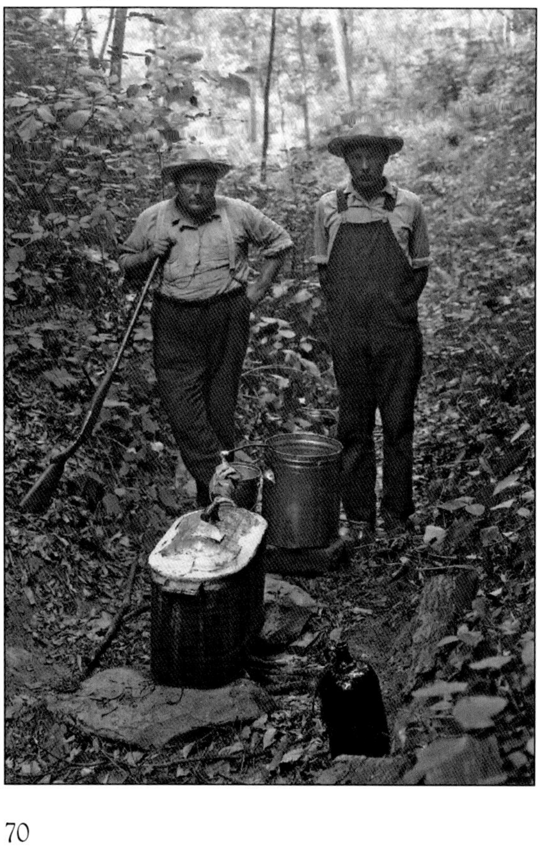

Stills were definitely part of country life in Brown County. This one is a captured still in the Weed Patch settlement, now part of the Brown County State Park. Oliver Neal, the sheriff of Brown County, is shown in this 1926 photograph. (Lilly Library, photograph by Frank Hohenberger.)

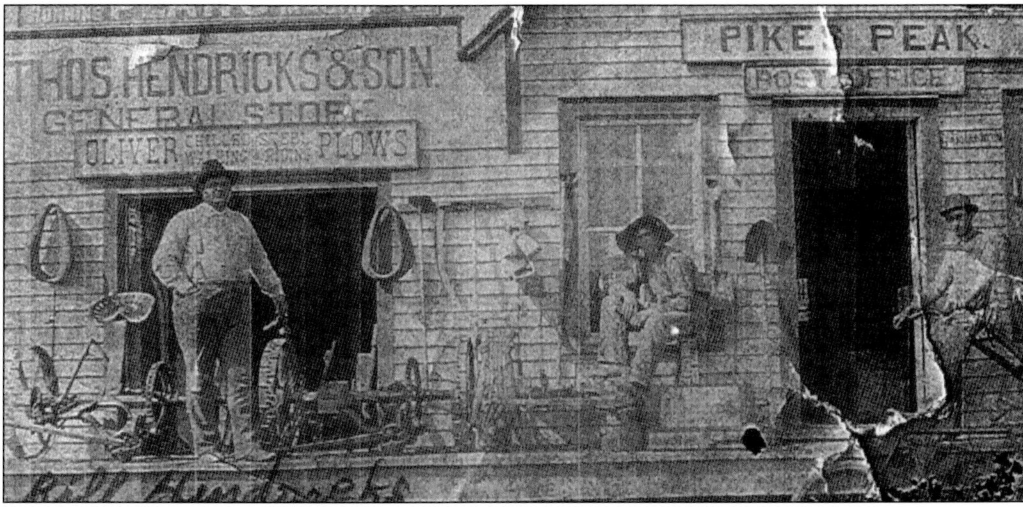

This is a Pike's Peak store in the 1800s. Now Crouch's Market is the only store left in Pike's Peak. It is a genuine country store selling food, clothing, plumbing parts, hunting licenses, gasoline, firewood, and electrical supplies. Owned by Harry and Norma Crouch, the couple has been in business for over 40 years. According to Norma, they are the fourth store in Pike's Peak. The store, formerly her husband's family garage, has grown over the years. (Brown County Historical Society.)

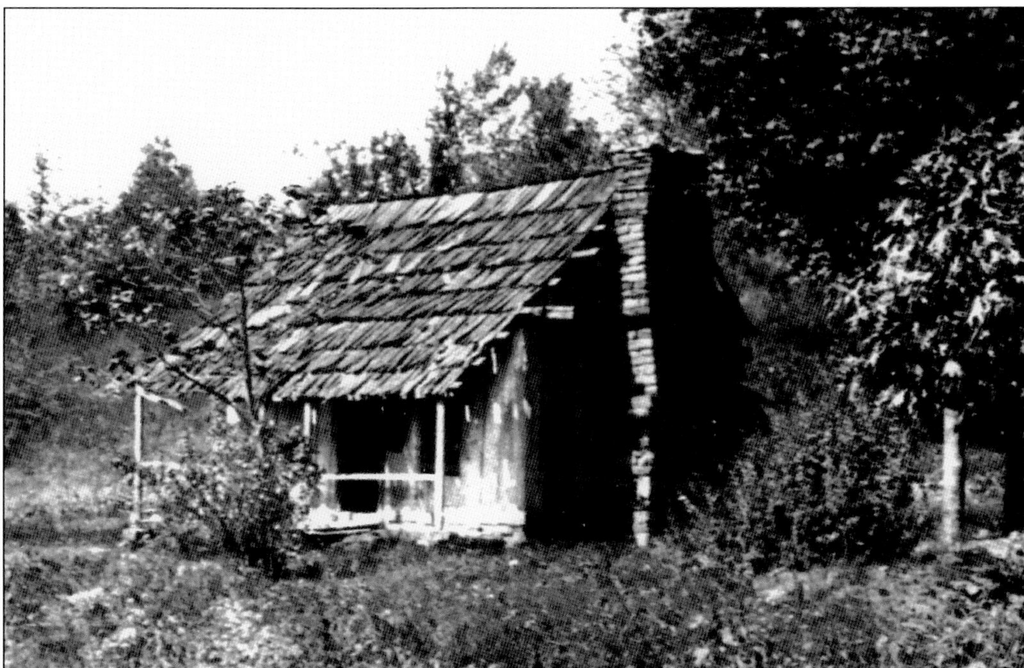

Life for many in Brown County was one of hard work and isolation, as evidenced by this small cabin where someone lived. According to Webb Waldrun, in his 1933 article on Frank Hohenberger, when the photographer first set out in search of the characters he had seen in photographs of Brown County with his camera and tripod, one native asked, "Who's that furriner?" The hardware dealer replied, "He's makin' a map uv the forterficashuns 'round here for the Kaiser." This is a classic Hohenberger photograph taken near Helmsburg. (Brown County Historical Society.)

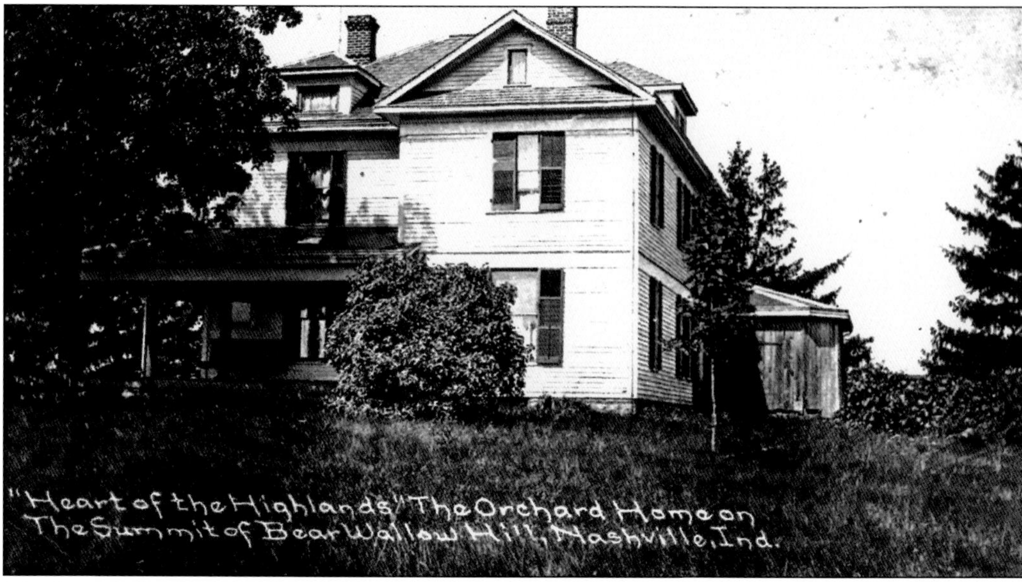

The home of Marcus Dickey, former secretary to famed Hoosier author James Whitcomb Riley, on Bear Wallow caused a number of rumors according to Joanne Nesbit writing for www.ourbrowncounty.com, "One of those was that Riley was going to make Bear Wallow his summer home. Actually, Riley never set foot on the property." Another rumor was that "James Whitcomb Riley is talkin' o' buildin' a sanitarium for incurable writers in the Bear Waller neighborhood an' it wuz th' all absorbin' topic et th' pust offis yisterday." (Brown County Historical Society.)

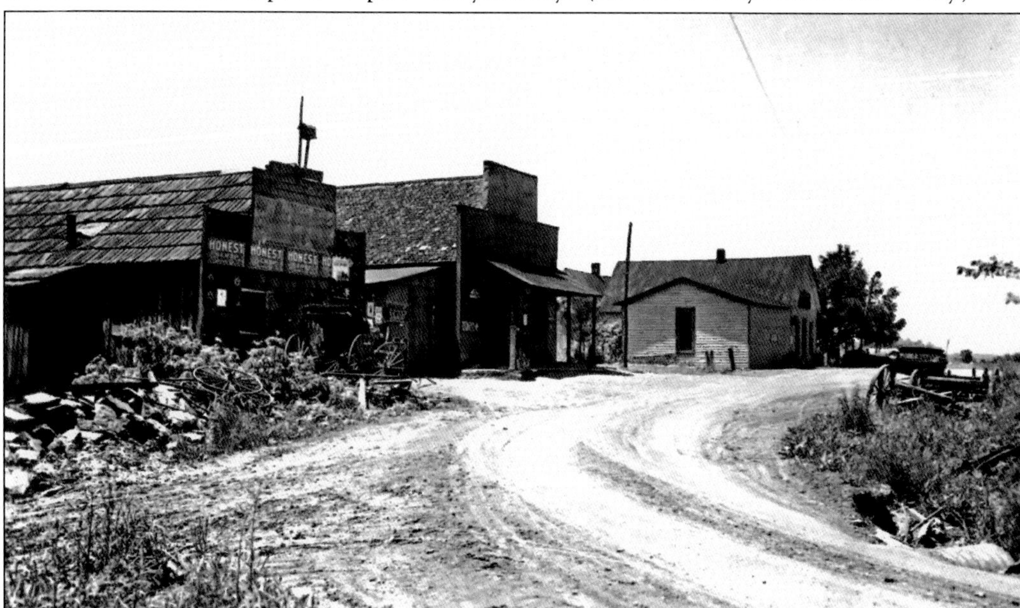

Brown County was so rural that well into the 1900s five out of six persons received their mail by rural delivery. "Our carriers total up better than 200 miles a day, most of it on back roads," recalled Henry Swain Jr. in *Brown County Remembers*. Swain notes that one mail carrier said, "You go up some of these hollows just as far as you can stick a knife and there is a house and a mailbox." (Brown County Historical Society.)

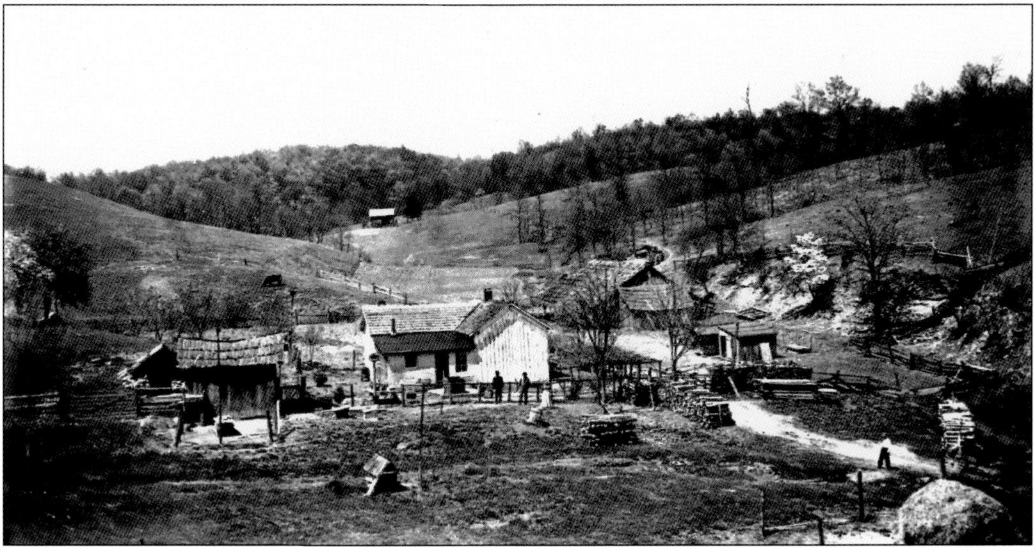

Selmeler Hill is pictured. Even in the early 1900s, actual cash money was nearly nonexistent for some. According to Helen Ayers, "Bartering for goods was the norm." It is easy to see why money would have little value compared to trading goods like vegetables, meat, and flour as well as other items for people living in such remote areas. (Brown County Historical Society.)

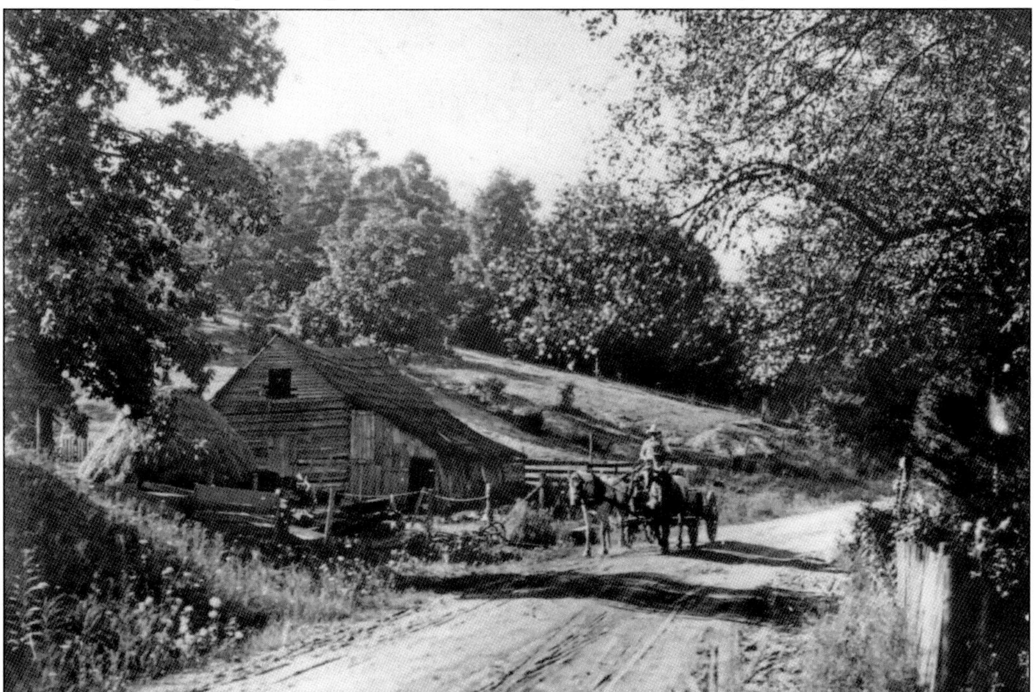

When Frank Hohenberger snapped this photograph near Helmsburg, parts of Brown County seemed more like the 1800s than the 1920s and 1930s. Dorothea Webb Cline said in *Brown County Remembers* that it often took too long for doctors to arrive on horseback, so women depended on midwives. She recalled, "Their fee was less than the doctors', sometimes being a donation of home-grown vegetables, meat or fruit." (Brown County Historical Society.)

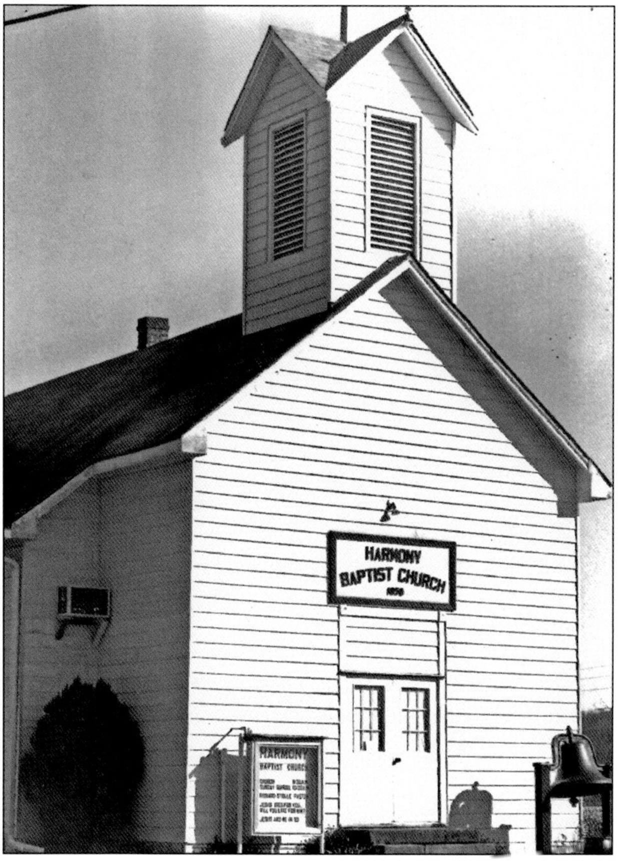

The Harmony Baptist Church, built in 1850, is typical of the simple white country churches found in Brown County tucked away on winding country roads. It is not unusual to be driving down a country road and come across a church that dates back to the 19th century. (Brown County Historical Society.)

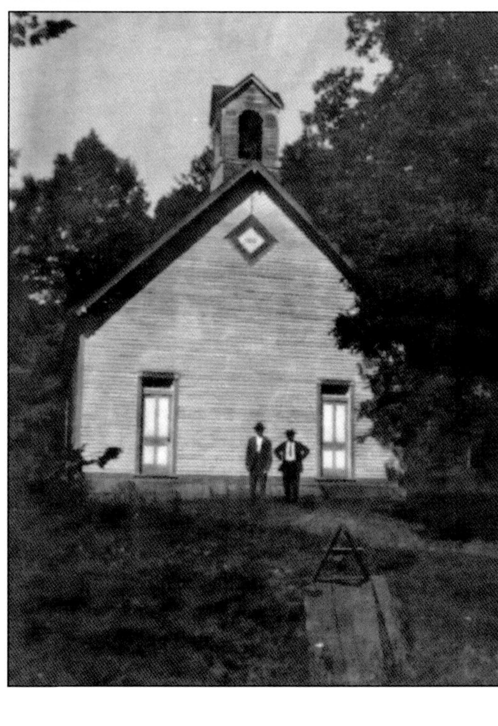

Here is the North Salem Methodist Church. Brown County has over 50 churches, including many dating from the late 1800s. According to Ray Mathis, early settlers of the area were mostly Methodist and Baptist. (Brown County Historical Society.)

This is a Methodist Episcopal church. In 1881, there were 20 doctors in the county and 37 churches, including Methodist, United Brethren, Baptist, Christian, Presbyterian, and New Light in Brown County. (Brown County Historical Society.)

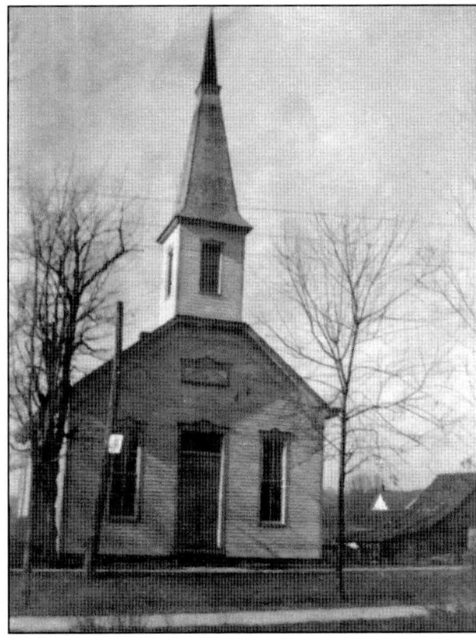

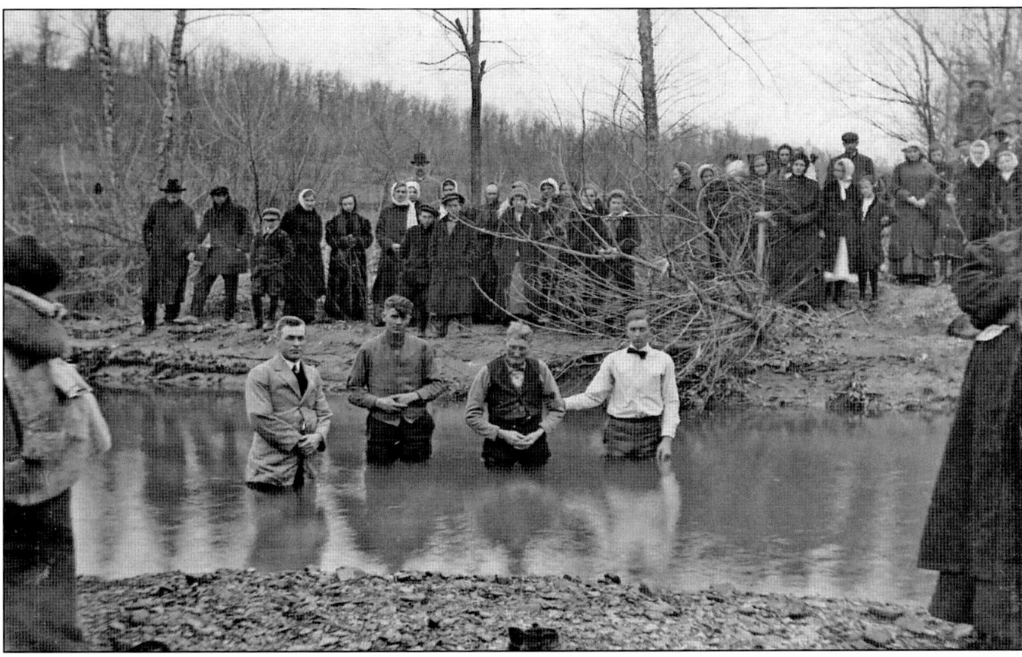

In a photograph taken by Frank Hohenberger, note that the people standing on the river bank near New Bellesville at the Lon Clark Bridge are bundled up for the cold on this March day in 1915. Pictured here are from left to right are (in water) Reverend Merrill, Lewis J. Deaver, Aquilla Deaver, and Borcil Deaver; to the far left front is Lucretia Deaver; those standing on the bank include Henry Seitz, Walter Henderson, Clarence Williams, Mae Stewart Clark, Mamie Tipton, Nell Clark, Fern Moore, Dr. A. J. Ralphy, Deaver Wilson, Stella Clark, Fred Lemley, Sara Ann (Mrs. Coon) Butler, Earnie Ping, Gillie Moore, Ima Moore, Bunell Deaver Hedrick, Dollie Hendricks, Ruey "Dude" Henderson, Matt Bradley, John Truex or Charlie Hovis, Viola Truex, Thelma Williams, Minnie Clark Hurley, and Fern Helms, Staussie Clark, and Olive Tipton. (Brown County Historical Society.)

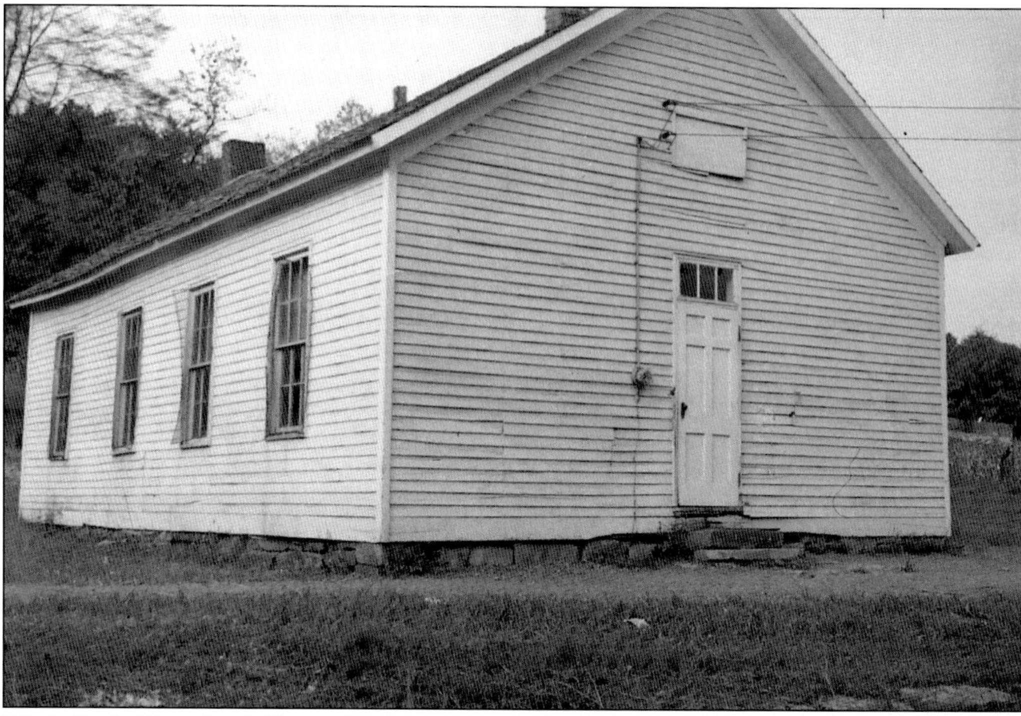

Pike's Peak Church of Christ, built in 1891, still stands at the edge of Pike's Peak, a small community tucked away on Bellesville Pike 1 mile east of Stone Head. According to the church's Web site, Pike's Peak Church of Christ has been in existence since the 1850s. Pike's Peak still has a general store, Crouch's Market, making it a community that retains its rural historic heritage. (Brown County Historical Society.)

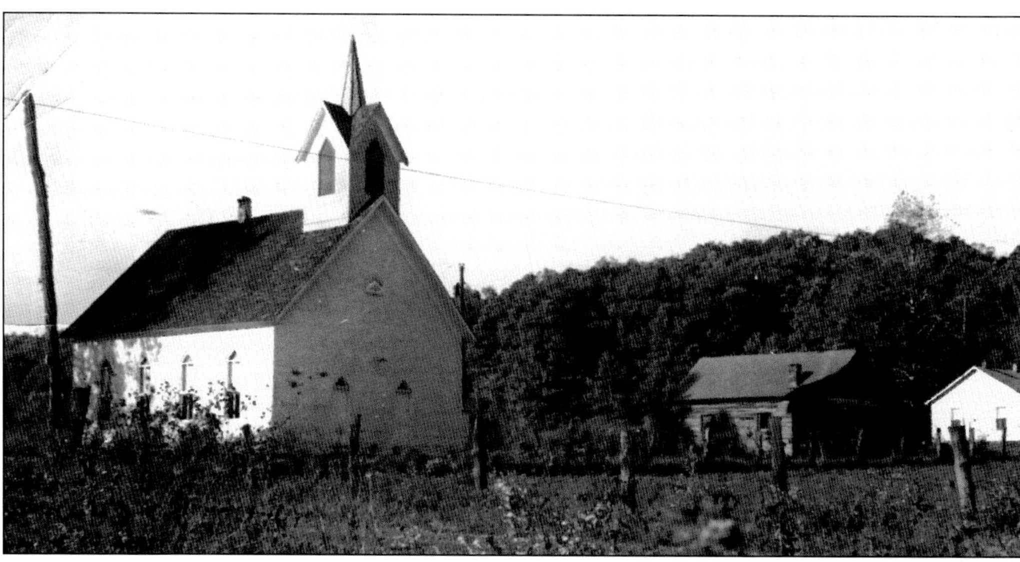

The Christianburg United Methodist Church still stands along a country road at the southern end of Brown County. According to notes, at the time this photograph was taken the home in the background was owned by William and Martha Wordsworth. (Brown County Historical Society.)

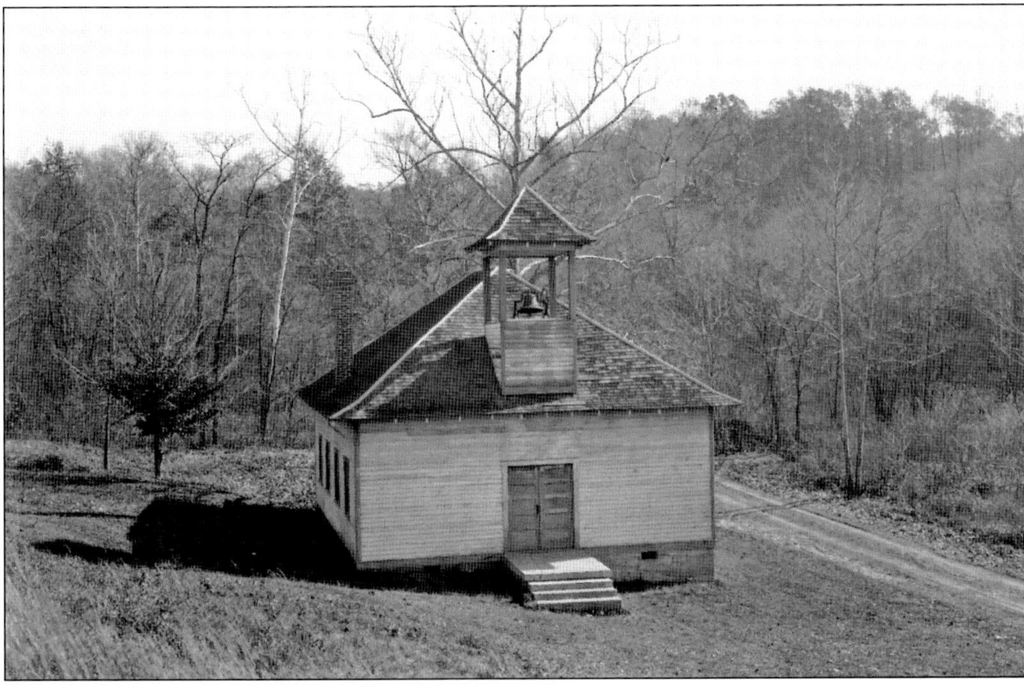

Located on Bear Creek Road, this 1927 photograph shows one of many of Brown County's country churches, several of which are still standing and continue to be used for worship. Religion is an important part of life in Brown County communities. Carol Lucas Cummins, who went to church in Elkinsville, remembers that her mother and grandmother were "prayer warriors." She recalls, "When someone was really sick, they would go to their home and pray and pray, sometimes for what seemed like days." (Brown County Historical Society.)

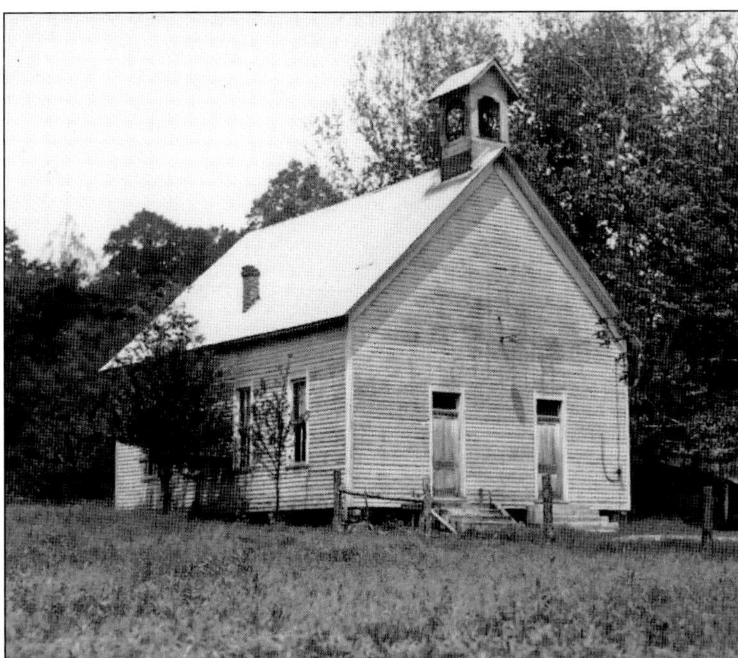

The Cottonwood Christian Church on Lick Creek Road, with its gable front, was built in 1892. One of the reasons that Brown County entranced many visitors was that its rural charm continued on throughout a good part of the 20th century. (Brown County Historical Society.)

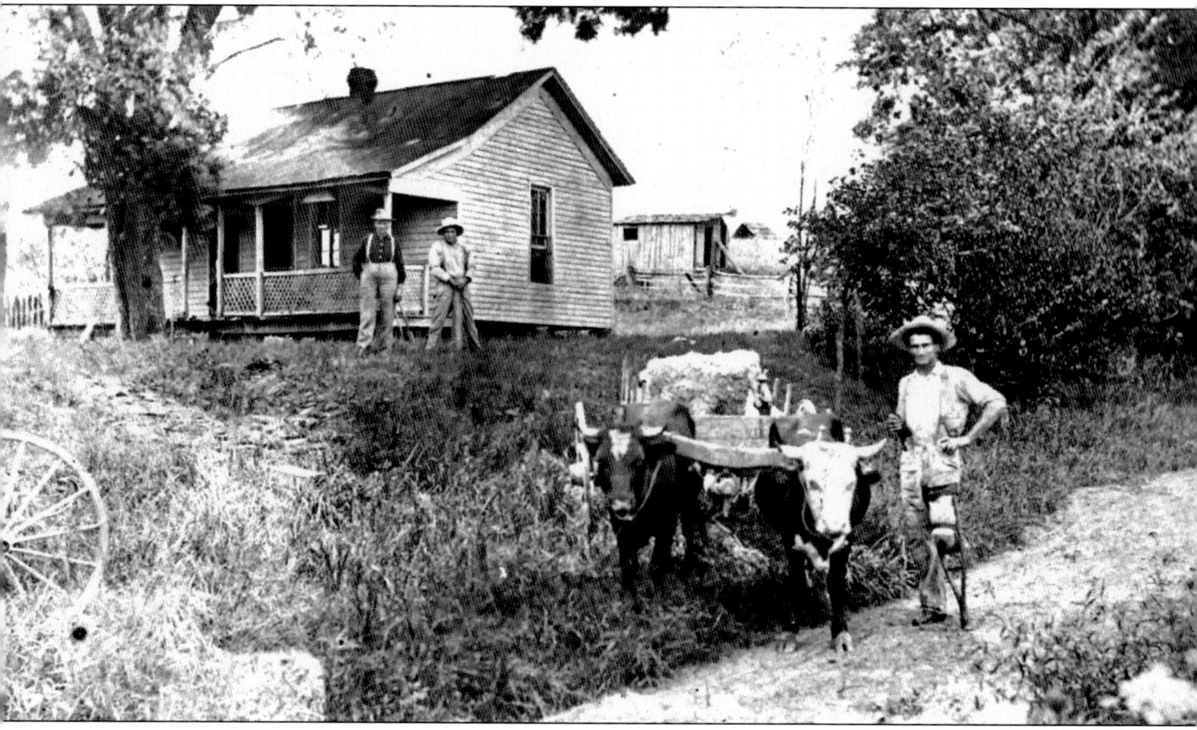

A 1913 photograph shows the A. E. Banson Scott residence. According to the Brown County Historical Society, "In 1900, villages were still the centers of Brown County life. Travel by horseback, wagon, or carriage was exceedingly limited due to deeply rutted, rocky roads. There were people in remote areas who never made a trip to Nashville their entire lives. Many a family's only contact with the outside world was the huckster's weekly visit with his horse and wagon. As a result the pioneer way of life continued long after other counties had adopted a new pattern of living." (Brown County Historical Society.)

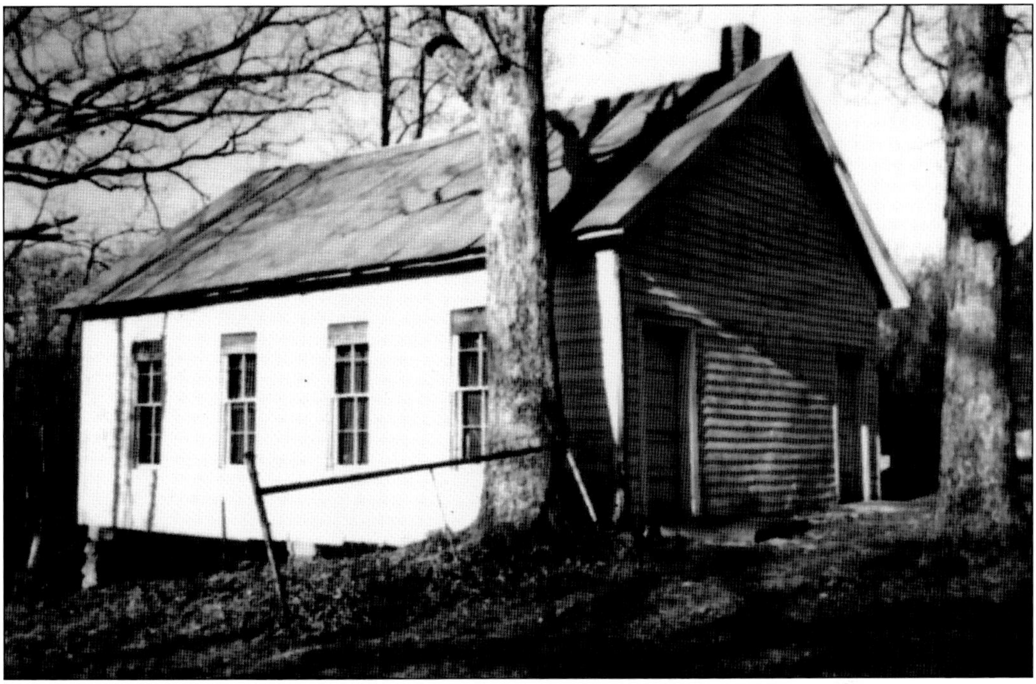

Country schools like Deckard School, built in 1890, were often heated with potbellied stoves and had only one room. Though he taught at the Story School and not this one, when Gladys Whitaker's father, A. J. Ralphy, started teaching in 1871 at age 16, he was paid $1 per pupil per school term. That might be one reason why he decided to become a doctor. (Brown County Historical Society.)

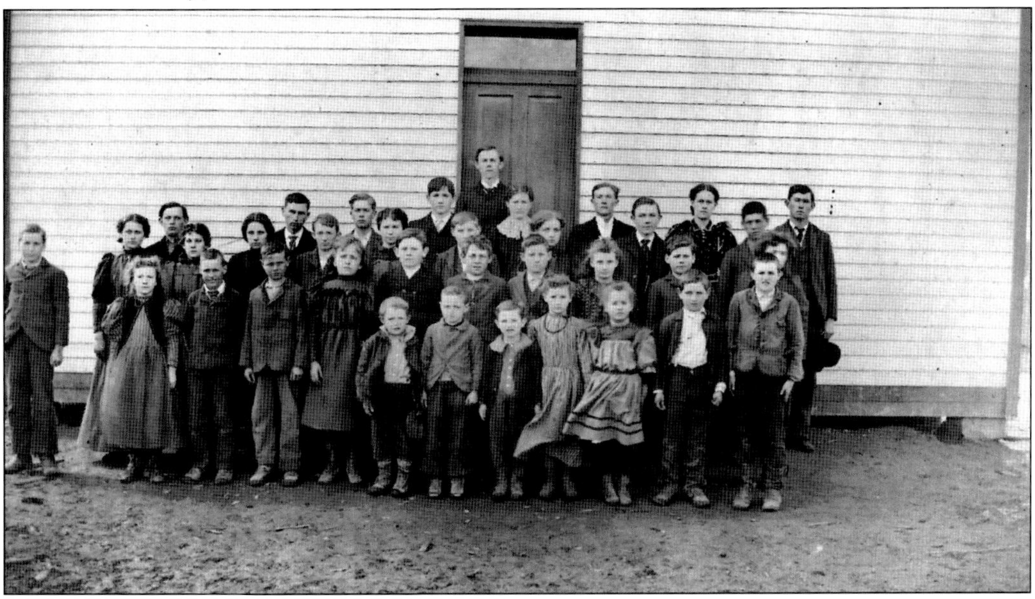

This 1985 photograph shows Greenwood School, located northeast of Bean Blossom. Students include (first row) Christopher Everling (age 6) and Hannah J. Everling (Castner, age 8); (second row) Maggie Everling (Taylor, age 6), and Linnie Everling (age 12); (third row) Lucinda Everling (Paulish, age 13) and William Paulish. (Brown County Historical Society.)

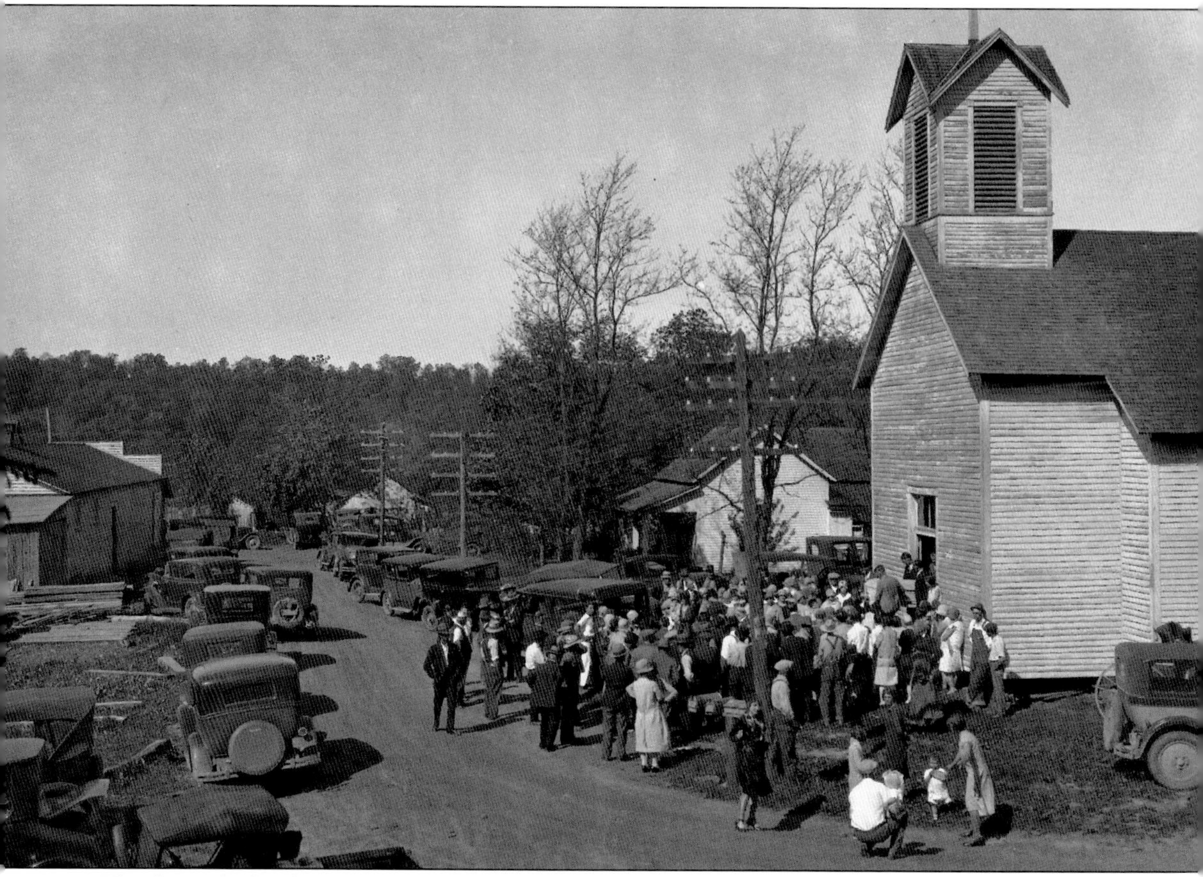
The funeral of Valentine Penrose in spring of 1930 drew many people and is representative of a community gathering in a time of grief in the small communities of rural Brown County.

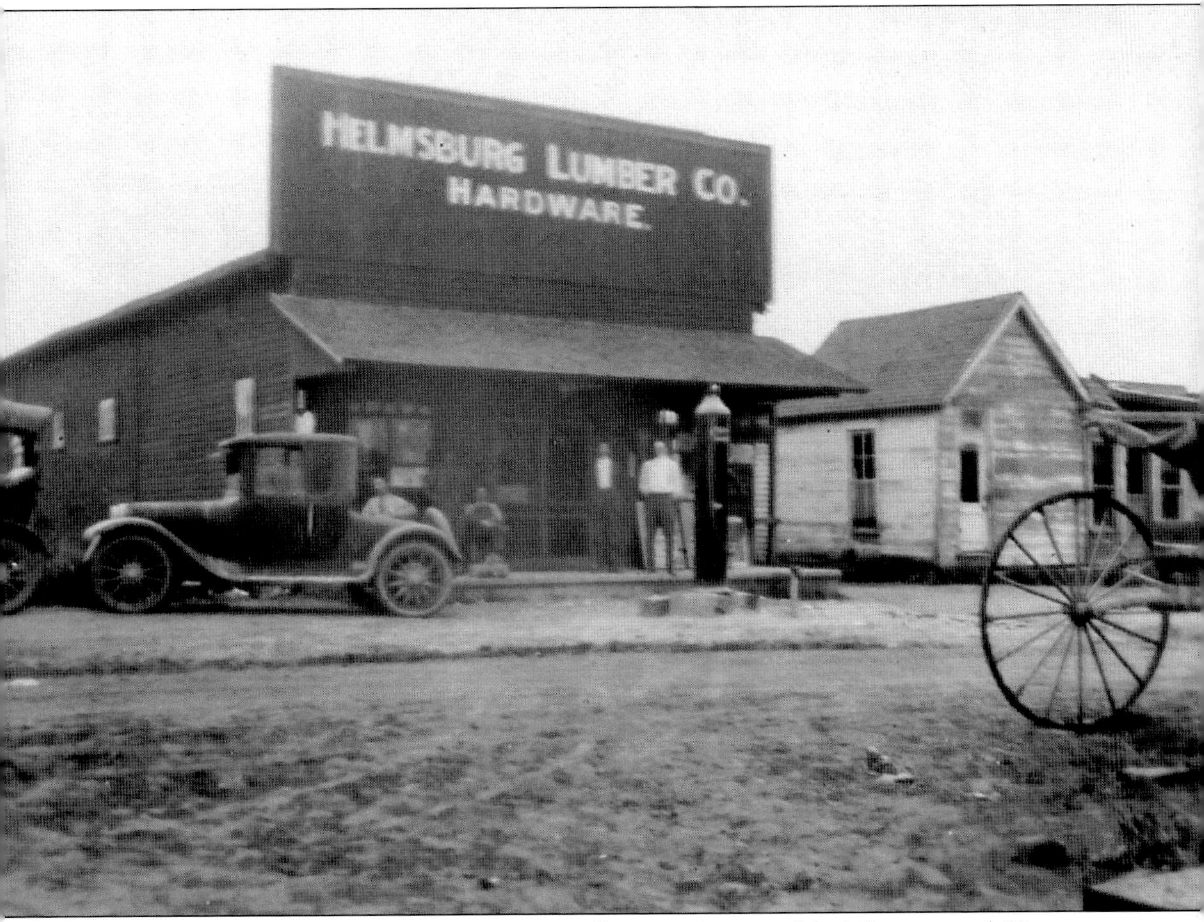

When automobiles came to Brown County, it really opened up people's ability to travel. "At some time during the early 1840s or 1850s a peddler who came from the east of south of Nashville traveled this road," recalls Chattie Wade Miller in *Brown County Remembers*. "His wagon was one of the old fashioned peddler's covered wagons, and of course, bumping over clay topped Brown County roads he drove a big strong team of horses. He made this trip every two or three months, carrying articles which were nonperishable." (Brown County Historical Society.)

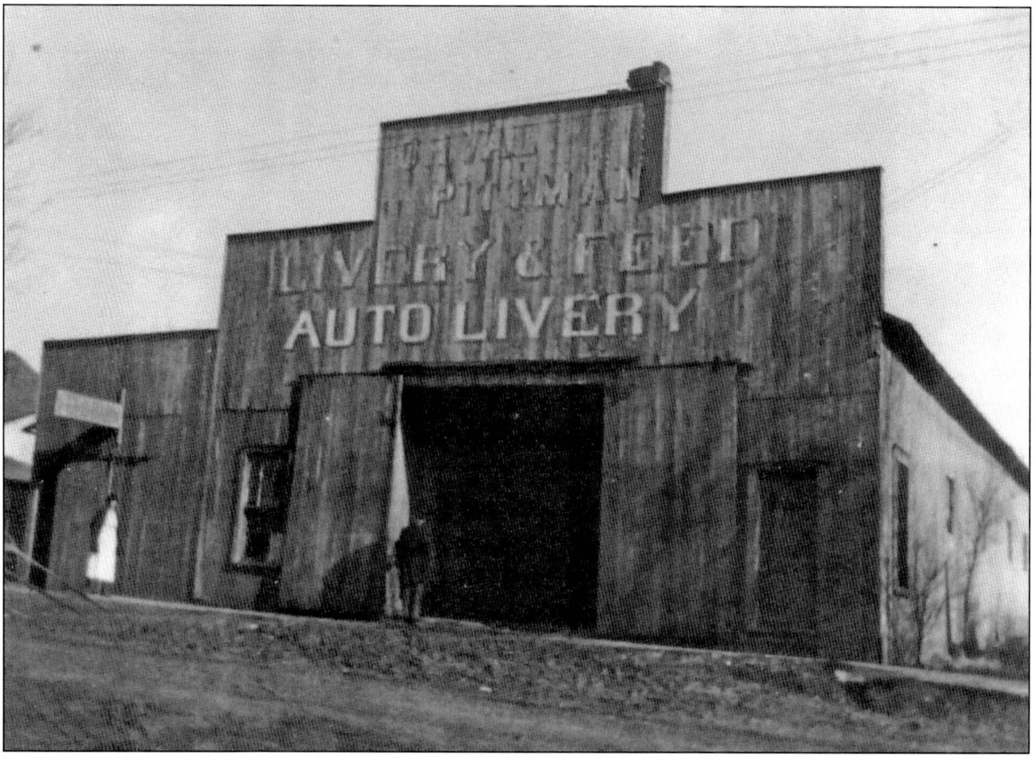

Susabel Bond Poling recalled in the book *Brown County Remembers* how her grandfather Joshua Bond bought a livery barn in Helmsburg, "My father worked with him there. Grandfather Joshua Bond became an undertaker in 1913 in Helmsburg. He used a horse-drawn hearse. After he moved the business to Nashville my father, Earl, took over the business with my brother Jack in 1937." (Brown County Historical Society.)

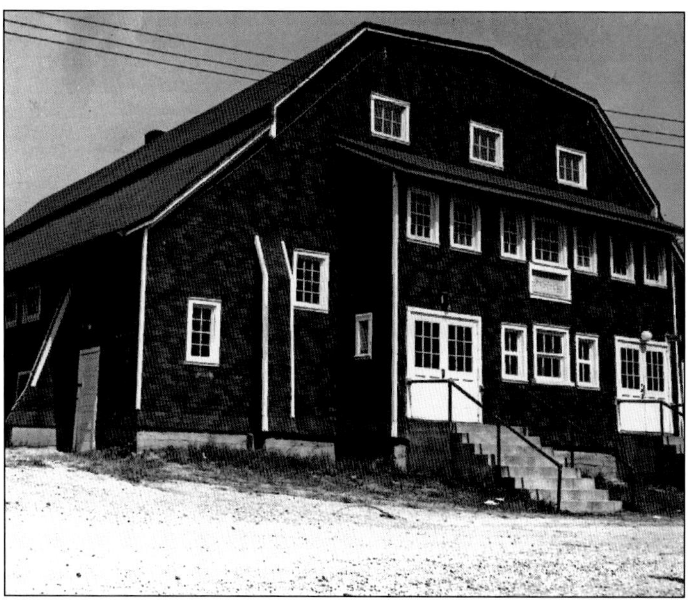

Chattie Wade Miller, a member of the first graduating class of Helmsburg High School (the gym is shown here) in 1915, recalls in *Brown County Remembers* that one evening while practicing the senior play, she and some friends walked to the old iron bridge over Bean Blossom Creek. They heard the sound of horses' hooves, a squeaking harness, and wagon wheels in the gravel. They stood back but no wagon appeared. "We had all heard it so distinctly," she stated, but there was no wagon. (Brown County Historical Society.)

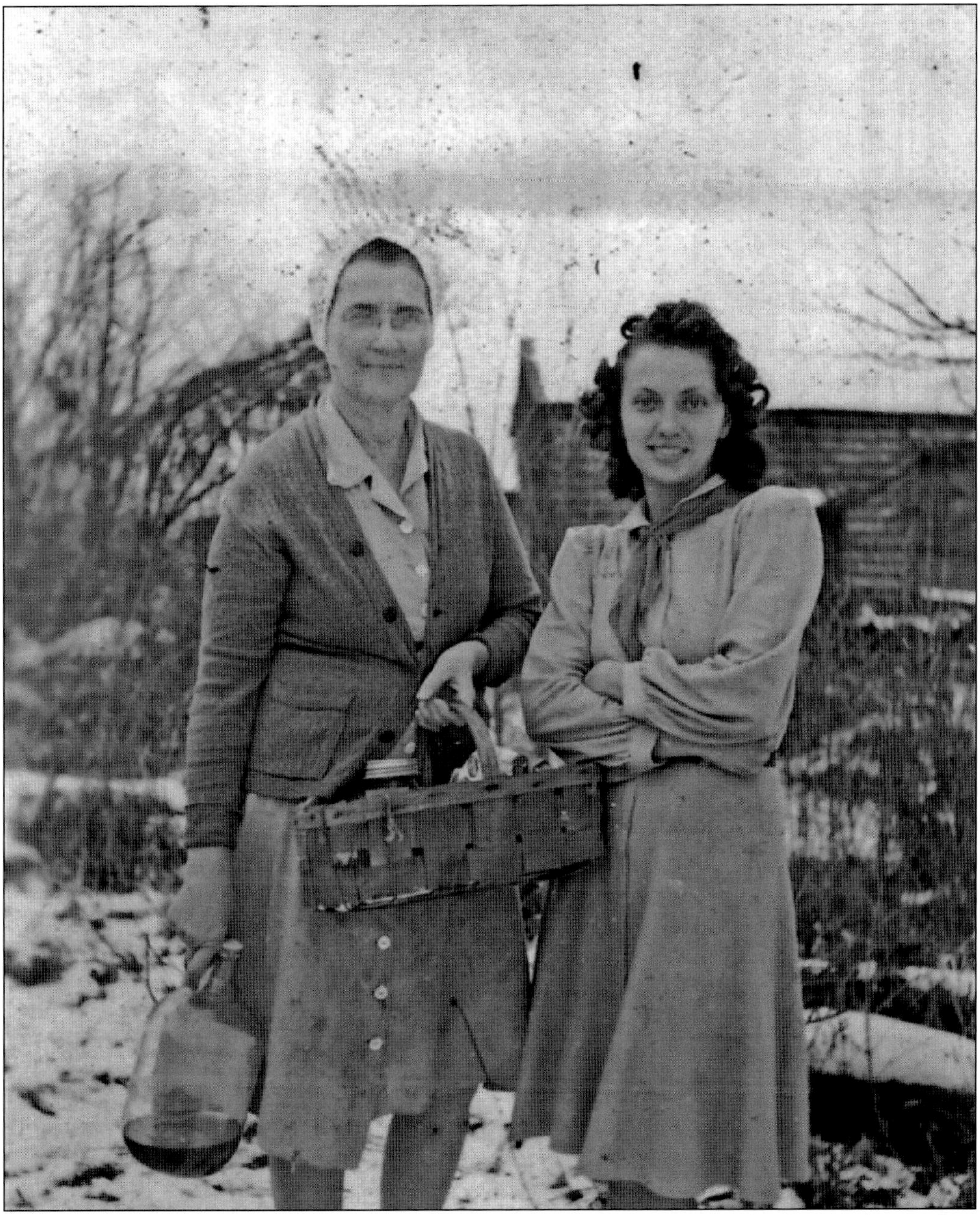

Exemplifying country life, Nellie Hendricks Wheeler Clark and her daughter-in-law Wilma Wheeler stand in front of the old log cabin where Nellie kept her chickens about 2 miles east of Stone Head on Grandview Road. Wilma lived between Stone Head and Story. (Sarah May.)

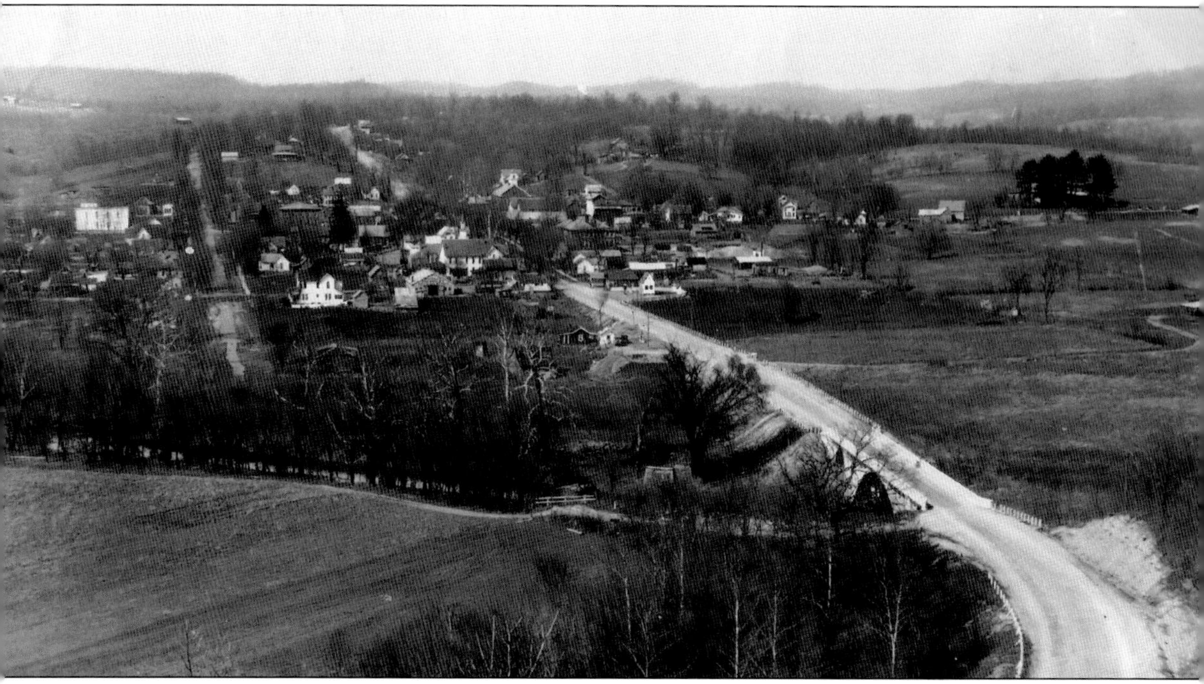

A dirt road leads into Nashville. Kin Hubbard, who created the character Abe Martin, stated in Fred C. Kelly's biography that the reason he chose Brown County as the setting for Martin's adventures was that Brown County was one of the most inaccessible places in the state. (Brown County Historical Society.)

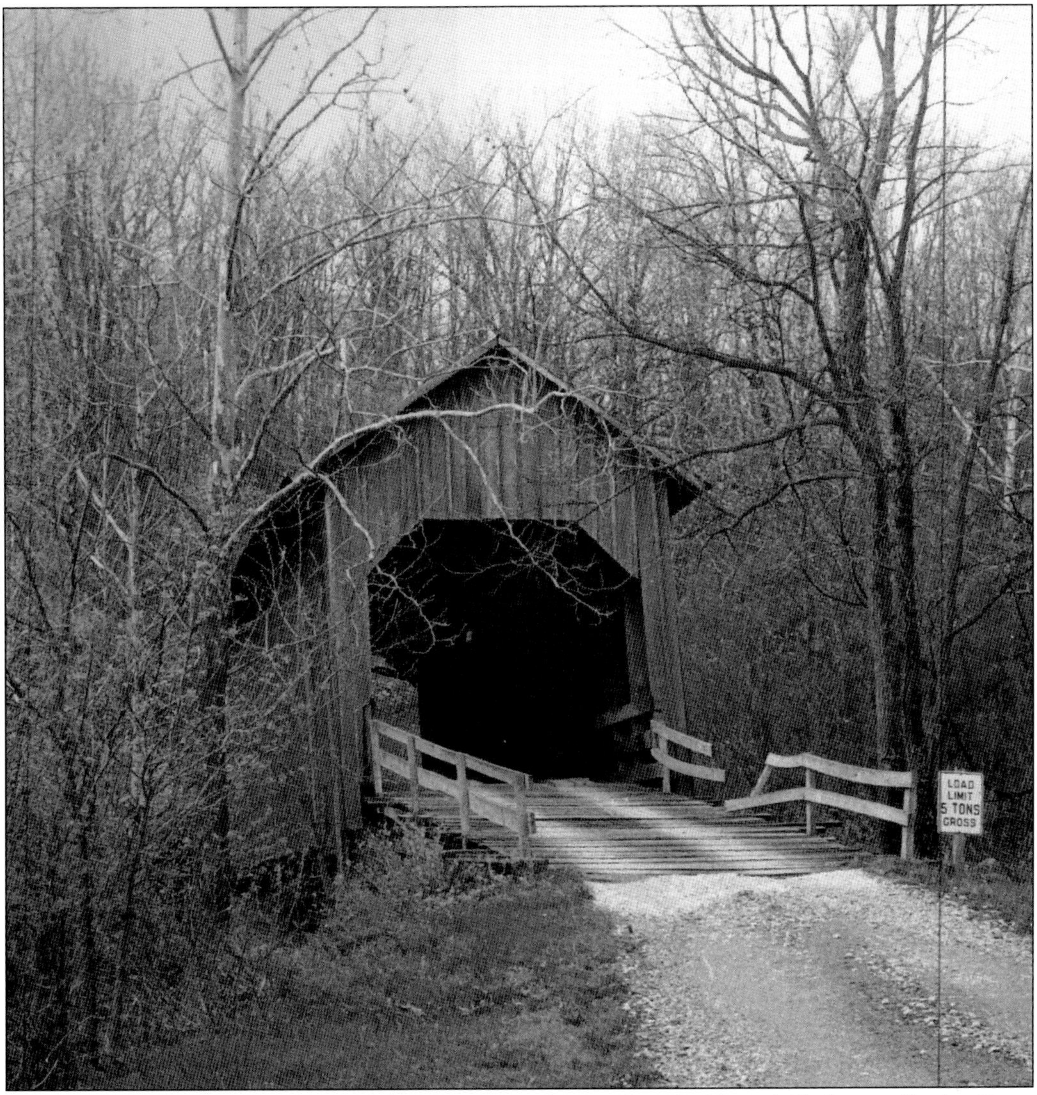

Located a half mile southwest of the junction of State Road 135 and Highway 45, the Bean Blossom Bridge was built in 1880 by Capt. Joseph Balsy at a cost of $1,200. Today the red-painted bridge, named a Rand McNalley Best of the Road attraction for 2003, crosses Bean Blossom Creek and is still open to traffic. (Brown County Historical Society.)

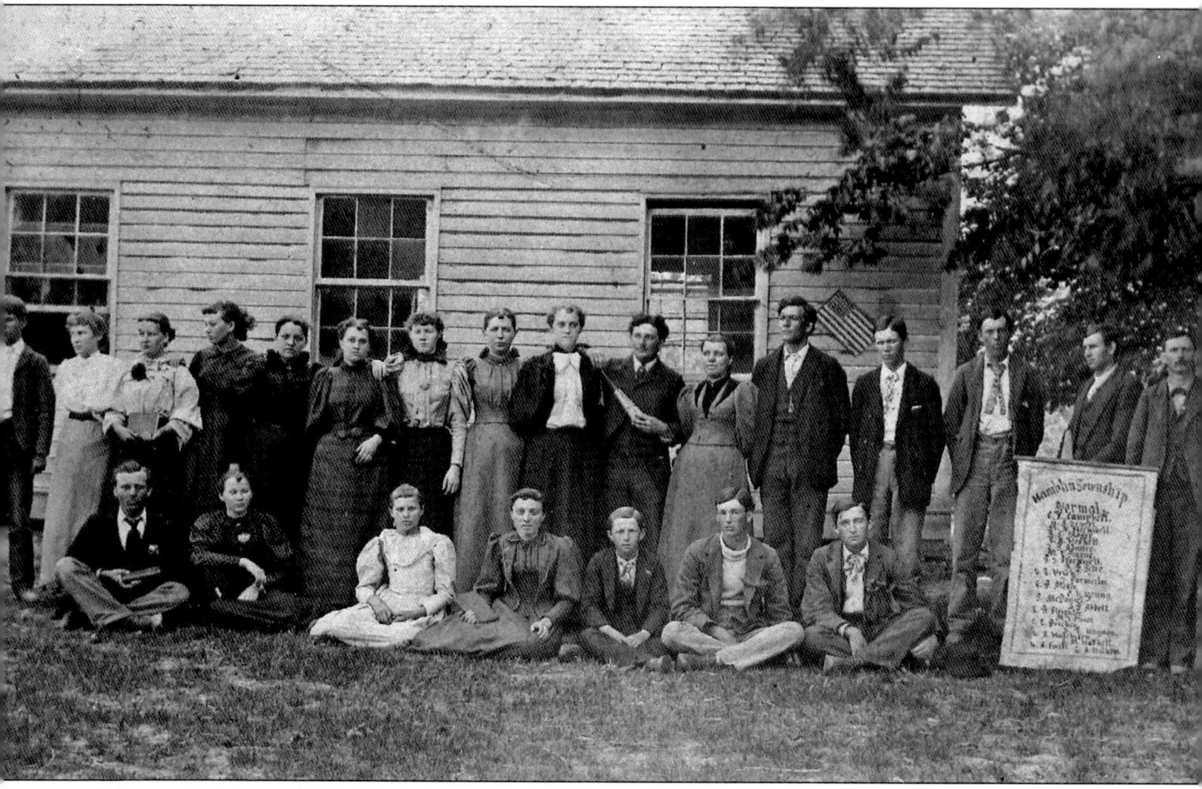

This is the Normal School in Hamblen Township. In the online Brown County history project, resident Jim Greedy recalled that in ways there were advantages to the old one-room schools. "You were sitting in the room with the first through fourth grade, so when you were in first grade you got to pick up on the things the fourth grade was learning," said Greedy, who became a Brown County social studies teacher. (Brown County Historical Society.)

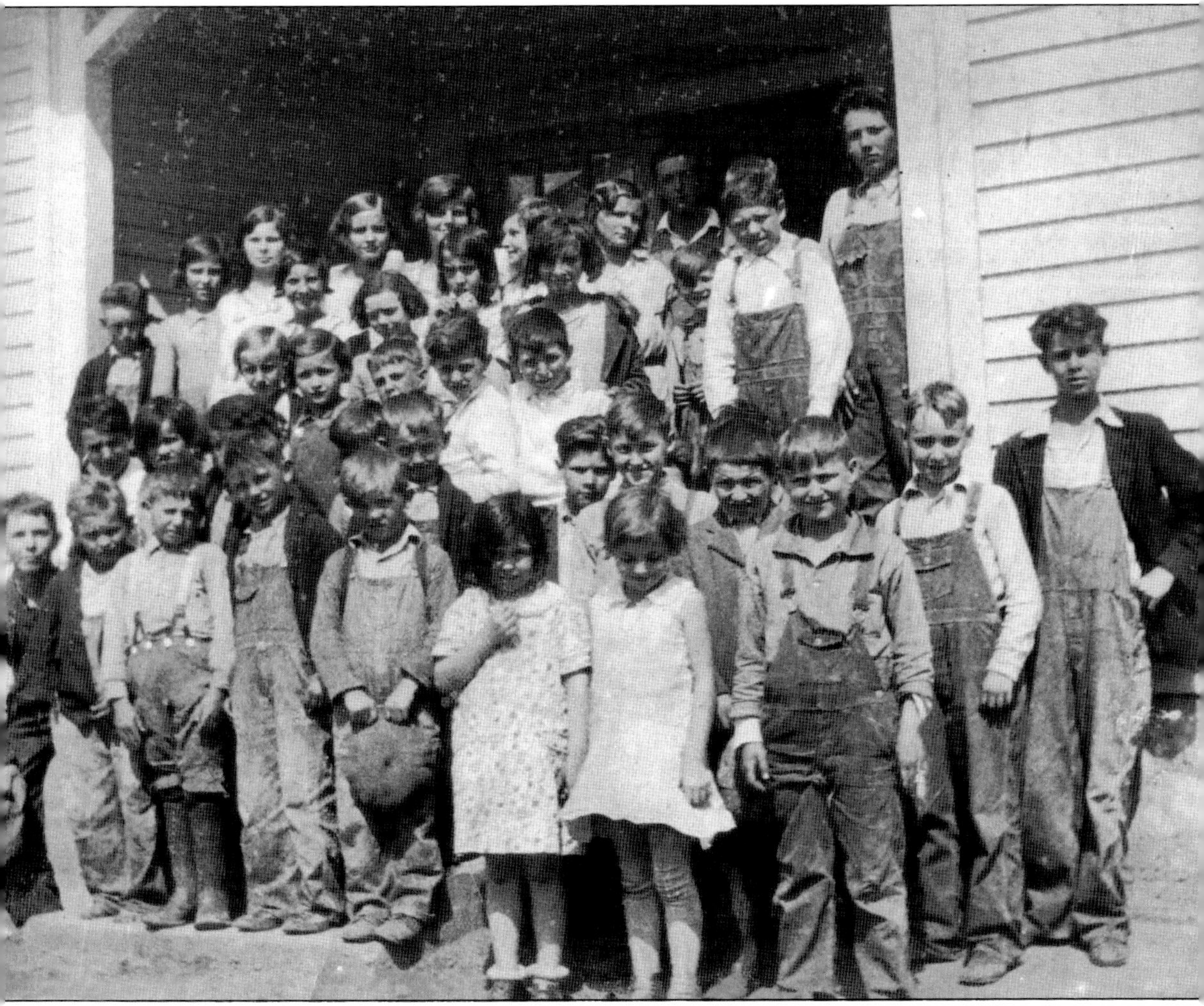

One of the first schools built in Brown County was on the Taggart farm in 1837 and was described as an "old log." Things had changed by the time this photograph of the Taggart School was taken in 1932 by teacher Walter Waltz. Pictured here from left to right are (first row) Frances Condon and Esther Pruitt; (second row) Thompson Gatewood, Andrew Reed, Robert Bell, Roscoe Stillabower, Harold Stillabower, Estelle Wheeler, Edward Pruitt, Dale Bell, Wayne Pruitt, Forrest Waltz, and Lem Wheeler; (third row) Malcolm Roller, Valentina Petro, Thelma Roller, and Orville Stillabower; (fourth row) Evelyn Stillabower, Ruth Bisel, William Sinkhorn, George Fox, and Robert Fox; (fifth row) Ruth Roller, Madeline Gatewood, Emma Line, Dorothy Shelton, and Joseph Bell; (sixth row) Virgil Stillabower, Nellie Gatewood, Beatrice Roberts, Lena Reed, Frances Roller, Opal Mead, Mary Ruth Campbell, Leon Shotts, Bryon Campbell, and Ralph Miller. (Brown County Historical Society.)

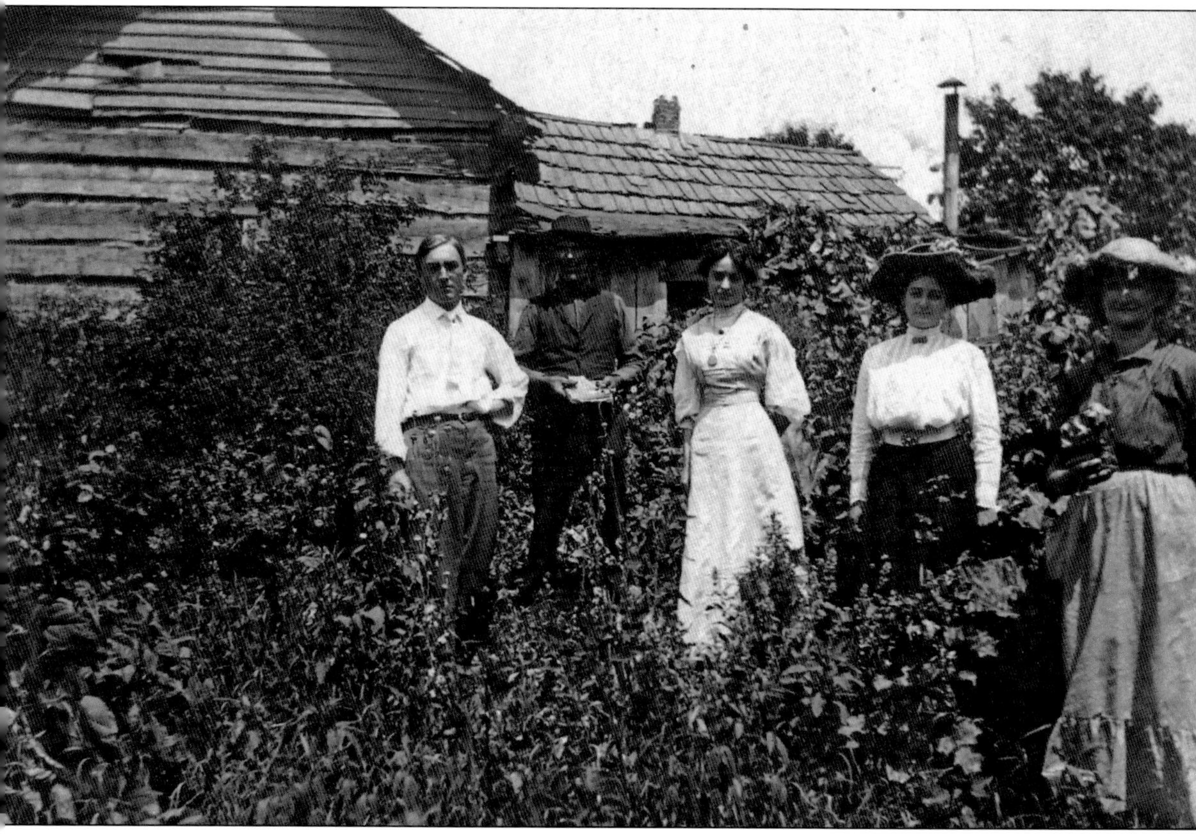

The original Barnes cabin on Owl Creek is shown in this photograph taken by Frank Hohenberger. An article written by Rachel Perry for the Brown County online history project states that "in August 1924, Hohenberger wrote, '(Artists) Carl Graf and (Marie) Goth called at the old Barnes cabin on West Owl Creek and wanted to paint the place but they were halted by a female voice who gave them to understand that they paid good money for the spot and if Graf wanted to paint it they would want money for it.' " Virgil Gregg is on the far left and Grandma Barnes on the far right. (Brown County Historical Society.)

Gnaw Bone is situated on state highway 46, between Nashville and Columbus. It is known for its flea markets and has been promoted as the "flea market capital of the world," as it is said to have one flea market for every five residents. How the town got its name is not known for sure. Some say it is named after Narbonne, which is in the south of France, and that the name was mispronounced by later English settlers who ended up with the much less flattering Gnaw Bone. (Brown County Historical Society.)

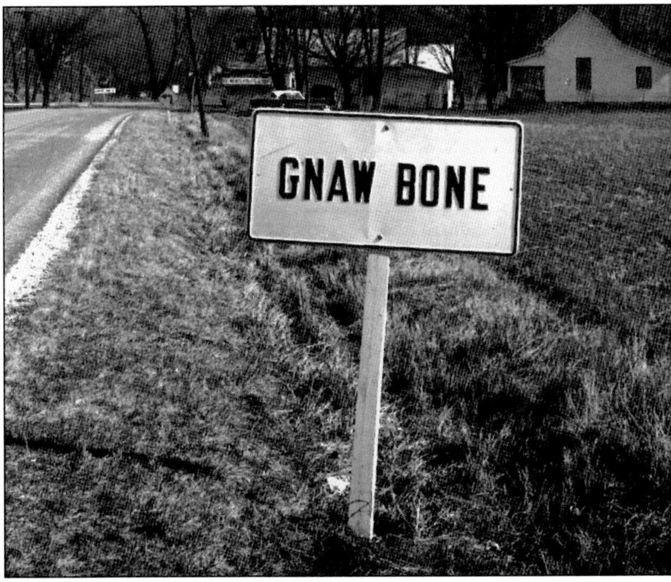

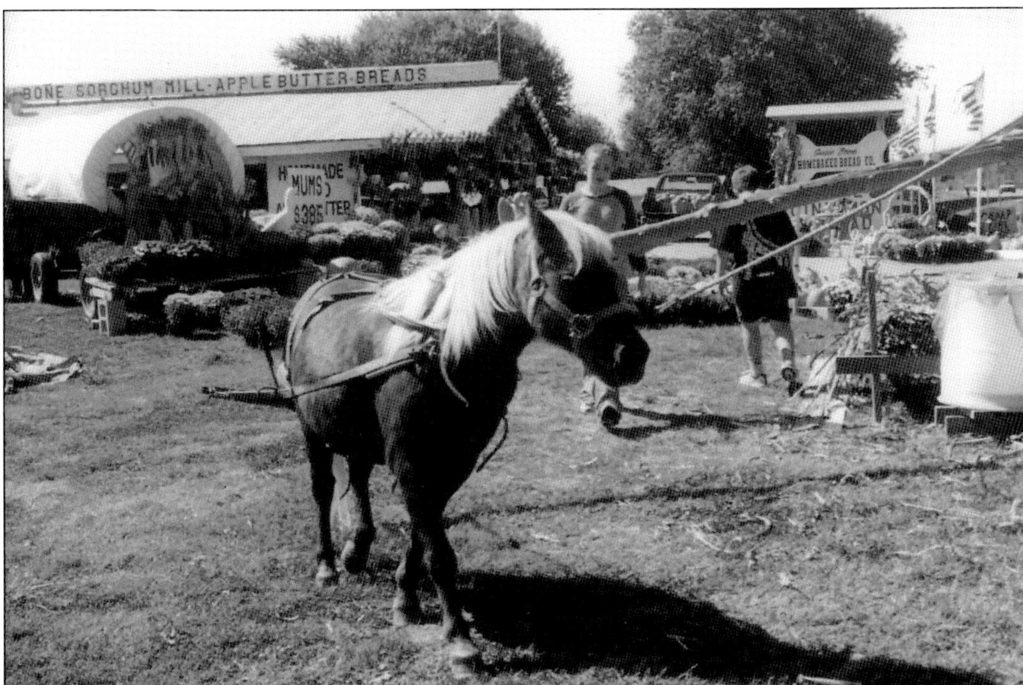

Now owned by Bill and Pat Watkins, Pat's Gnaw Bone Sorghum Mill was first opened by Roy Roberts in 1948 and then later run by his son. The Watkins, who bought the mill in 2007, are only the second owners. The old sorghum mill, which was run by horsepower, still stands in the front of the building. The Watkins sell the locally produced sorghum in their store. (Bill and Pat Watkins.)

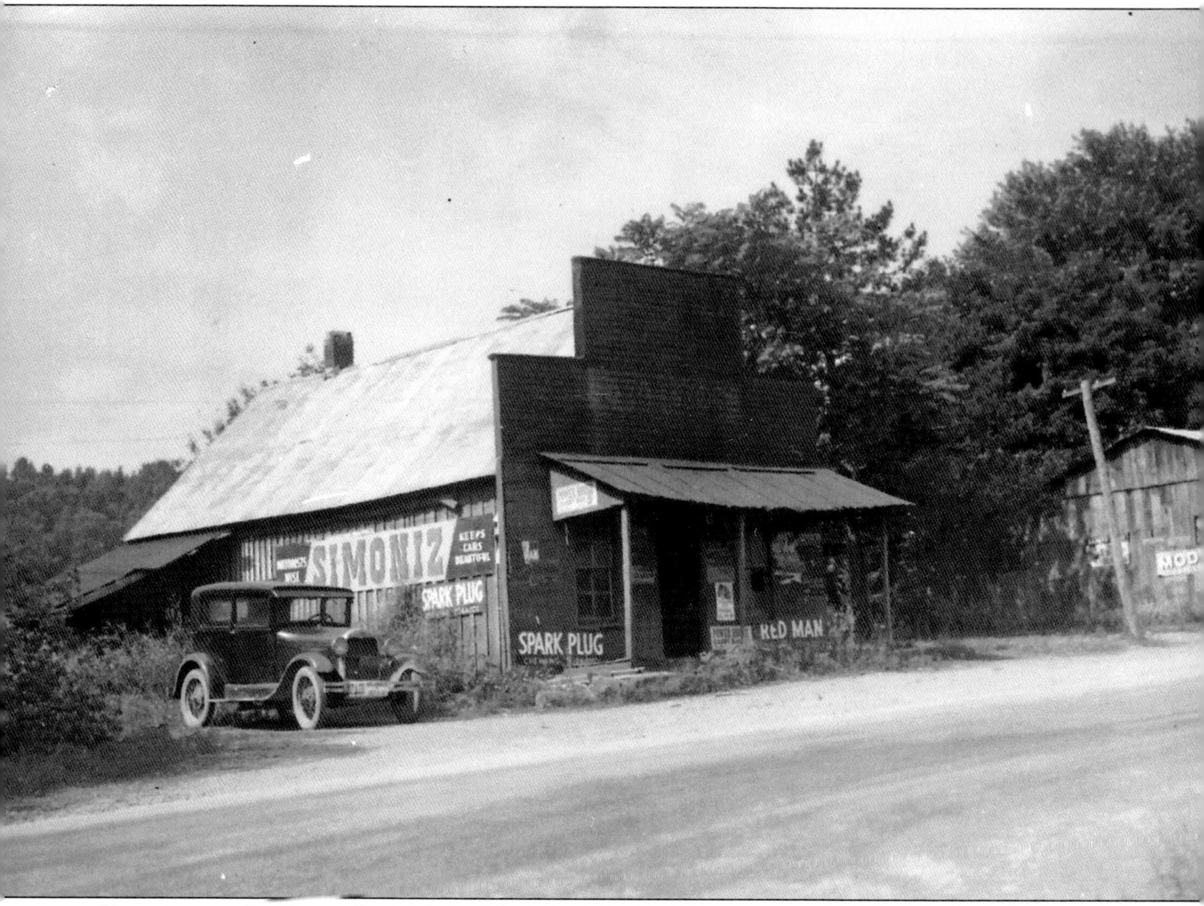

Seen here is the Gnaw Bone General Store. In *Brown County Remembers*, Christie McDonald shares this account of Gladys Mayne, "If Gladys wanted to get Herb home in the evening when a late card game was going on in the store, she would turn off the generator." (Lilly Library, photograph by Frank Hohenberger.)

Six

Old-Time Frivolity

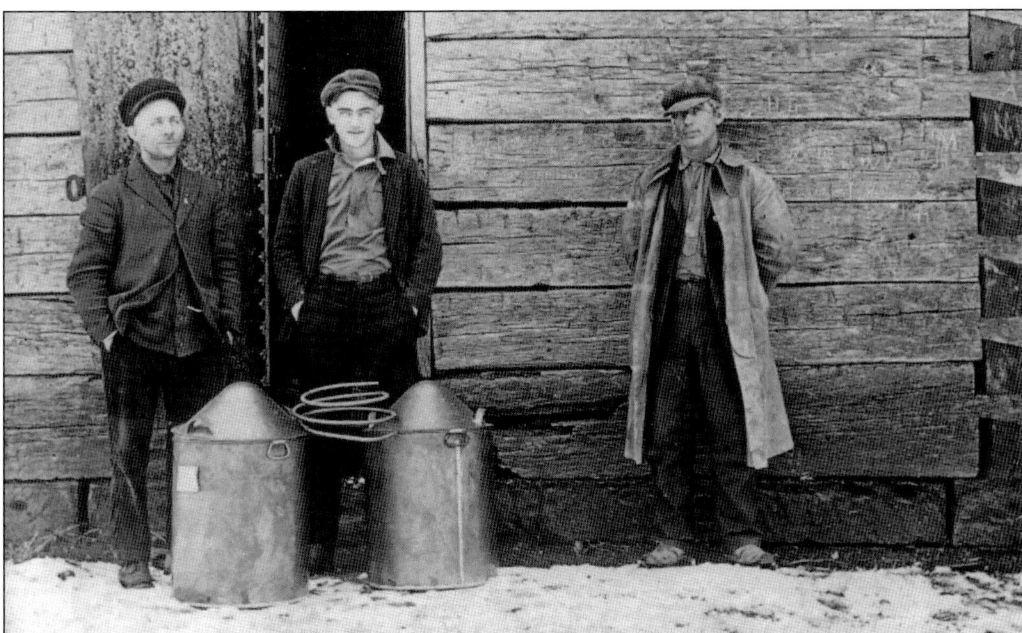

The caption on this photograph, taken by Frank Hohenberger, reads, "Hill McGee, Sol Wilkerson and Nub Moore, Glenn Hutchinson still." In *Brown County Remembers*, Taylor Wilson recalls, "There were stills all over Brown County during Prohibition and I only heard of one person being convicted and he soon got out. Persons that I never dreamed would make mule. G-men were always too late to catch anyone as they were notified to get rid of evidence." (Brown County Historical Society.)

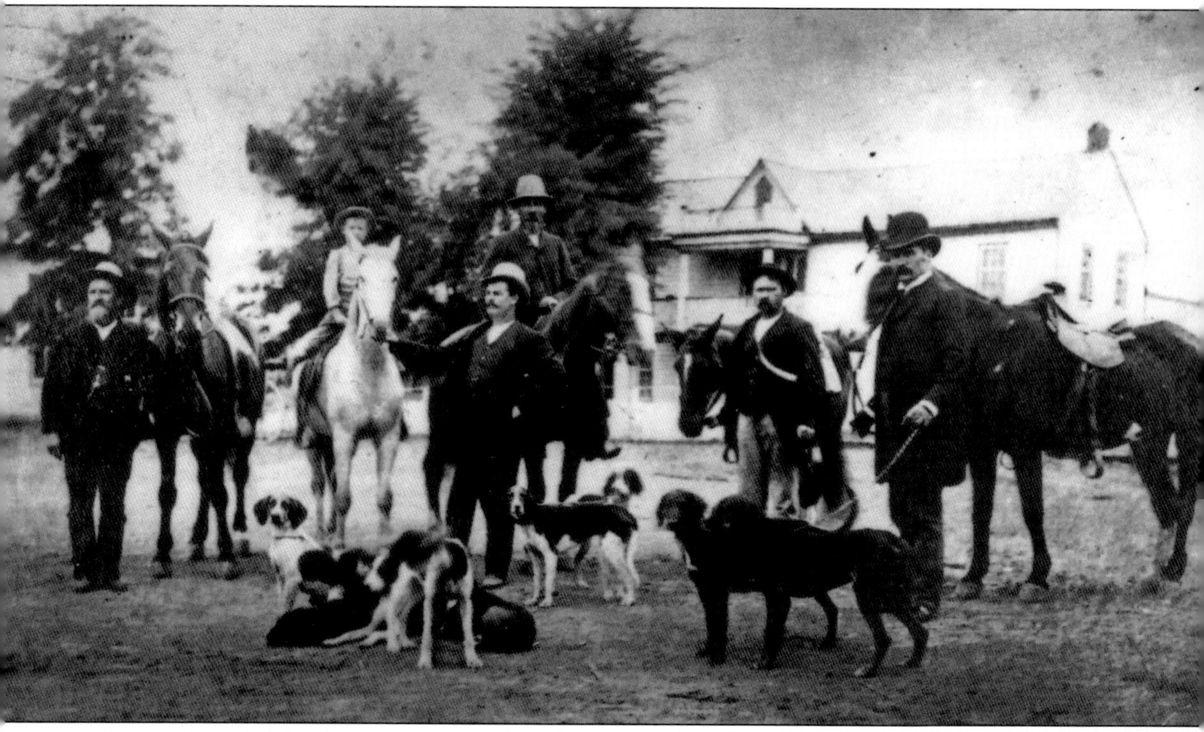

In this Frank Hohenberger photograph, taken in 1906, foxhunters gather in front of the Mason Hotel in Brown County. "The foxhunters' meet was so important that school was dismissed on Thursdays and Friday for the event," recalls Taylor Wilson in *Brown County Remembers*, compiled and edited by Dorothy Biney Bailey and indexed by Nancy Coulter. Pictured here are, from left to right, Frank P. Taggart, Dan Turner, William Kennedy, George Turner, Dan Gordon, and Anderson Percifield. (Brown County Historical Society.)

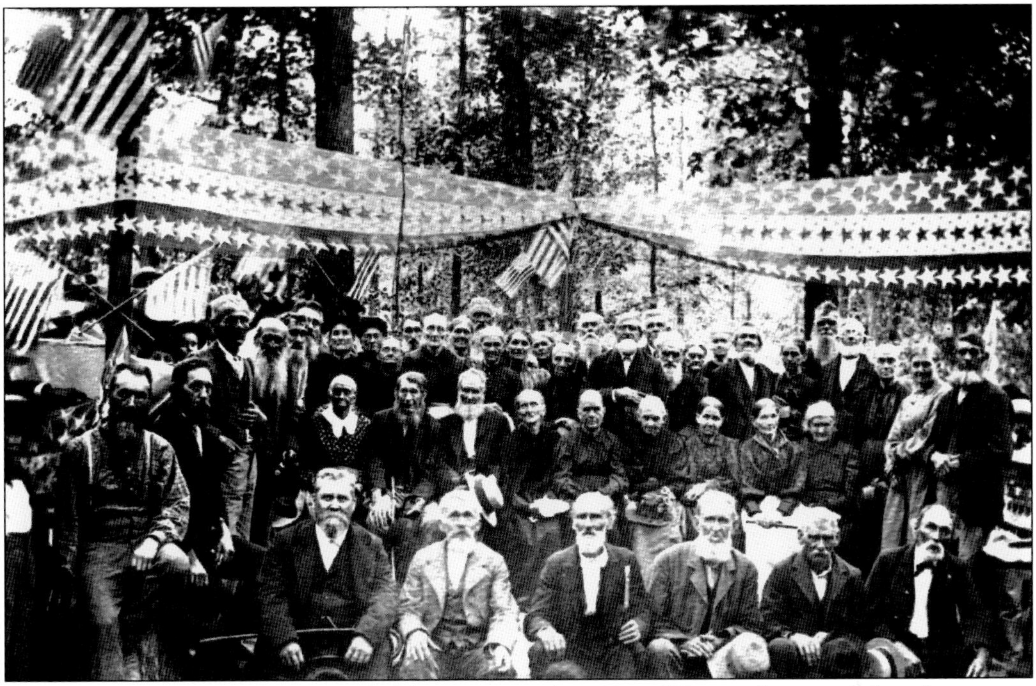

The first Settlers Reunion was held on September 22, 1877, at what was then known as Georgetown but is now the village of Bean Blossom. A hickory rocking chair was awarded to Margaret Graham in honor of her being the oldest woman living in Brown County. She was 80 at the time and had lived in Brown County for 63 years. The oldest living man, Edward David, age 92, danced a jig after being awarded with a cane. (Brown County Historical Society.)

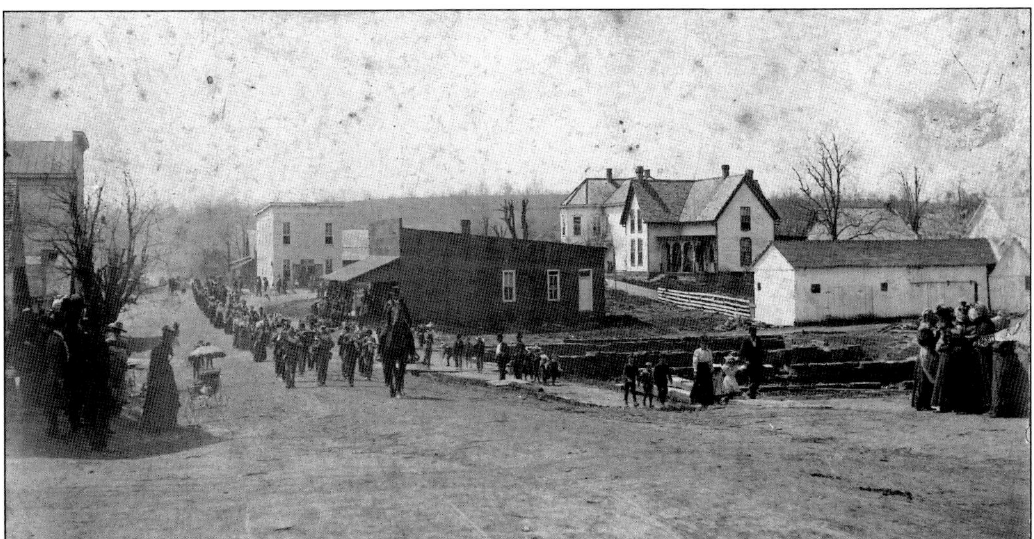

An Independence Day parade makes its way through Nashville in 1900. According to journalist Jackie Scheckler Finch, "There were parades, picnics and day-long speeches. Brass bands, drum and bugle corps and glee clubs from the townships furnished music." (Brown County Historical Society.)

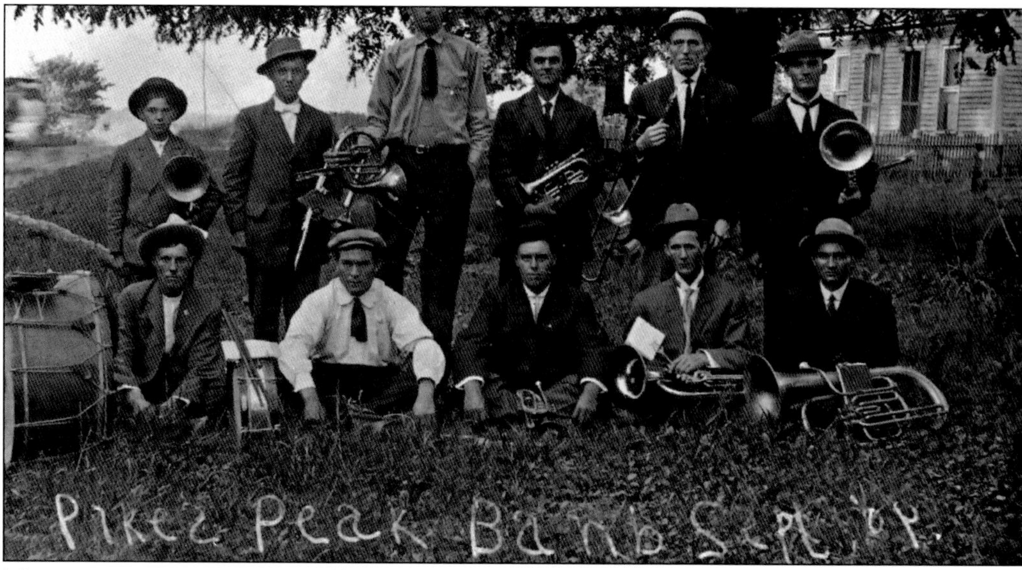

Music was an important part of life in Brown County. Even a town as small as Pike's Peak had its own band. One of the band members in the back row is James Hendricks, minister at the New Harmony Bellsville Baptist Church and first cousin to the Hendricks children. Another person in the photograph is John Hendricks, son of Thomas A. Hendricks, who built the House at Stone Head. John and his wife, Dottie, would live at Stone Head for most of their lives. (Brown County Historical Society.)

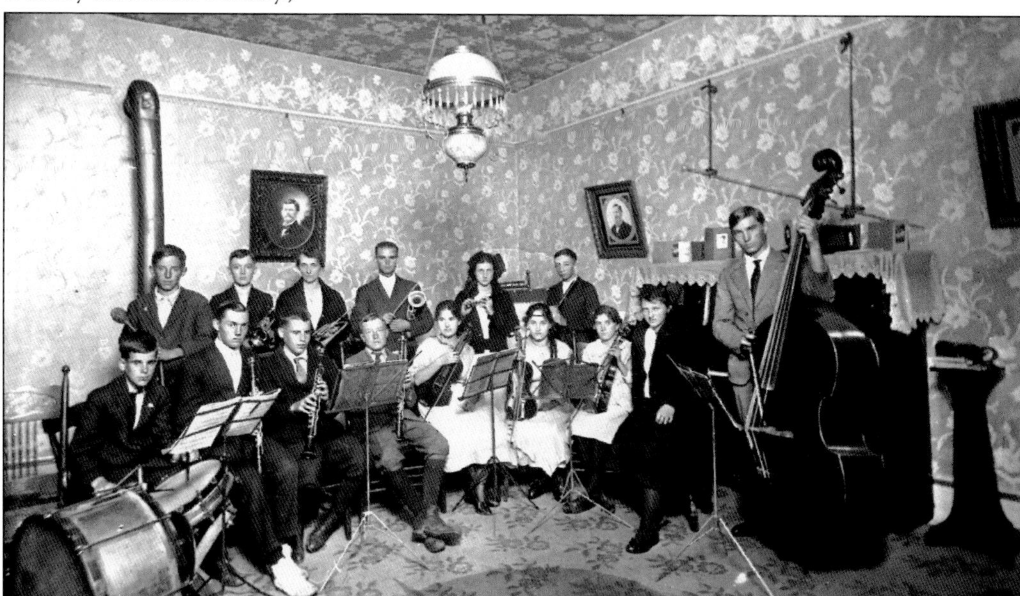

The Mart Hopper Family Orchestra poses in the Hopper family parlor. The Jefferson Street home was built by Mart Hopper's father-in-law, Frank Taggart, and photographed here in the early 1910s. Pictured are, from left to right, (first row) Myron Hopper, Earl Moore, Frank Hopper, Mike Street, Etta Hopper, Lucille Jones, unidentified, Gail Battin (?), and Harry Bitters on the bass viola; (second row) James M. Jones Jr., two unidentified, Rex Hopper, Olive Marshall, and Charles Kennedy. (Brown County Historical Society.)

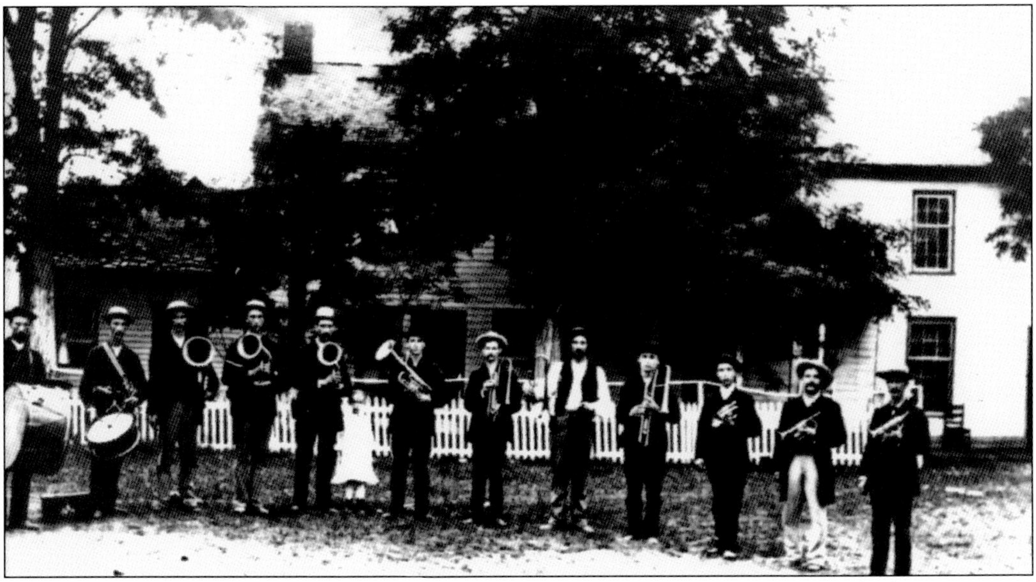

The Nashville Band poses in front of Mason Hotel. "One good thing about a little town—you kin git in th' band," wrote Brown County humorist Kin Hubbard. The Nashville Brass Band had gold-braided gray uniforms with red plumes in their hats. (Brown County Historical Society.)

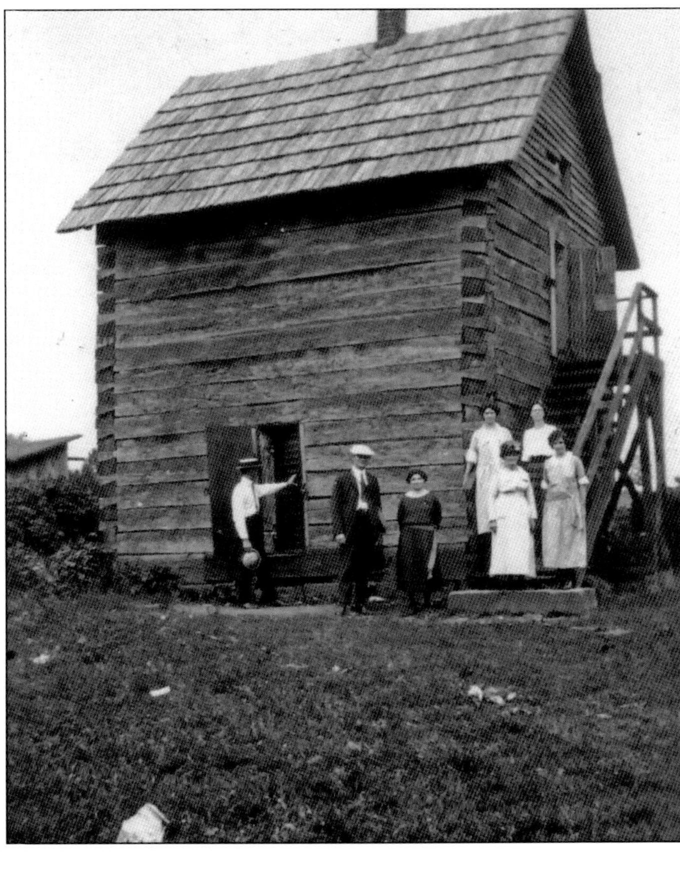

The Hamblen family visits the old 1879 log jail, which now is part of the Brown County Historical Society Museum in Nashville. The two-story log jail cost $1,500 to build according to the society's Web site and was "designed with two walls spaced one foot apart and one entrance consisting of three doors, one of which required a key that was 10 inches long." The Hamblens are an old, established family in Brown County; Eliakim Hamblen built a water mill here in 1838. (Brown County Historical Society.)

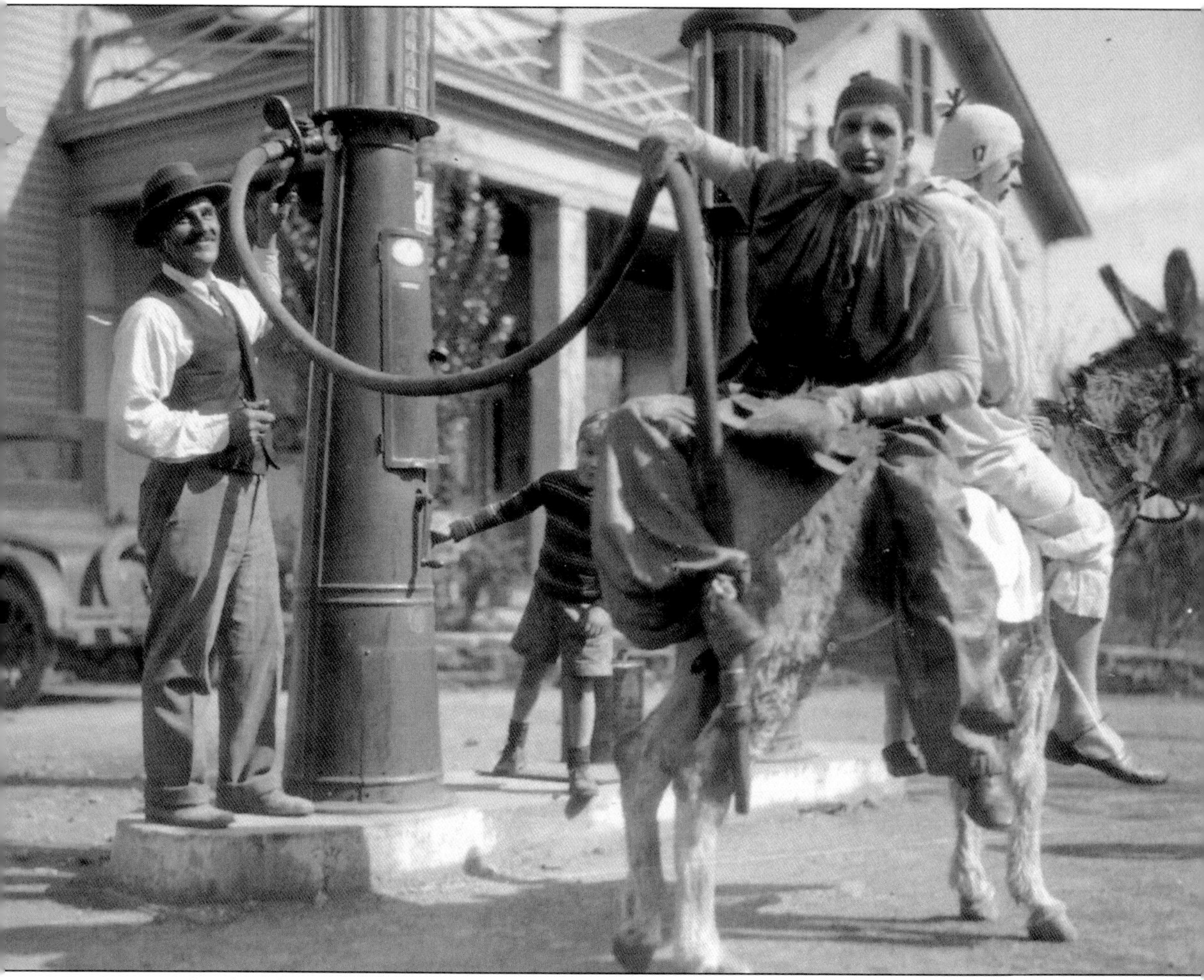

Carey Cloud and Lane Bond stop to "gas up" a mule during the 1930 Spring Blossom Parade at James Clovis's gas station. Though Bean Blossom may seem like a sleepy town, there are plenty of interesting stories about the place. (Brown County Historical Society.)

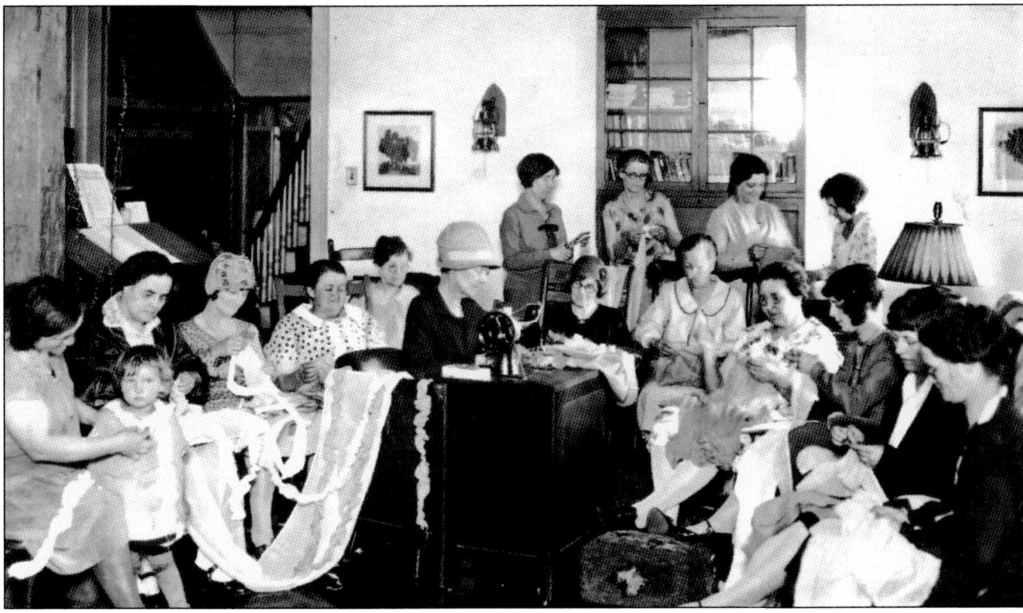

Women prepare for the Bean Blossom Festival. Though Bean Blossom is a sleepy little town now, according to Ralph Burkholder's history of the Nashville Masonic lodge, "As early as 1839, it had one of the largest and finest tanneries in the state, a jewelry manufacturing plant, a newspaper, grist mills, taverns, churches, schools, and a population that had reached 100 by 1875." (Brown County Historical Society.)

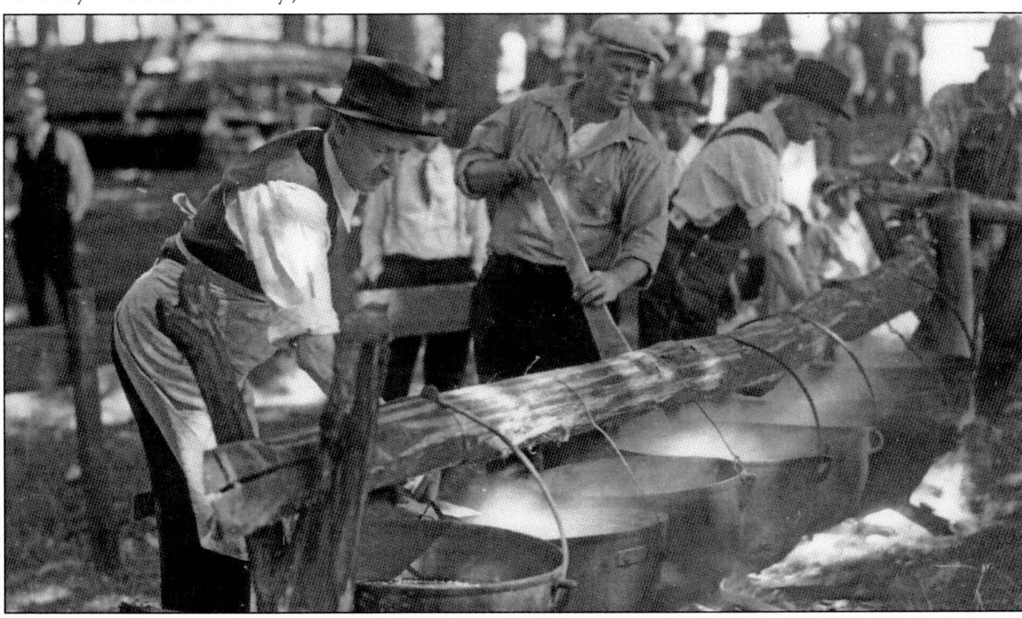

Frank Hohenberger took this 1930 photograph of the 44th annual Schooner Valley Bean Dinner. When he was 87, Seralvo McGuire described Schooner Valley as a happy hunting ground for the Native Americans who lived in this area back in the early 1800s in a conversation. But McGuire also remembered a less happy place, a battle that happened on Jade Floyd Place. According to McGuire, the Native Americans who died in the battle were buried vertically. (Brown County Historical Society.)

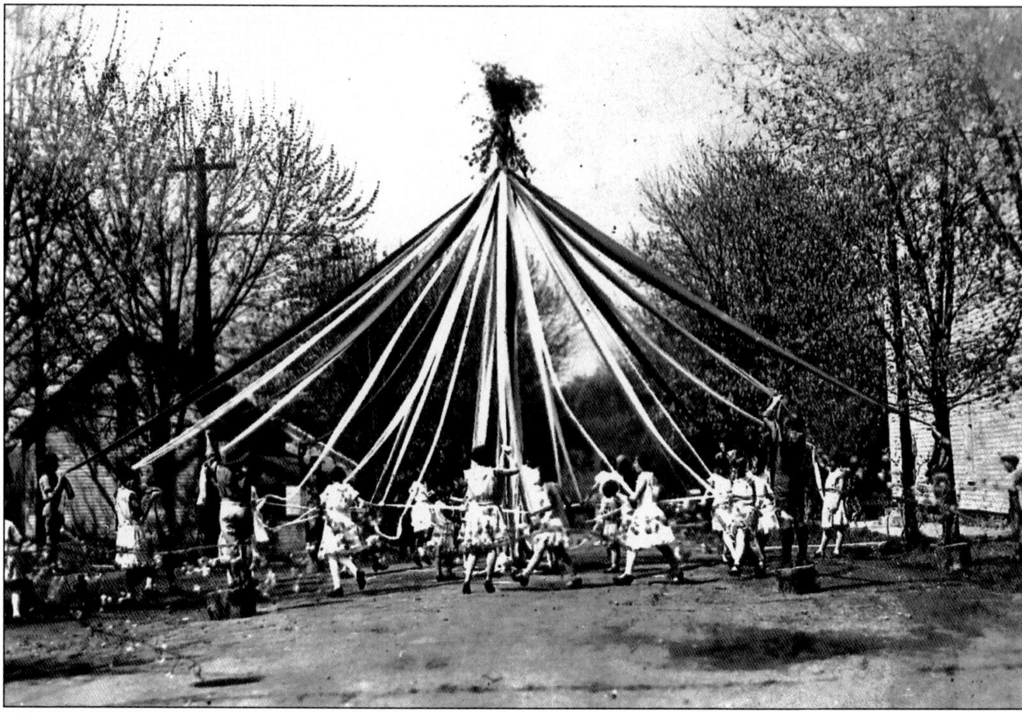

This is the Dance of the Unfolding of the Blossoms at the Bean Blossom Festival in 1930. Once called Georgetown, Bean Blossom was famous for its horse racing in earlier years. The movers and shakers of Brown County, including William Snider, Matthew Mathis, Edward David, the Brummets, and the Grahams, owned fast horses. Amid discussions on the merits of their steeds, they also would imbibe and bet—sometimes indulging in both to an extreme. (Brown County Historical Society.)

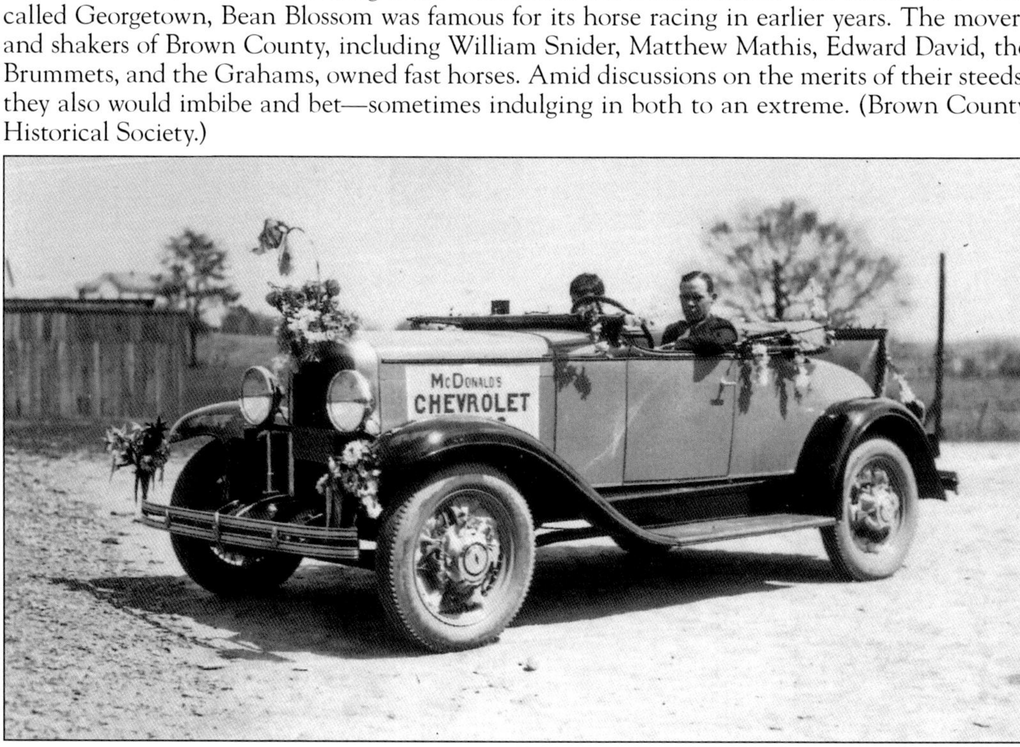

A new Chevrolet from MacDonald's is one of the entries in the Bean Blossom Festival in 1930. (Brown County Historical Society.)

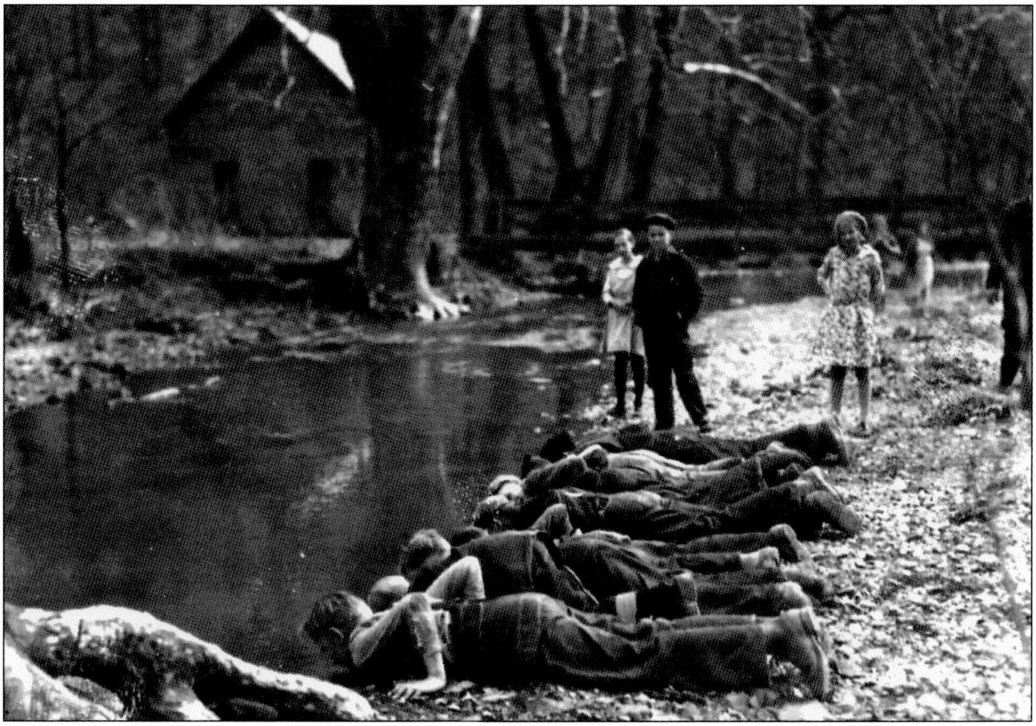

Young boys drink from a creek in front of Deckard School in what looks like a nice afternoon break from learning. (Lilly Library, photograph by Frank Hohenberger.)

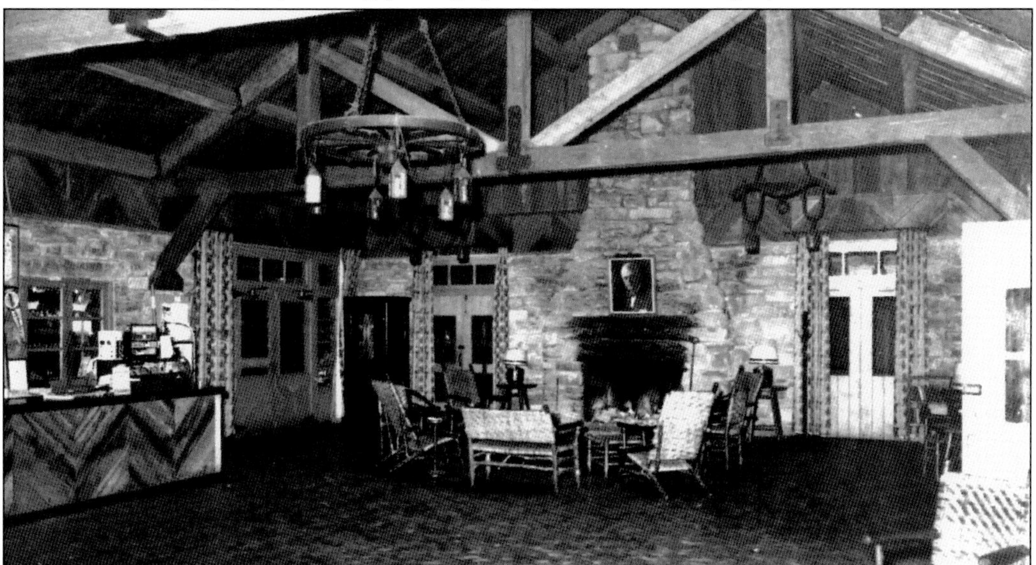

Abe Martin Lodge at the Brown County State Park was named after the Kin Hubbard character who, for many, epitomized the country wisdom of the area. The park's creation was inspired by Richard Lieber, head of the state conservation department, who owned a summer home in Brown County and wanted people to enjoy its beauty. The central portion of the park is Weedpatch Hill, which at 1,152 feet, is one of the highest points in Indiana. (Brown County Historical Society.)

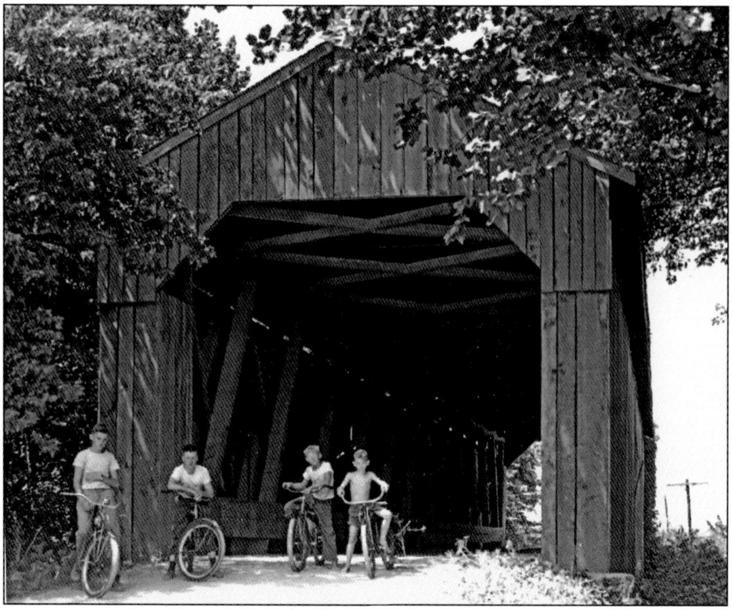

Frank Hohenberger took this photograph of four young boys on their bikes at the Bean Blossom Covered Bridge. The 1880 bridge, which spans Bean Blossom Creek near the town of Bean Blossom, is still open to automobile traffic. It is the only one built in the county that is still standing. A two-lane, covered wooden bridge marks the north entrance of Brown County State Park, but it was brought from Fincastle, Indiana, in the mid-1930s.

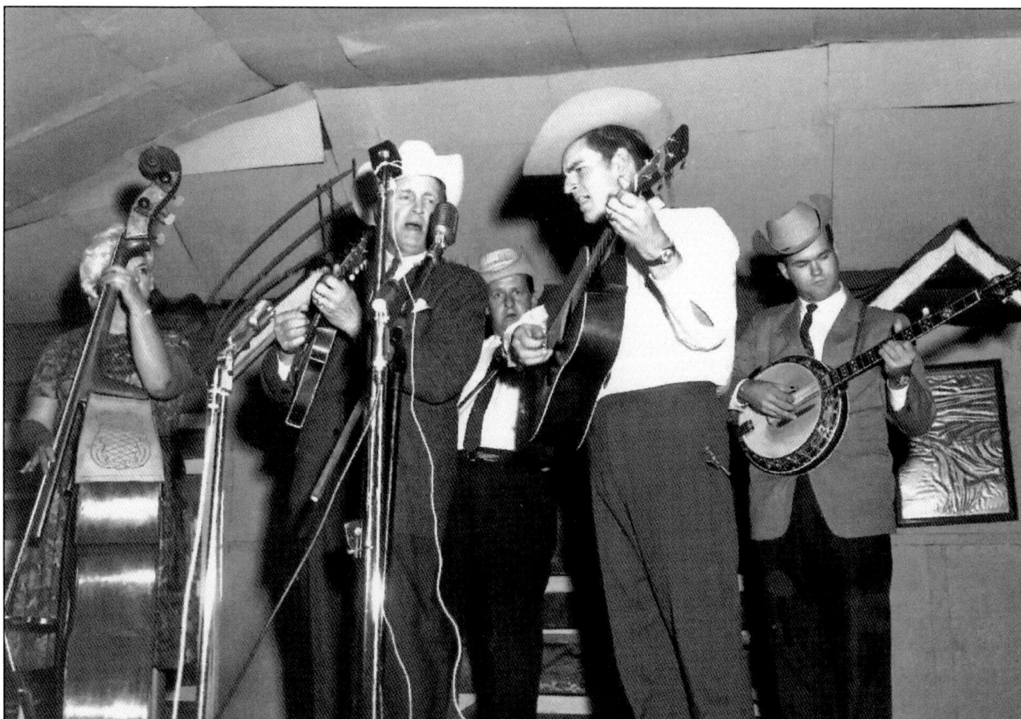

Legendary musician Bill Monroe discovered Bean Blossom when performing in the Brown County Jamboree. The jamboree started in 1941 and morphed into the Bill Monroe Bluegrass Festival. It is now the oldest and largest continuously running outdoor festival in the world. It is held on the 55-acre Bill Monroe Memorial Music Park and Campground. Pictured are Bessie Lee Mauldin, bass; Bill Monroe, mandolin; Joe Stuart, fiddle; Del McCoury, guitar; and Bill "Brad" Keith, banjo. This photograph was taken at the jamboree barn in 1963 by Jim Peva.

Seven

WORKING

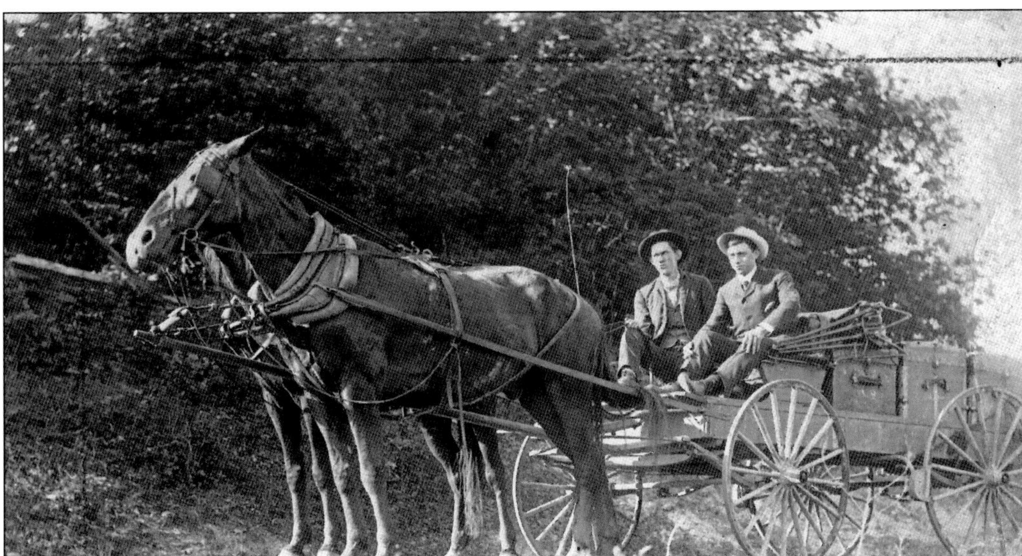

"John Pruitt Drives Drummer" is the title of this photograph that appeared in the *Brown County Democrat* in 1930 with the following caption, "Back in the Drummer Day: When a Drummer kept good track of his trunk—the traveling salesman being driven over a gravel road when there was little paving in the state. Pruitt of Freetown." John Pruitt (left) drives his spring wagon with a drummer (salesman) and his trunks. (Brown County Historical Society.)

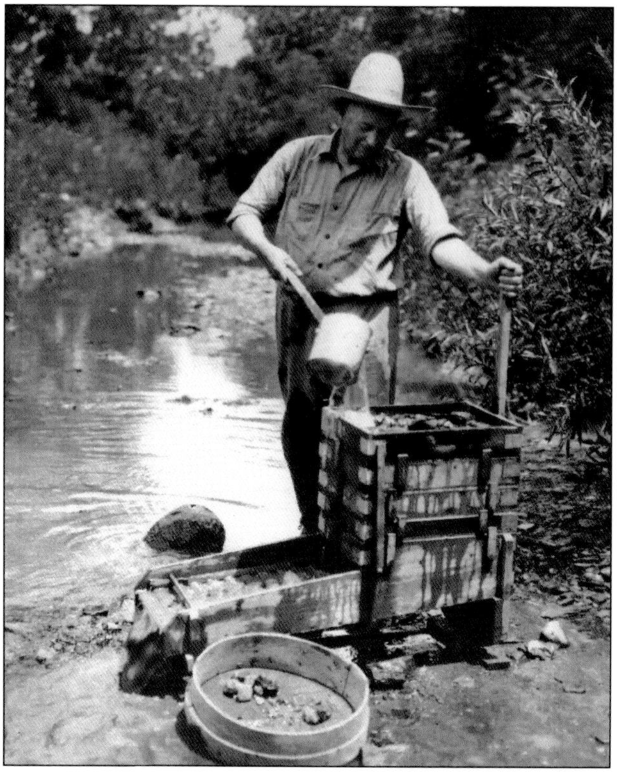

In his 1936 book, *A Brown County History*, author Ray Mathis states that in 1875 the Brown County Company Mining was incorporated and 14 years later so was the Indiana Gold Mining and Investment Company. Gold was occasionally found but not enough to spark any sort of gold rush. Instead, according to Mathis, most people panned for recreation, as he estimates that the two mining companies "did not average in gold more than twenty-five cents a day." (Brown County Historical Society.)

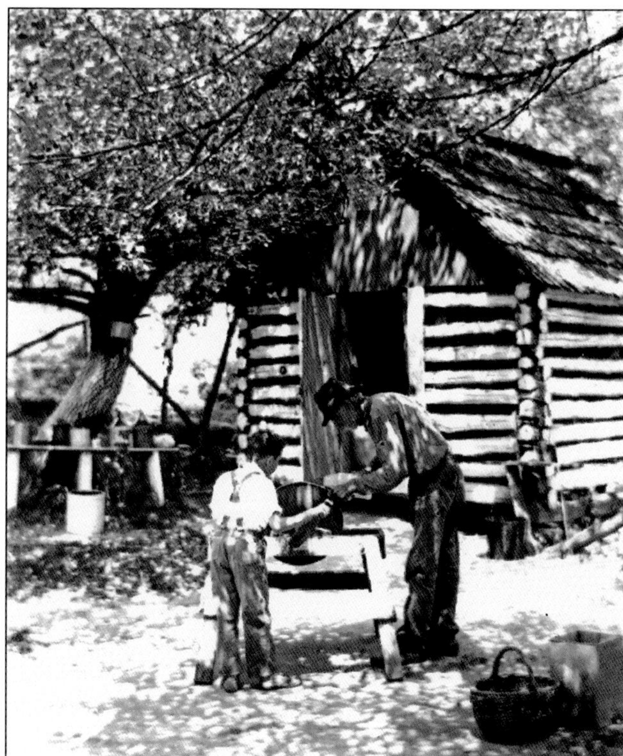

Alex Mullis and George Turner are shown grinding, but Mullis has also been described as a stave maker. According to Mathis, stave factories flourished in Brown County for a time until the timber supply was practically exhausted. Other Brown County businesses included wagon making, furniture and cabinet making, and of course distilling. Salt mining was also a big industry for a while. (Brown County Historical Society.)

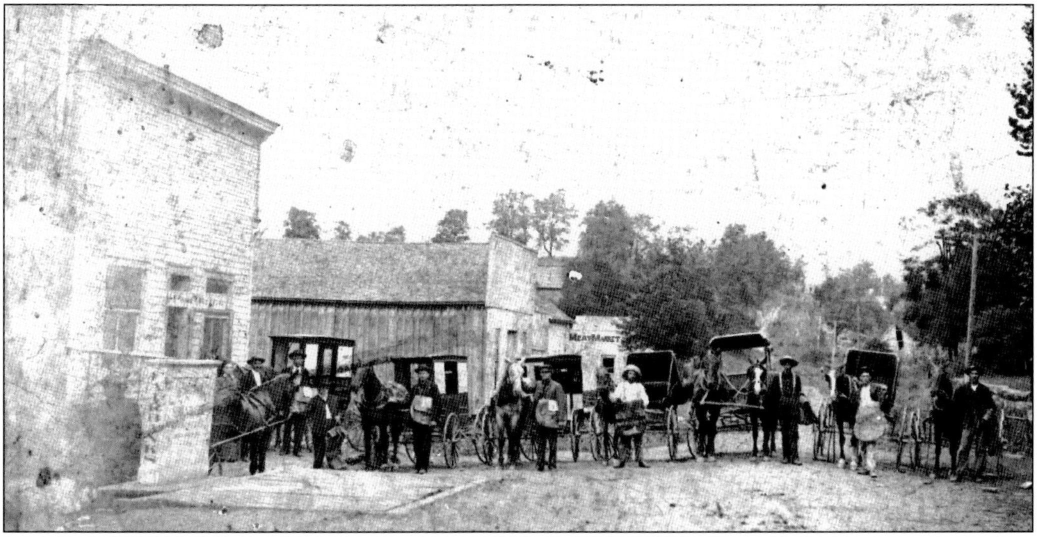

The inscription on this photograph, labeled "Nashville Carriers," notes that the third man from the left is Billy Gale, who brought mail from Columbus, Indiana. In the book *Brown County Remembers*, Henry Swain Jr. recalls mail carrier George Howard, stranded in the middle of a creek while delivering mail, "George looked up to see a big log rushing down the current straight for his car. Climbing out on the hood, he kicked the end away clearing the car, but the rest of the log swung around broadside against it. Blowing the horn finally roused Toby Kirts, who waded out as far into the current as he dared and caught the mail sacks George threw to him." (Brown County Historical Society.)

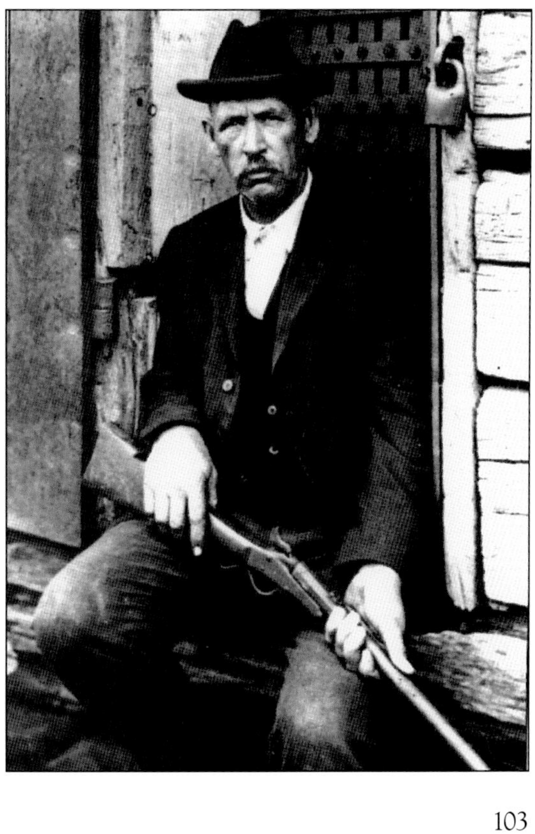

A Brown County sheriff is pictured. Besides law enforcement, there was also a group of local men called "Whitecappers," who meted out justice when they thought it was due. According to Chattie Wade Miller in *Brown County Remembers*, a man thought to be a chicken thief was "taken out of his home one night and in no uncertain terms was told what would happen to him if any more chickens were missing." (Brown County Historical Society.)

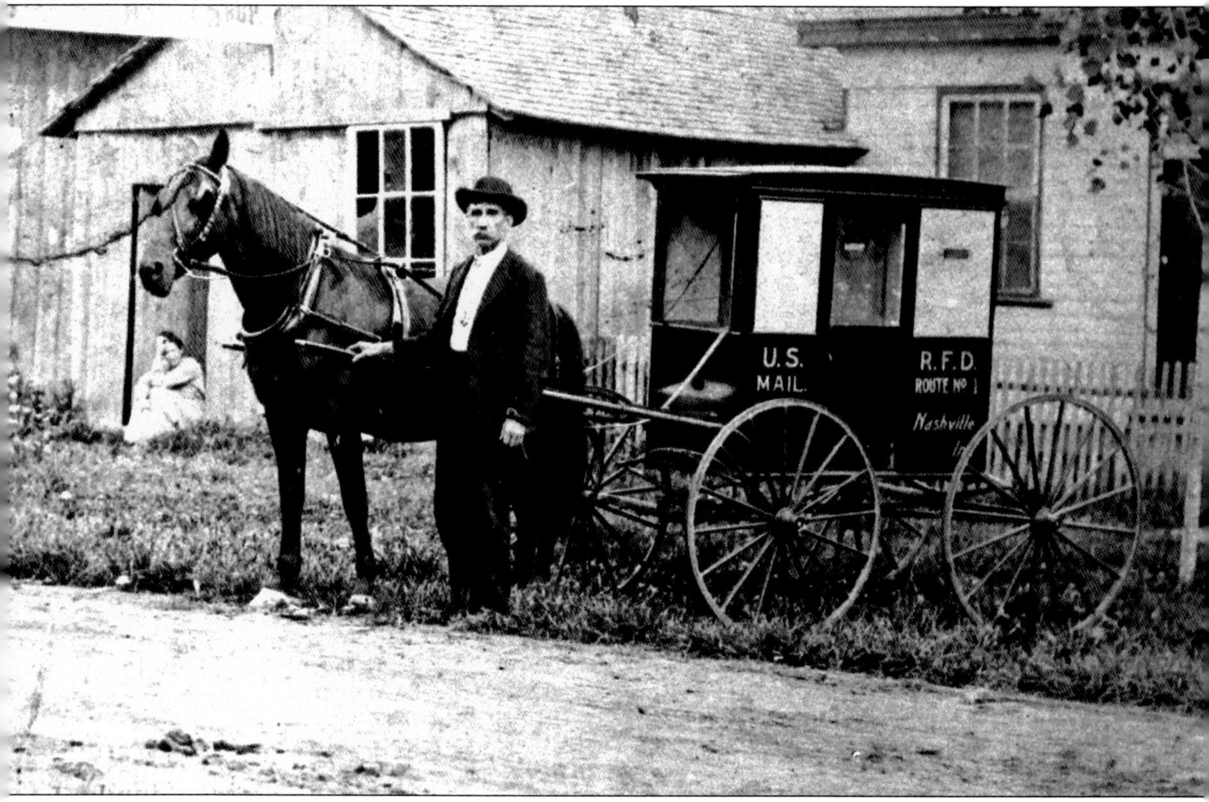

Collins Calvin is pictured in 1907 on his RFD (rural free delivery) route. He and Hugh Tom Adams were each given 30-mile routes. "There was no hard-top or so-called gravel roads," writes Adams's son Harold in *Brown County Remembers*. "The little creeks had no bridges over them. The winters were so cold my dad bought a closed-in rig pulled mostly by two horses. He also had a foot warmer that burned charcoal and a small wood-burning stove which made it almost too hot." (Brown County Historical Society.)

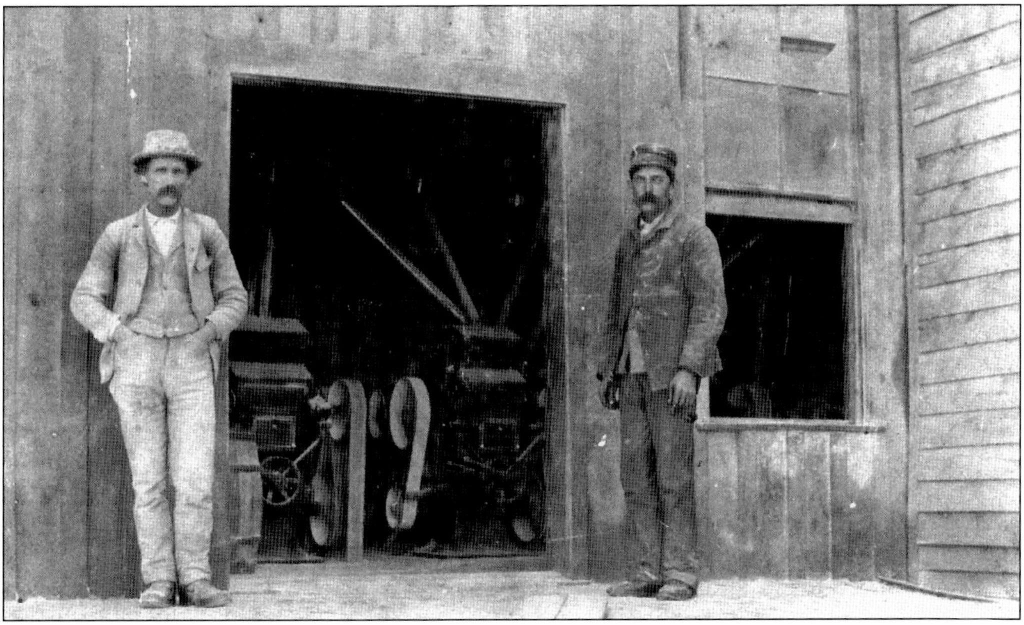

The Nashville Flour Mill, pictured here in 1900, burned down nine years later. "One night I was awakened by the ringing of church bells—a warning of fire," recalls Ruth Tilton. "My west window looked out upon our barn. The sky was alight and our barn appeared to be on fire. The next thing I remember is standing with the crowd watching the flour mill burn down. When I saw that my grandmother was crying I asked Mother why. She told me that Grandpa had an interest in the mill." (Brown County Historical Society.)

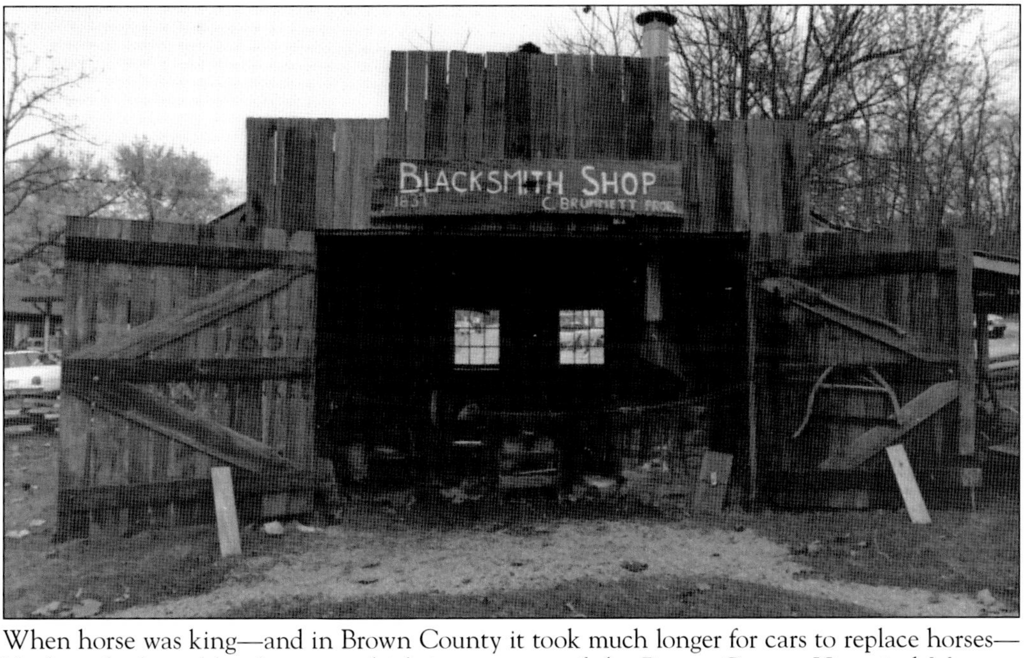

When horse was king—and in Brown County it took much longer for cars to replace horses—blacksmith shops like this one, which is now part of the Brown County Historical Museum (a wonderful collection of historic buildings in downtown Nashville), were a vital part of the community. (Brown County Historical Society.)

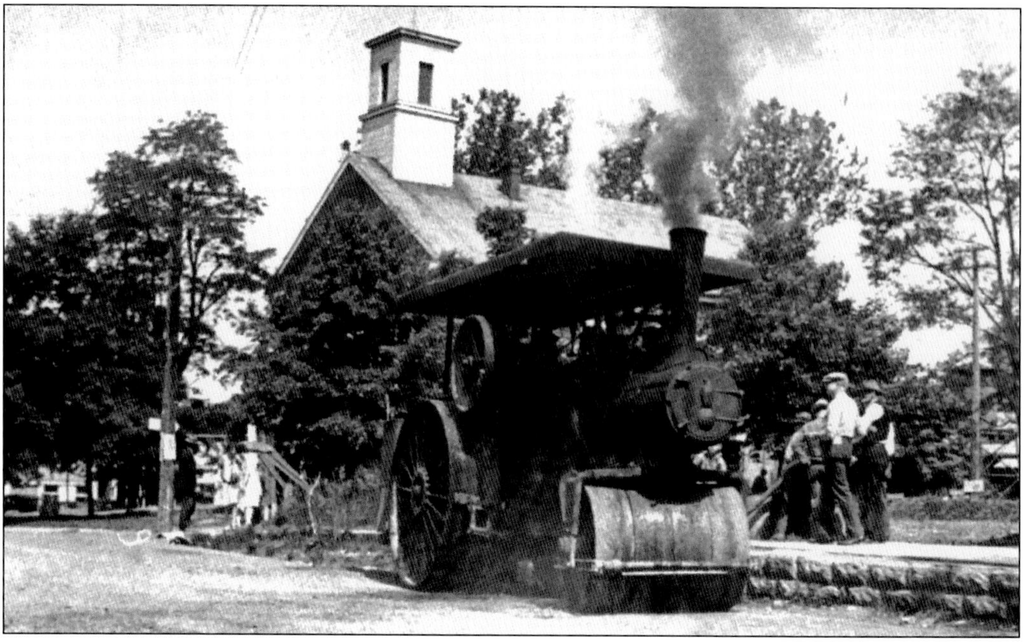

Oiling the streets of Nashville, as shown in this photograph, was important for keeping down the dust from the dirt and gravel. Kin Hubbard, in his book *Short Furrows*, writes about communities, "In oiled street towns, there are many varieties of the E-flat sport besides the one that lolls in the whittled chairs of the pool bazaar. There's the craps shooting sport that hangs about the livery, feed and sale stable and smells like a goat." (Brown County Historical Society.)

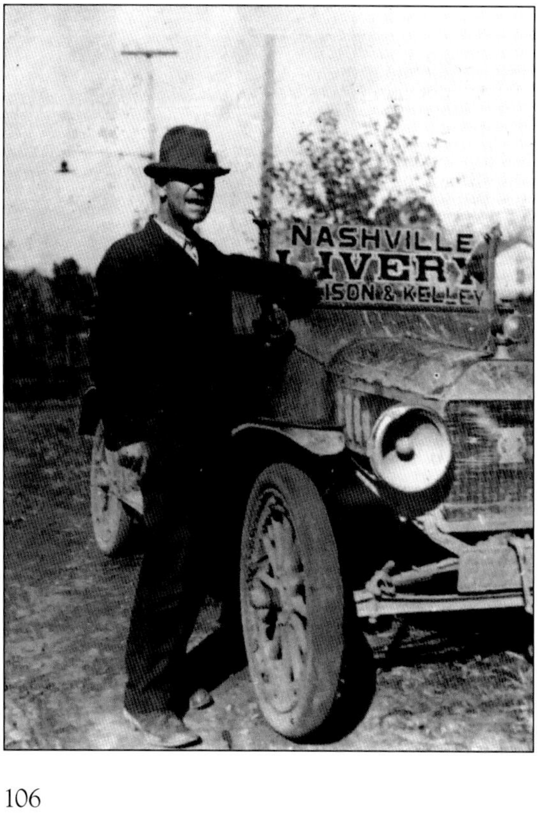

Clark Campbell stands at the side of a meat wagon. (Lilly Library, photograph by Frank Hohenberger.)

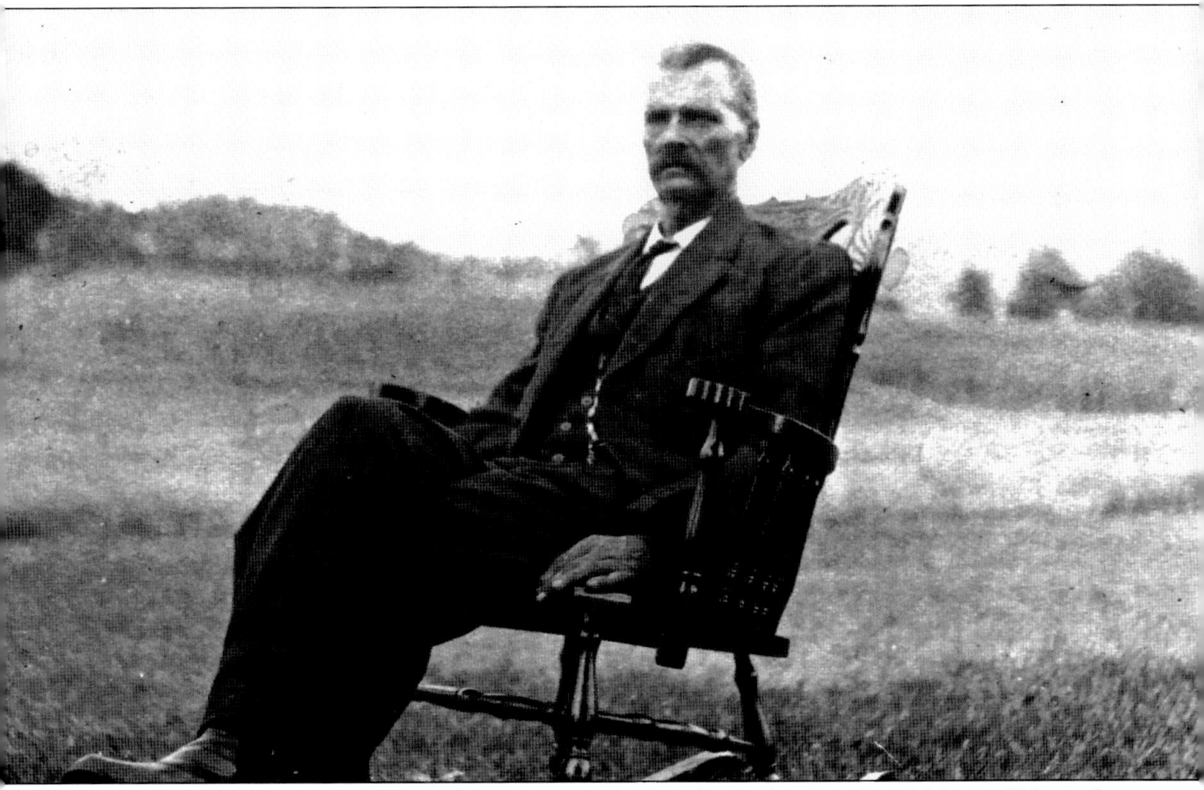

Alfred J. Ralphy studied medicine in the office of his brother-in-law Dr. Arnold S. Griffith, and the two were partners for about a year, according to his daughter Gladys Ralphy Whitaker in *Brown County Folks* by Richard Reed, in the early 1870s. Ralphy later studied at the Cincinnati School of Medicine and Surgery, then at the Kentucky School of Medicine, before returning to practice in Nashville. He moved to New Bellsville in 1891, and the office he had there is now part of the historic complex in downtown Nashville. In the 1890s, Brown County had at least 28 doctors and also several midwives. But despite the number of doctors, it was a hard and busy life. "When father practiced at Nashville he kept two drivers and two teams busy taking him on calls night and day," stated Whitaker. "What little rest he got was when he was being driven on calls." (Brown County Historical Society.)

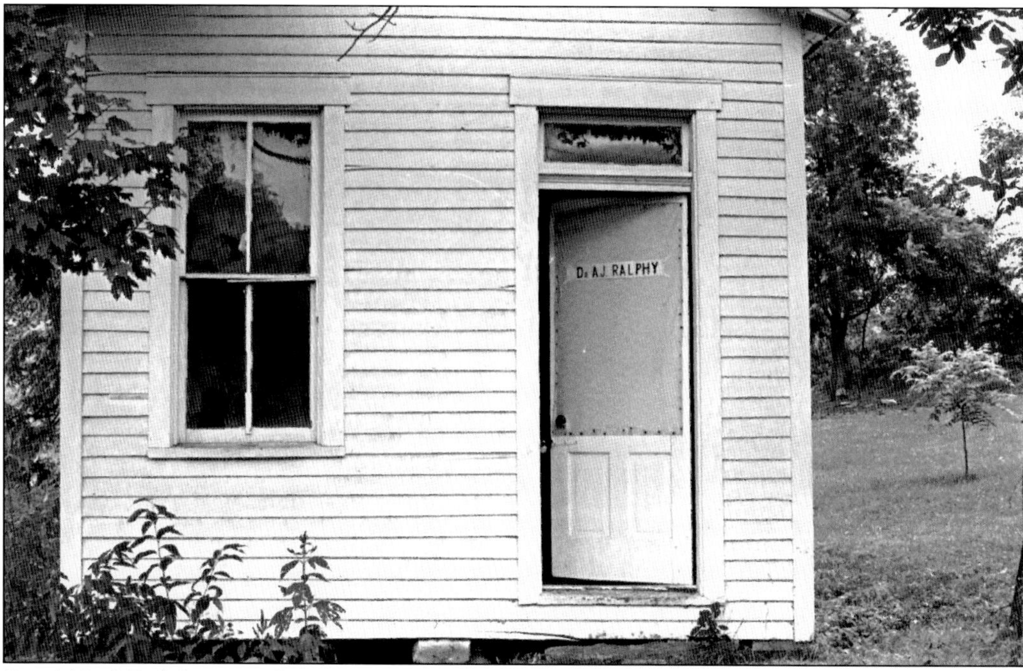

Dr. Alfred Ralphy was the epitome of a country doctor, riding to visit patients often in a buggy pulled by his horses, Bess and Fred. In 1907, a flash flood down a creek near Pike's Peak overturned the buggy and swept the horses off their feet, drowning them. Ralphy tried to save them and almost drowned himself. The horses washed ashore near Stone Head and were buried the following day. Residents attended a funeral for the horses just as they would have for the burial of a friend or neighbor. (Brown County Historical Society.)

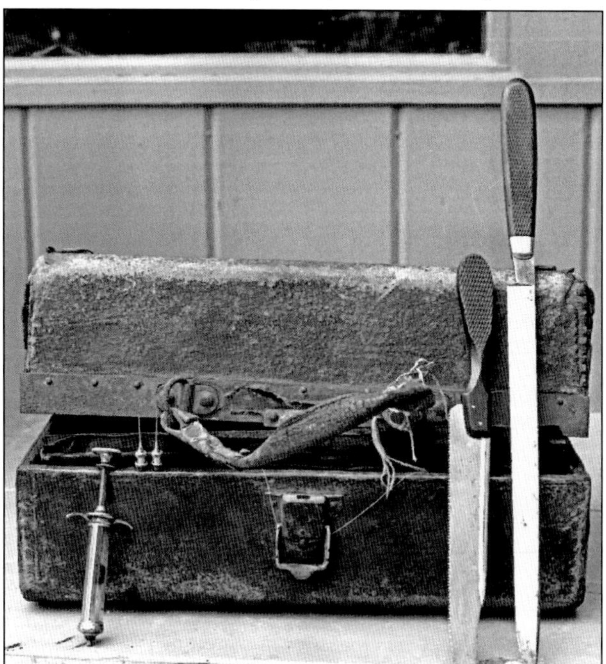

Dr. Ralphy delivered 2,049 babies during his career and, according to his daughter Gladys Whitaker, no mother died in childbirth (very rare back then) and very few of the babies. Ralphy charged about $5 for a delivery and $10 if instruments had to be used. "When he was riding horseback in the winters, many's the time he had to be lifted off the horse and thawed in some cabin before he could administer to the patient," Whitaker stated. (Brown County Historical Society.)

During the bad influenza epidemic of 1918, Whitaker remembers that her father, Dr. Ralphy, whose interior office is shown in the photograph (it is now part of the Brown County Society Museum Complex in Nashville), "never lost even one patient. He didn't get the flu himself but the strain weakened him for the rest of his life." Ralphy died in 1928 at age 74 after a five-year illness. (Brown County Historical Society.)

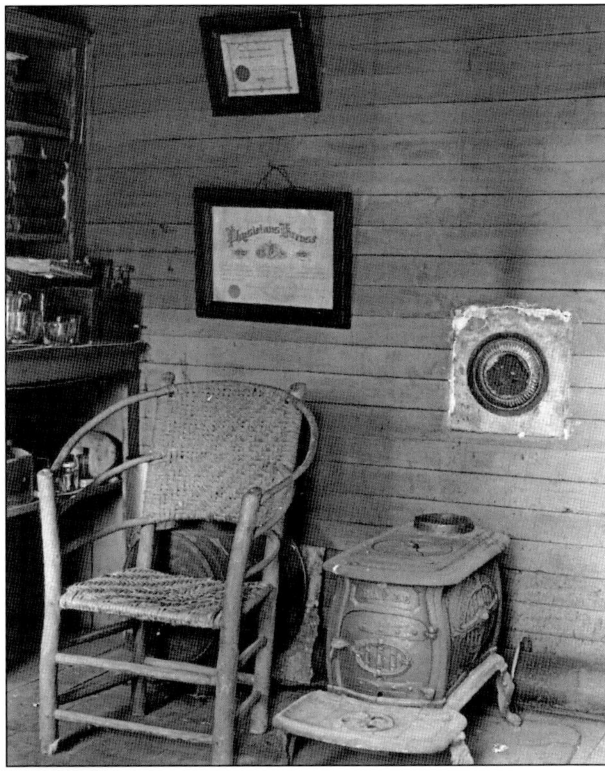

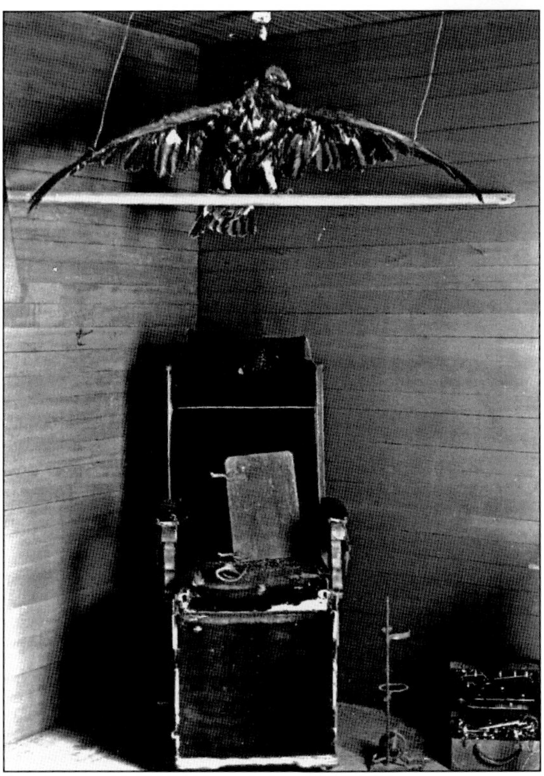

Here is another shot of the interior of Dr. Ralphy's office. Because it took doctors who lived in Nashville four or more hours to reach a patient in the outlying areas (before telephones, someone first had to be sent to get the doctor), midwives were sometimes called. "Their fee was less than the doctors', sometimes being a donation of home-grown vegetables, meat or fruit," recalls Dorothy Webb Cline in *Brown County Remembers*. (Brown County Historical Society.)

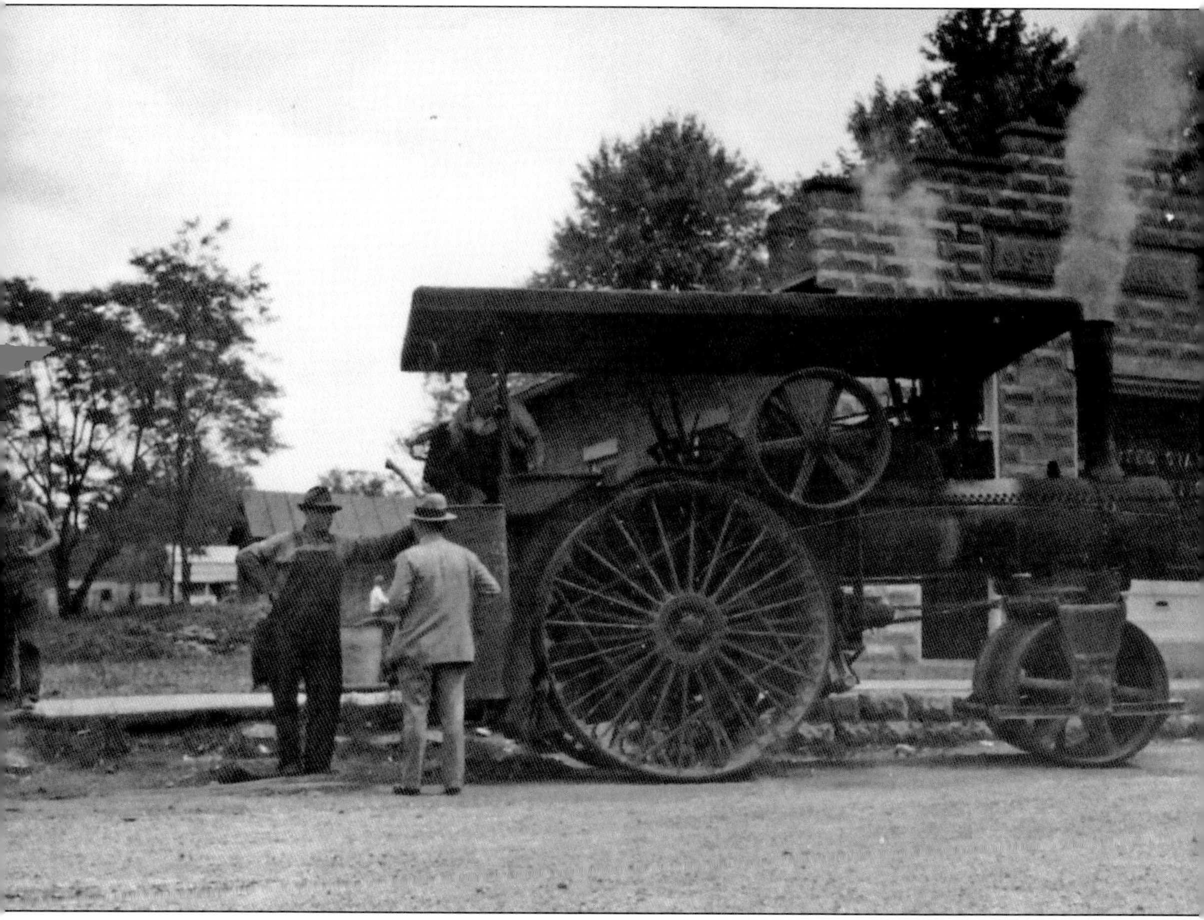

Keeping the gravel and dirt roads common in Brown County even up to the middle of the 20th century required such equipment as this steam roller, which sits in front of the Nashville Post Office on a summer day in 1928. (Lilly Library, photograph by Frank Hohenberger.)

Eight

TRAVELING

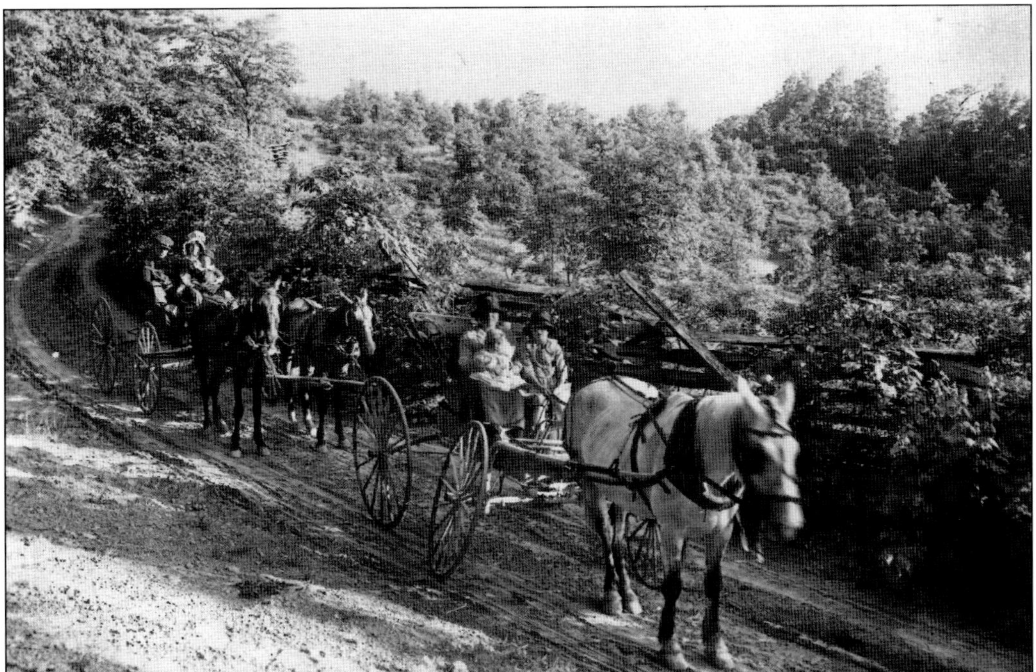

At one time, all roads in Brown County seemed to be back roads, and there were often ghost tales; one such tale was recalled by Chattie Wade Miller in *Brown County Remembers*. The story was about a peddler who disappeared when making his routes. In one of the ravines, a reclusive man lived, and he was suspected of murdering the peddler. After that, people often would hear the sound of a peddler's wagon, but though they would turn around and wait, no one appeared. (Brown County Historical Society.)

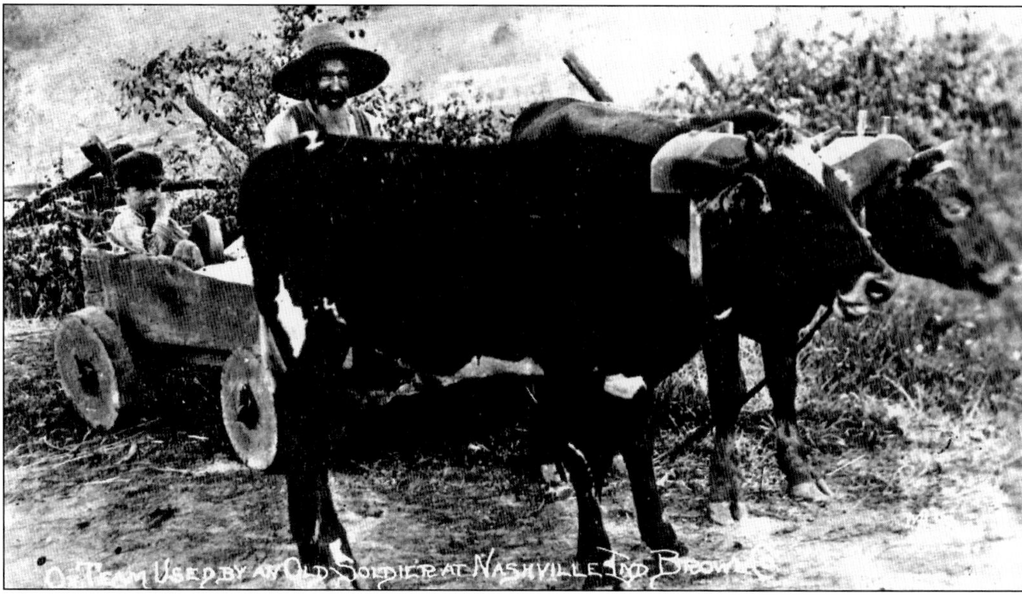

Note the wooden wagon wheels in this photograph, which is titled "Ox Team Used by an Old Soldier in Brown County." Ralph Burkholder wrote in his history of the Nashville Masonic Lodge, "Transportation in the earliest days usually was by wagons drawn by oxen, with carriages coming in shortly after the settlers had gained a firm foothold and could raise grain and grass to feed horses and other livestock." (Brown County Historical Society.)

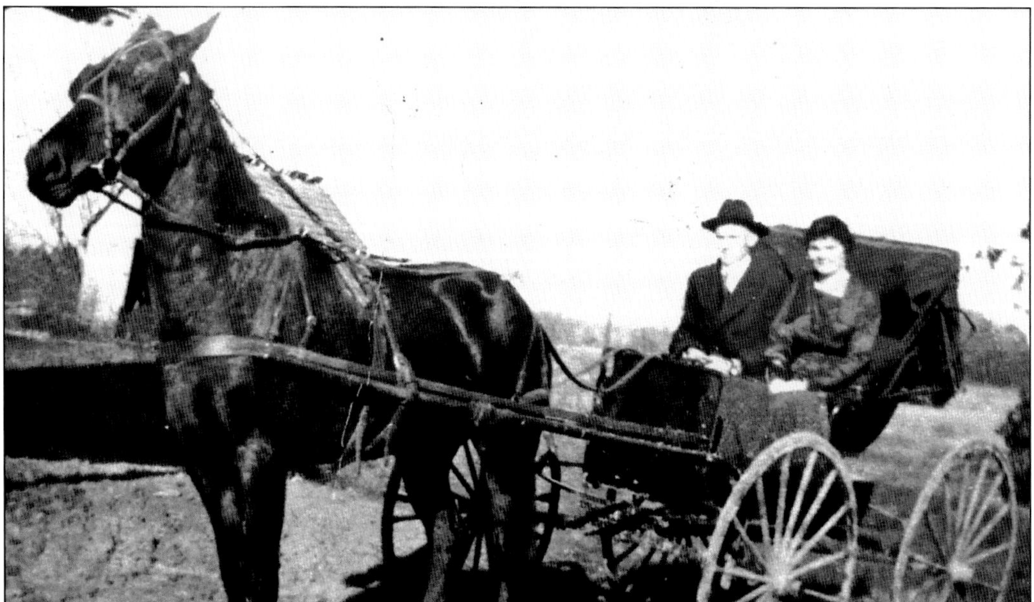

George Ray Fleener and Anna E. Campbell were courting when this photograph was taken in 1920. "Queen the horse was afraid of trains, was very excitable and moved slowly," writes Dorothy Biney Bailey in *Brown County Remembers*. Fleener recalls meeting Anna on the lawn of the courthouse where a Teachers' Institute was being held, "We sat close and listened some." Anna's father, Cornelius, was the Brown County superintendent of public schools. Including Anna, 5 of his 10 children became teachers. (Brown County Historical Society.)

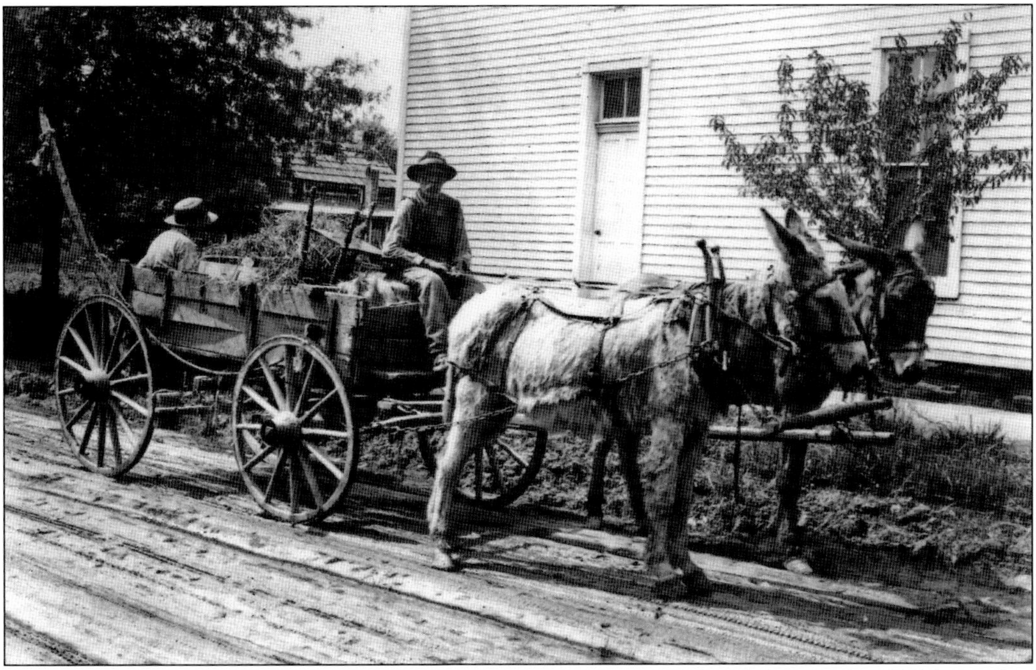

Dave Harden and his wife, Liza, travel in an open wagon stuffed with hay and pulled by mules. It was this quintessential rural life that inspired humorist like Kin Hubbard who helped make Brown County famous with his *Abe Martin* cartoons and witticisms such as "She who hesitates is saved" and "Nobuddy works as hard fer his money as th' feller that marries it." (Brown County Historical Society.)

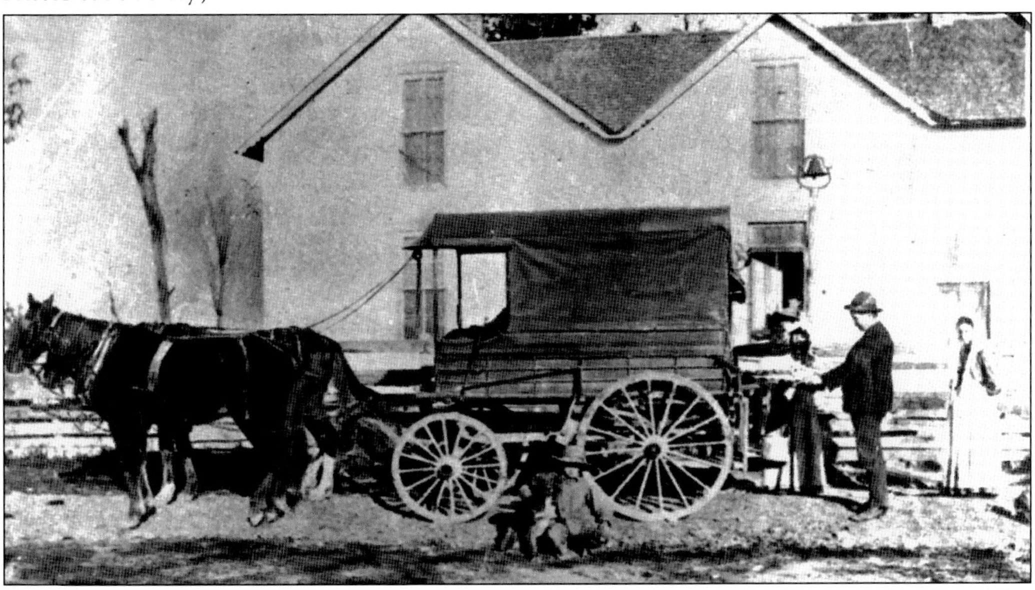

Hucksters called at the farmhouses tucked along the winding roads of Brown County. "The hucksters might trade a bag of flour to a woman in Story in exchange for three or four dozen of her chicken eggs," says Helen C. Ayers, explaining the barter system that existed back then. "Then further down the road, a woman might have needed a dozen eggs. She in turn might exchange a peck of sweet potatoes or a live goose, duck, or a roasting chicken for the eggs."

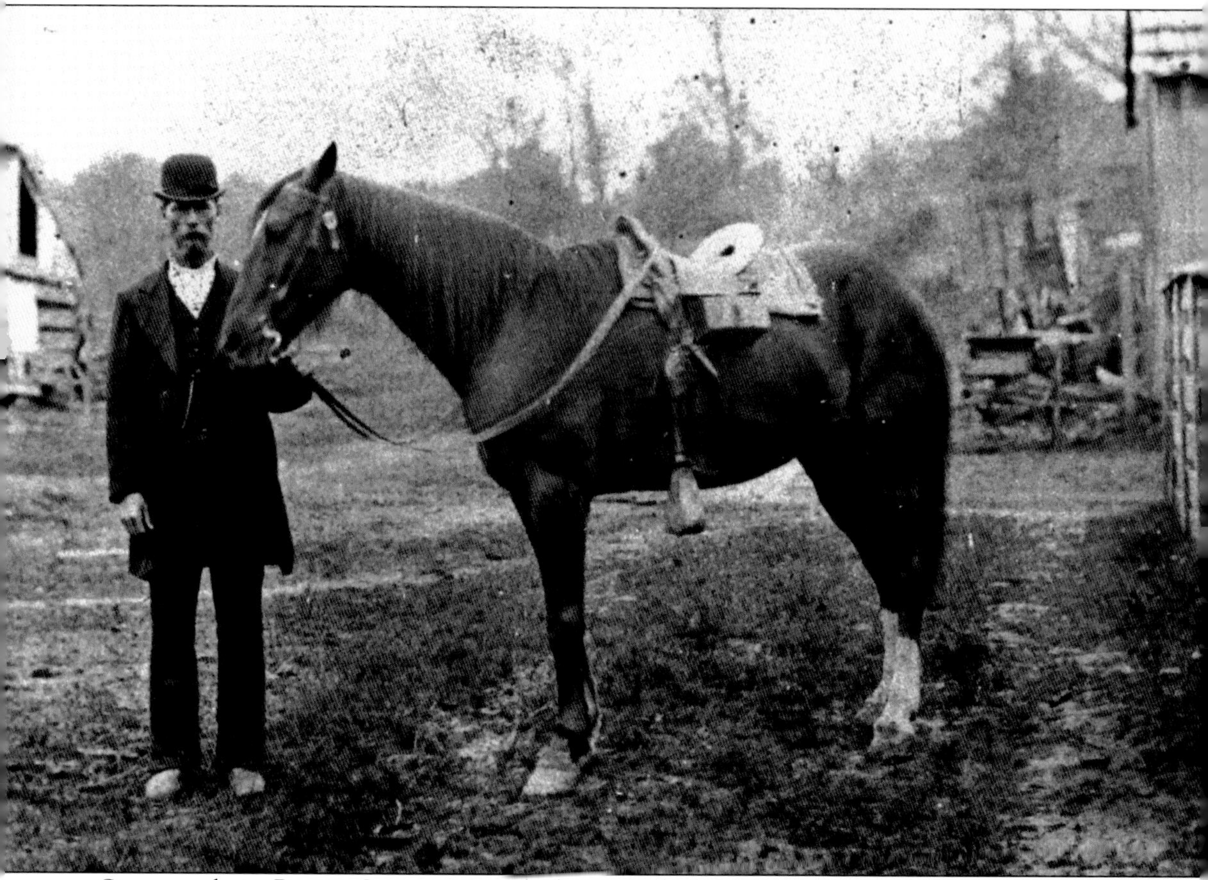

Since roads in Brown County were "little more than bridle paths through the forest," Dr. Ralphy made his calls on horseback and carried his medicine and surgical tools in saddlebags, his daughter Gladys Ralphy Whitaker recalled in *Brown County Remembers*. (Brown County Historical Society.)

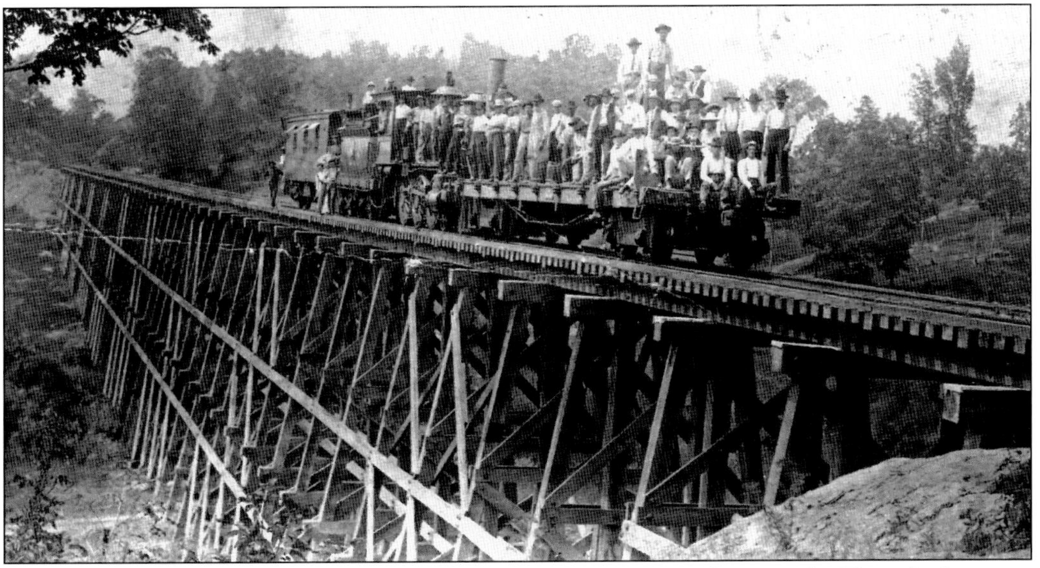

Workers travel along the trestle over Bear Creek in this 1912 photograph. Though the train made travel easier, travelers still had to contend with the dirt roads. For those disembarking to go to Nashville from the Helmsburg station, if the roads were deep mud, it took four horses to pull the hack and take passengers to their destination. (Brown County Historical Society.)

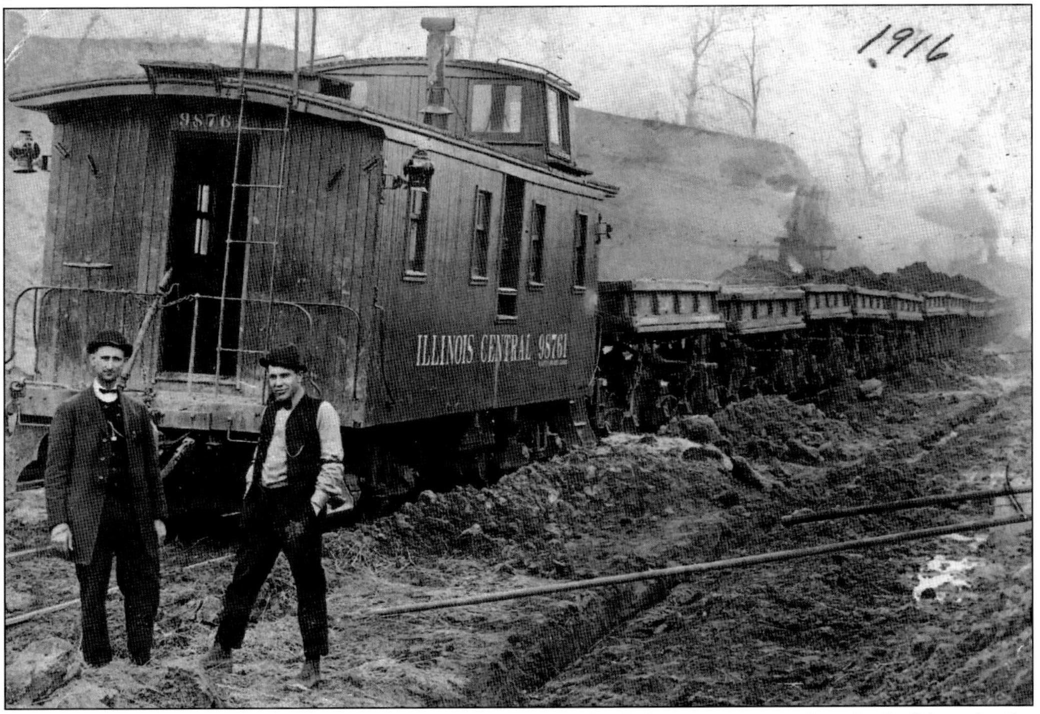

In the small towns dotting Brown County, the arrival of the train was a big deal. "Everybody, it seemed, turned out to see the train come in," Helen Jane Helms Strode recounted in *Brown County Remembers*. "The only experience like seeing the train come in is to live in an out of the way place and join with the other natives in going to the post office twice a day to meet the mail." (Brown County Historical Society.)

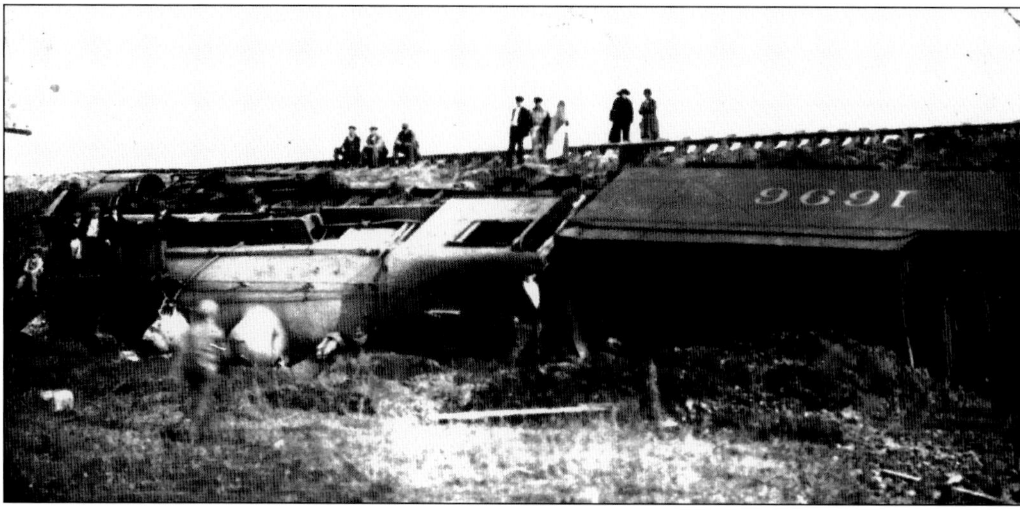

Historian Ray Mathis wrote, "It was quite interesting an event at Helmsburg when the train came in." The trains delivered people and goods, including coal, lumber, gravel, and road machinery and produced a lot of activity. Next to the station a stockyard enclosed cattle, hogs, and sheep. Logs, wood products like railroad ties and hoop poles, canned fruits, vegetables, and other farm products passed through Helmsburg Station. This undated photograph shows a train wreck that occurred along the line. (Brown County Historical Society.)

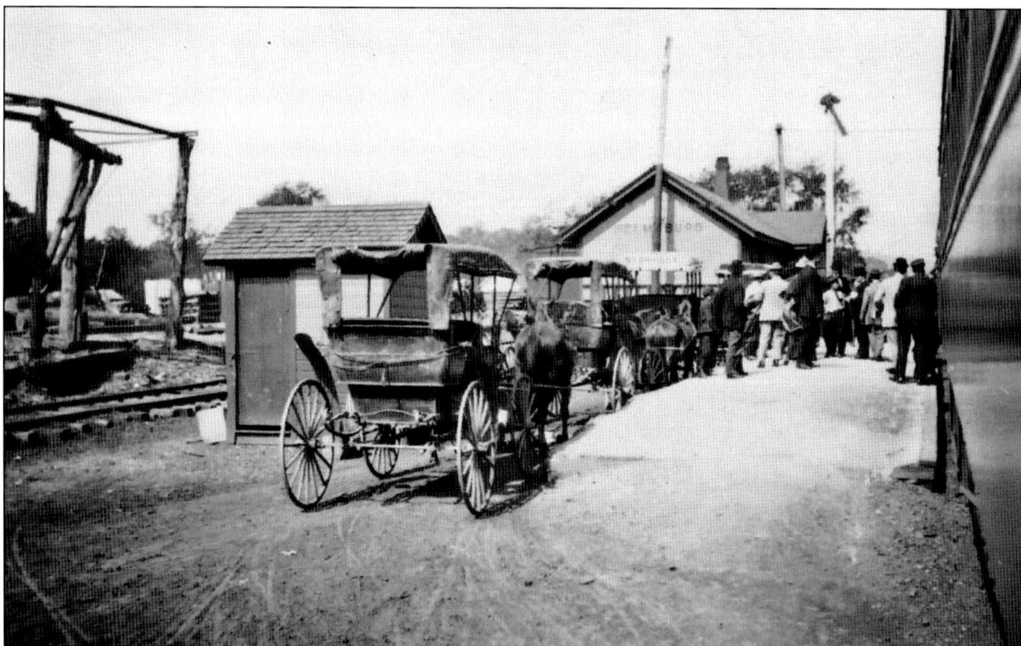

The arrival of the Helmsburg Train Station helped move Brown County into more modern times. According to the Web site of *Our Brown County* magazine, "Helmsburg quickly grew into a town with its own sawmill, flour mill, cannery, feed store, restaurants, hardware and grocery stores, storage facilities, post office, doctor's office, Methodist Church, Masonic Lodge, and undertaker supply store. Liveries competed to take passengers and freight to Nashville. The Rains Hotel served those whose business kept them in the county overnight." (Lilly Library.)

Driving along the road from Columbus to Nashville, as can be seen in this 1915 photograph, was both beautiful and daunting. "Old State Road 46 was clay," recalls Martha Snyder Weddle in *Brown County Remembers*. "The dust clouds in summer were so bad that side curtains were put up on the open car. I always held a handkerchief over my nose and mouth."

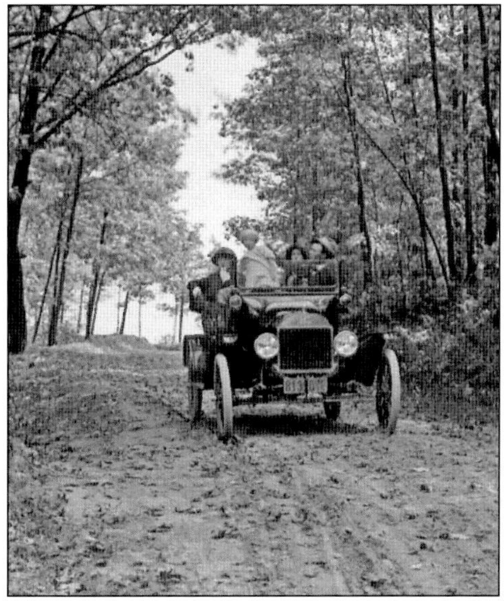

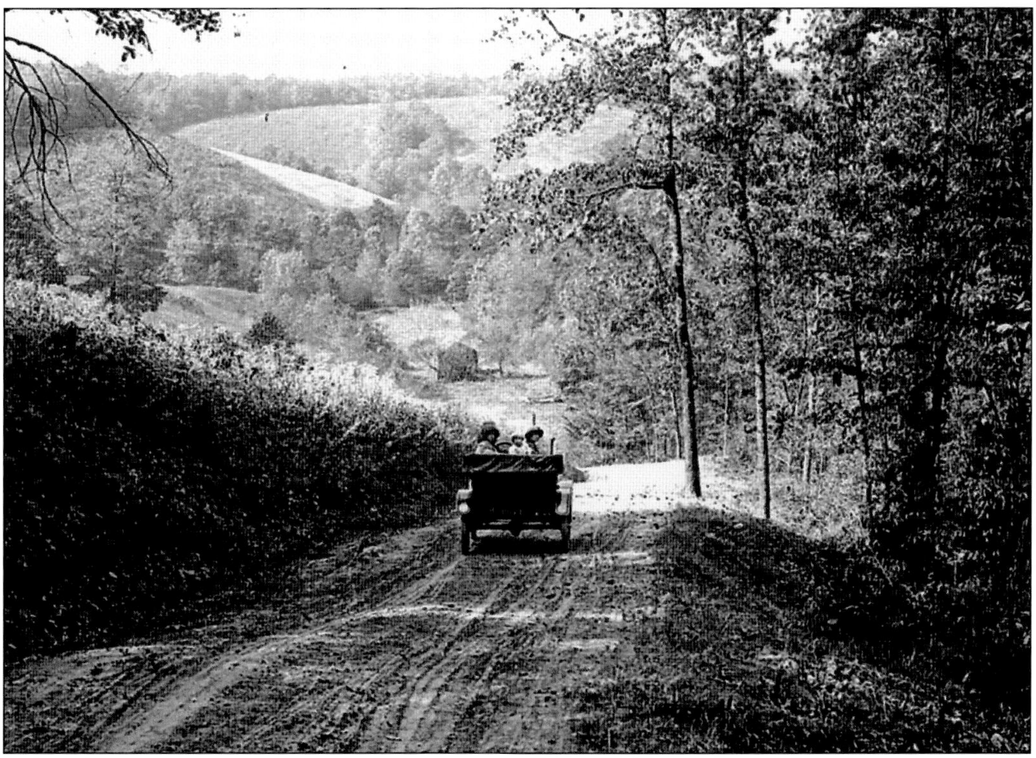

"Many times in winter, ruts were so deep that when two cars met in the same rut there was difficulty for at least one car in getting out of the rut," recalls Martha Snyder Weddle in *Brown County Remembers*. "In winter, bus passengers sometimes had to get out and walk up every hill on the Columbus Road."

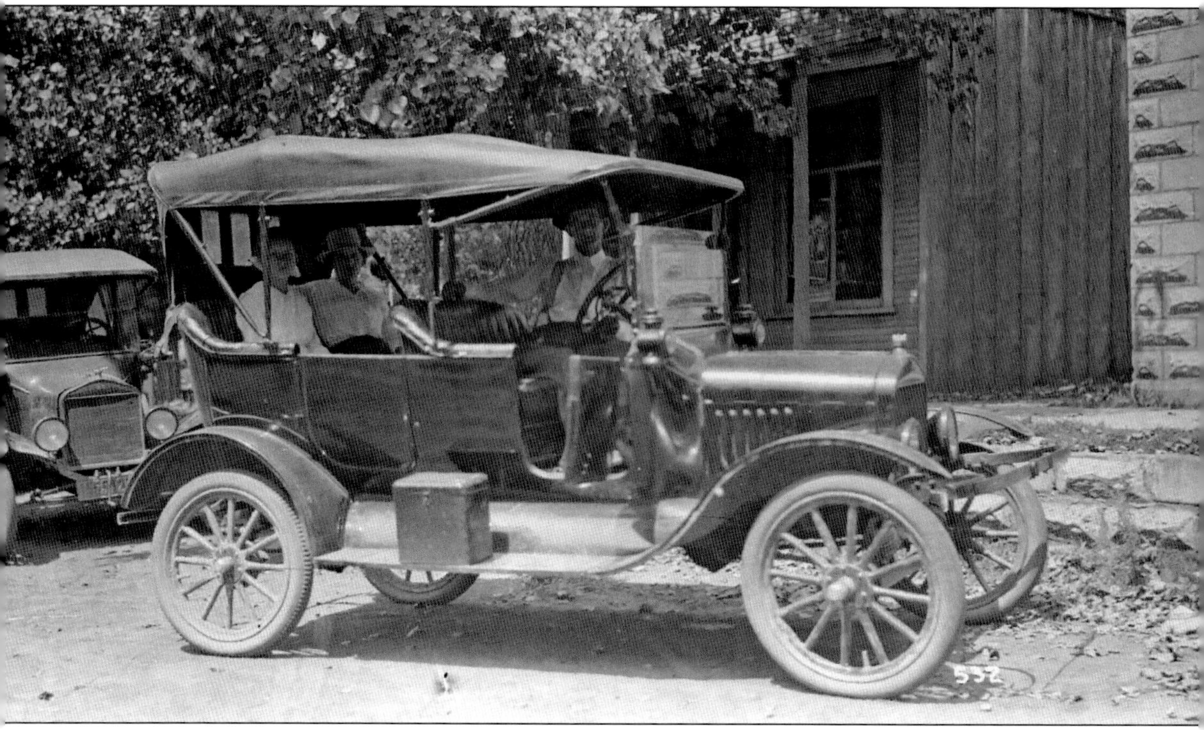

The Lures family sits inside their taxi. When automobiles first started traveling along Brown County roads, it caused difficulties for horseback riders. "Those autos frightened horses they met on the road," recalls Gladys Whitaker. "They'd shy and rear and had to be held by the bridles until the car had passed." (Brown County Historical Society.)

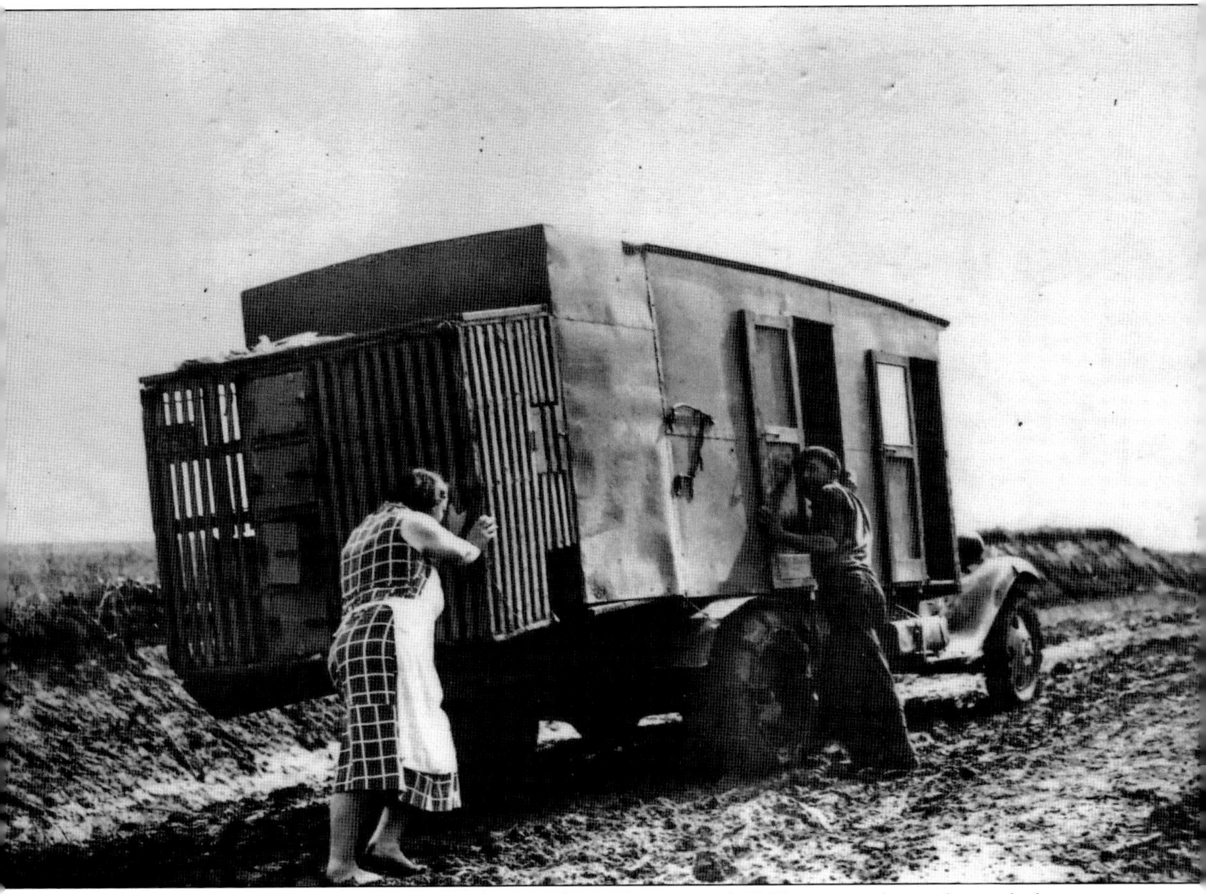

"There were few vehicles in the area during the 1930s to mid 1950s so residents depended upon huckster wagons for many of those years to bring groceries to them," writes Helen Ayers. "There was a Monday peddler and a Thursday peddler who came every week to Story and other small towns bringing necessities to these little homesteads. One peddler was Mr. Hamblen and the other was Mr. McDonald of Bean Blossom." Mary Ford and Herbert McDonald have the daunting task of pushing his huckster's wagon out of the mud in this 1933 photograph. According to Gladys Mayne, McDonald bought an old school bus, mounted it on a new truck base, removed the seats, and had shelves built along each side for his stock of merchandise, the same as he stocked in his store. (Brown County Historical Society.)

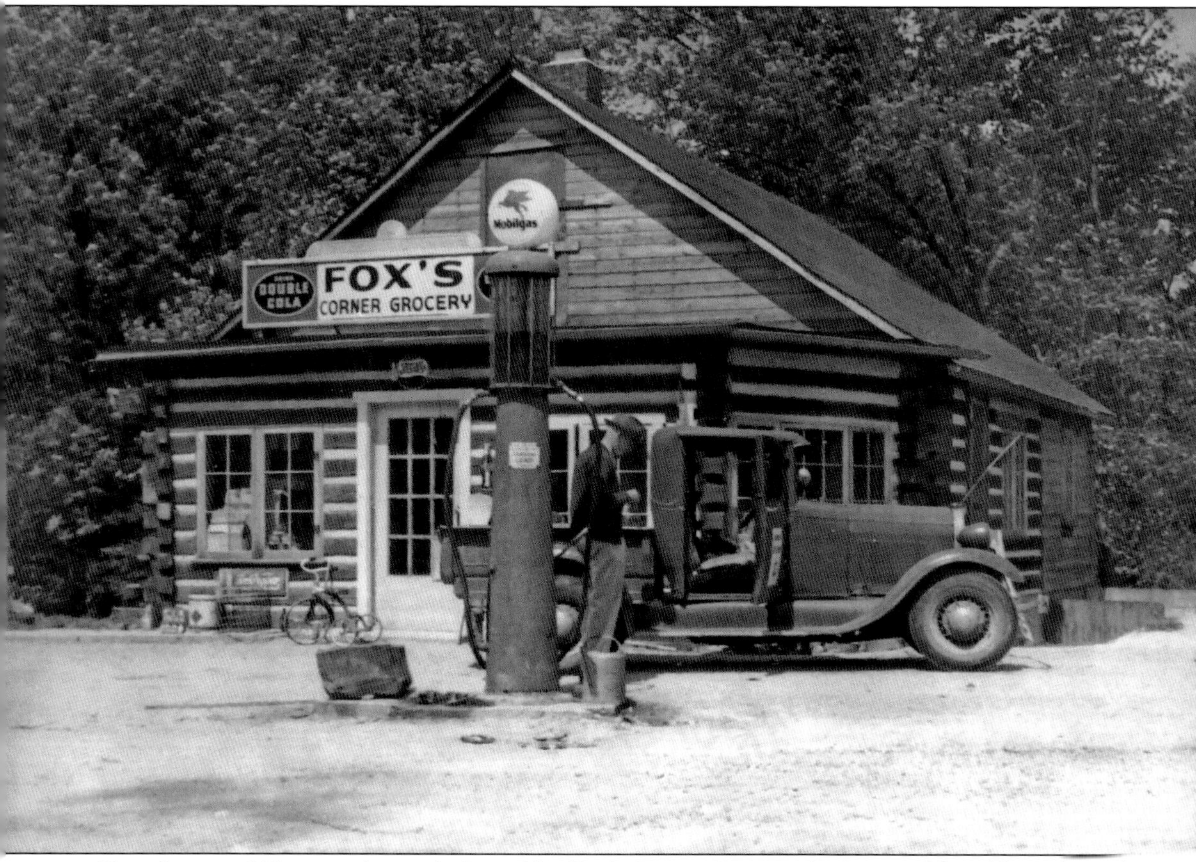

Travelers would have welcomed places like Fox's Corner Store, which served Double Cola and sold Mobil Gas. Before electricity reached the rural areas of Brown County, sometimes not until the 1940s, gas pumps had to be cranked by hand. (Brown County Historical Society.)

Nine

ELKINSVILLE
THE TOWN BENEATH THE LAKE

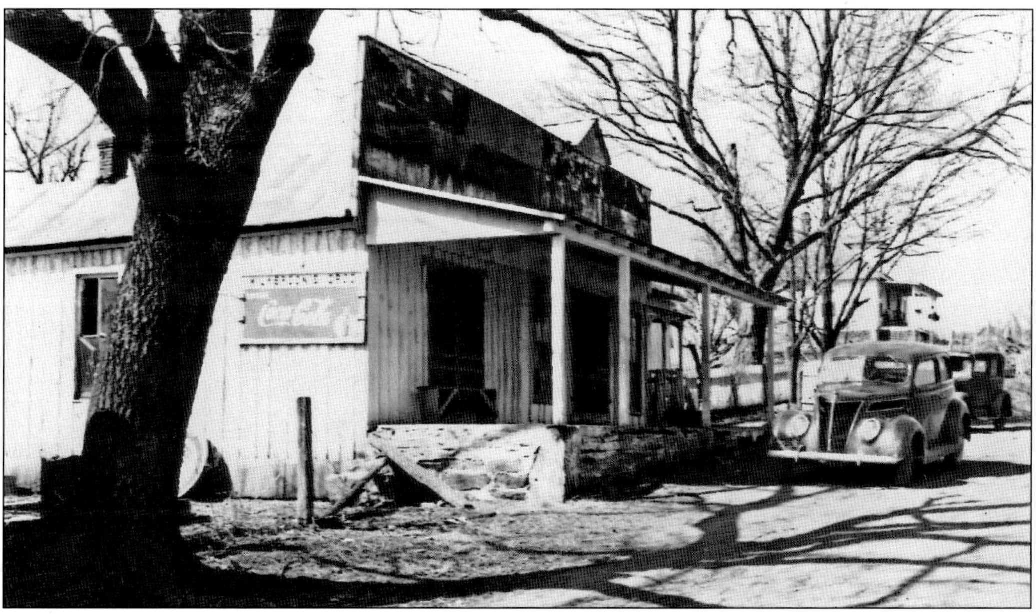

This is the general store in Elkinsville in a photograph taken by Frank Hohenberger. Even with it, some things couldn't be bought, either because they weren't available or were too expensive. "My mom would make sure we had enough chicken feed sacks to make us clothes," recalls Carol Lucas Cummins, whose family lived in Elkinsville for several generations. "There was also a tinker, something that has disappeared, who would come by in his rattle trap odd truck selling odds and ends like threads and needles." William Elkins was one of the first settlers in Brown County, and the story of the town named after him, Elkinsville, is in some ways a sad one as the town's people were made to give up their homes so that the land could be flooded for the development of Lake Monroe. Today there are still a few homes and abandoned buildings left. (Lilly Library.)

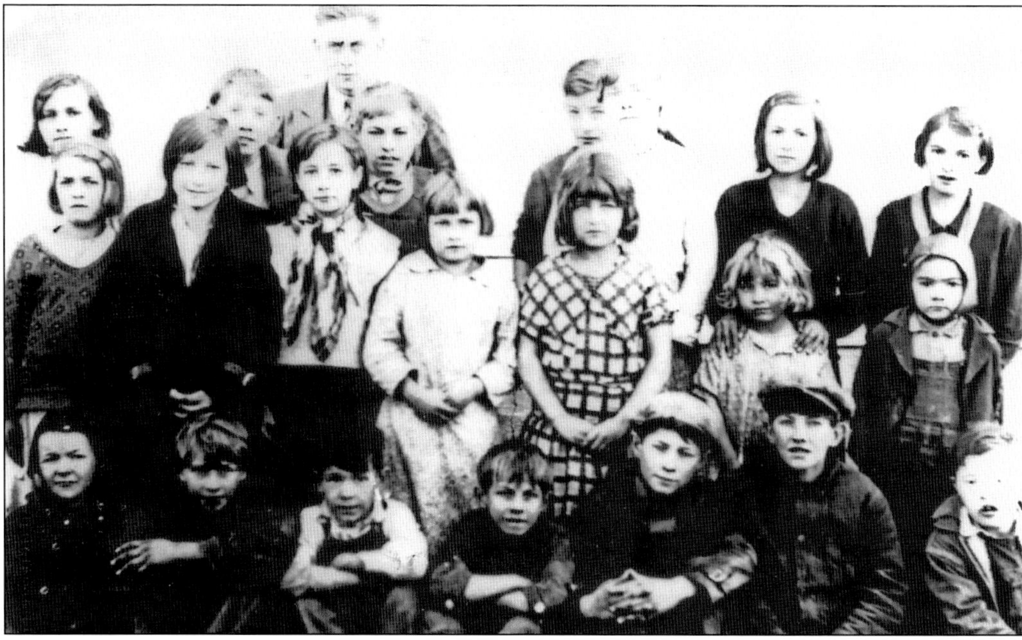

Pictured here are Elkinsville schoolchildren in 1932. They include (first row) Howard Crider, Burdine Bridgewater, Elza Lucas, Estol Bridgewater, ? Blackwell, and Ford Wilkerson; (second row) Ruth Ferguson Deckard, Irene Lucas Hatchett Fields, Jeraldine Wilkerson, Greedy Alonzo, Ella Mae Ferguson Miller, Maxine Lucas Trecker, Alphodean Lucas Miller, and Acie Crider; (third row) Katherine Ferguson Lucas, Chester Followell, Irvin Robertson, Goldie Robertson, Wilma Rayburn Hudson, Lordia Crider Deckard; (fourth row) teacher Frances Lutz and Raymond Lucas. (Lucas family.)

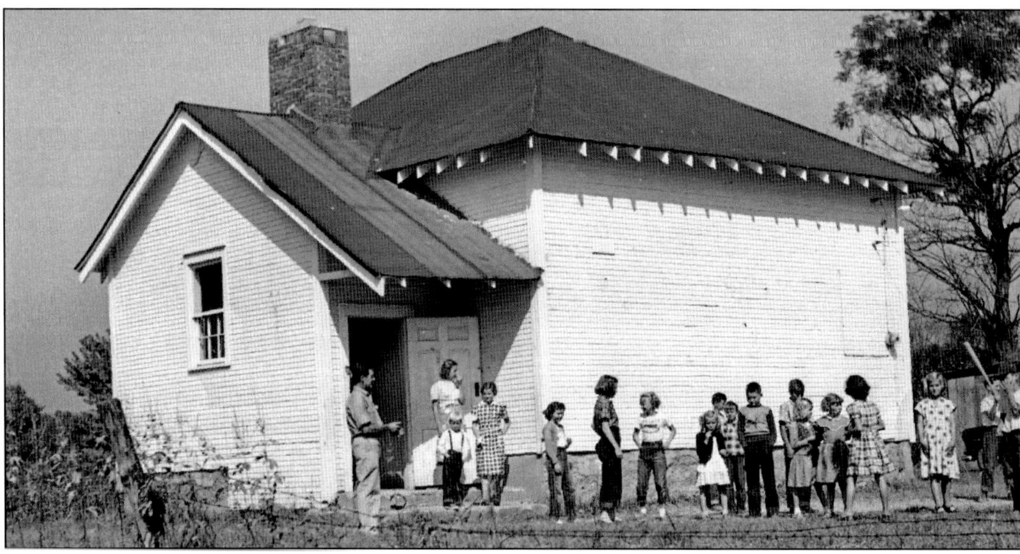

Elkinsville was so remote that in many ways life there was 20 or so years behind the rest of the country says Carol Lucas Cummins, who remembers riding in a Model T well after those cars were obsolete. Cummins's grandmother washed clothes in a big three-legged iron pot set over an open fire. In warm weather, children would go barefoot to save shoe leather, and kids walked to where they wanted to go. (Brown County Historical Society.)

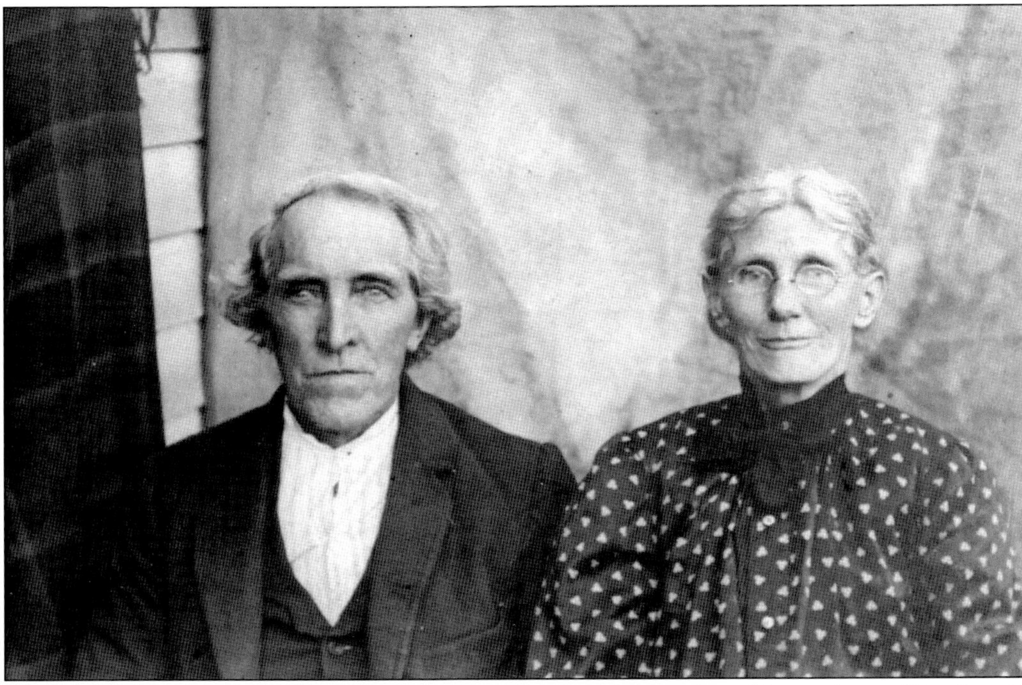

James Lowery Lucas (March 28, 1842–May 3, 1919) and Julia Ann Moore Lucas (October 16, 1847–August 6, 1919) were the great, great grandparents of Carol Lucas Cummins. (Lucas family.)

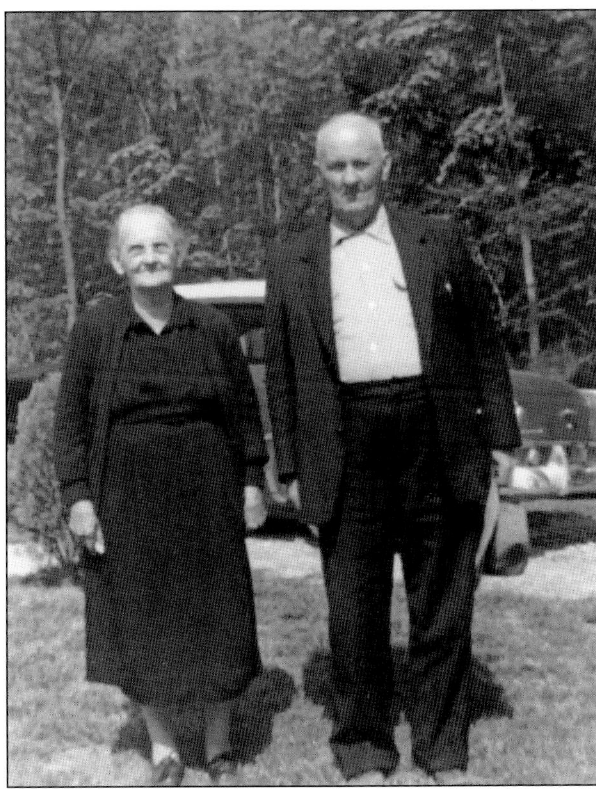

Pictured here are Elza Ambrose (July 14, 1882–June 29, 1965) and Sarah Ethel Hensley Lucas (December 1, 1882–May 29, 1958). Elza was the minister of Elkinsville's only church. The couple had 13 children. (Lucas family.)

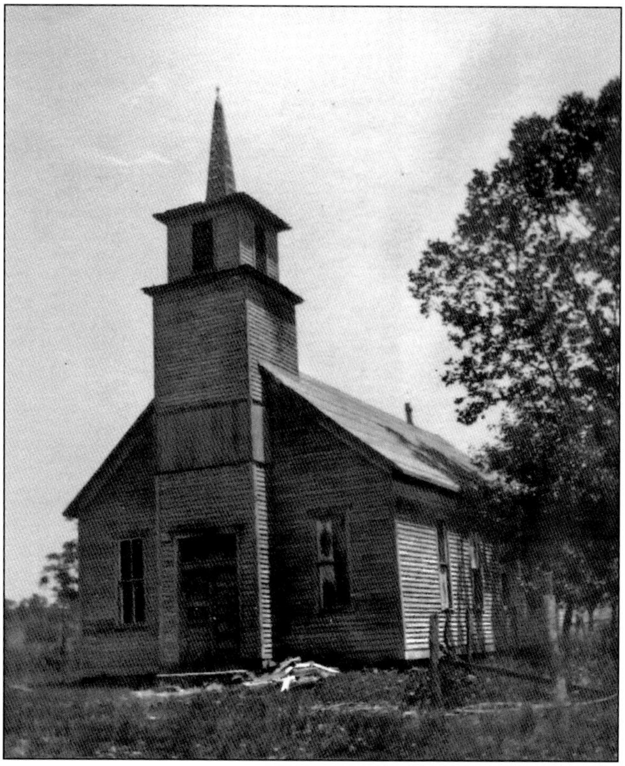

This is the Elkinsville Church. There were few public buildings, and former Elkinsville resident Carol Cummins recalls that the post office was often in someone's home. "One time it was in my grandfather's house," she says, "We truly lived a life beyond the time; a generation separated us from most people. We were still in the Depression era even though that had been more than 20 years before." Cummins remembers having to cross a swinging bridge to get to a friend's house from Elkinsville School. "It was frightening," she says. But there were fun times too, including revivals and school and church socials. "You would take your finest cake and it would be bid on," Carol recalls. (Brown County Historical Society.)

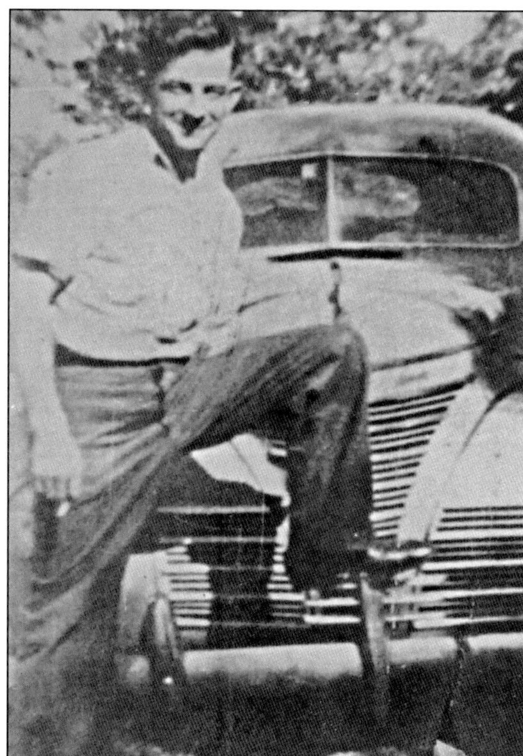

Pictured is a very dashing Raymond Deckard Lucas before he married Marie Fleenor. The father of four daughters and one son, Raymond would open his house to those who had no place to go on holidays. "We'd plan for 40 or 50," says his daughter Carol Lucas Cummins, noting that they often had to make emergency runs to the store to get more groceries. According to Forrest Lucas, Raymond's son, the group even included ex-spouses. "If we didn't get along that was our problem," he recalls, "He'd say that they might not be members of your family, but they sure do belong to mine." (Lucas family.)

Pictured here are Marie Fleenor Lucas and her daughter Carol Lucas Cummins. Marie was a very dedicated mother and homemaker. She canned vegetables that she grew in her garden, sewed, and cooked delicious dinners from what was available. She also was a prayer woman and would go into the homes of her neighbors who were sick and sit day and night, praying for them. Prayer women were not uncommon in the rural communities of Brown County. (Lucas family.)

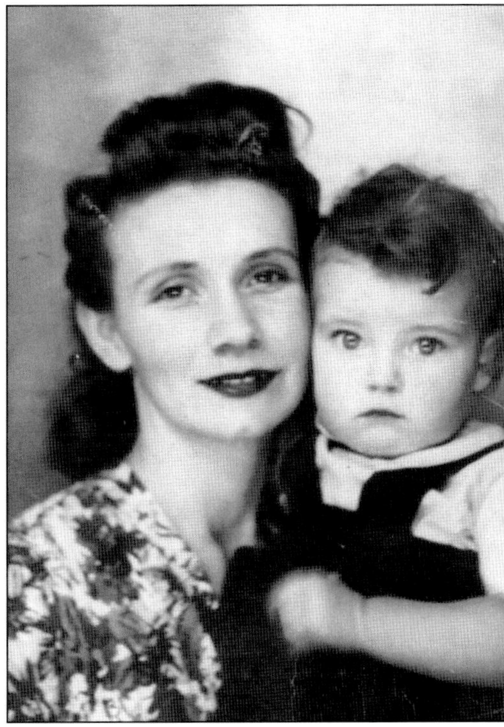

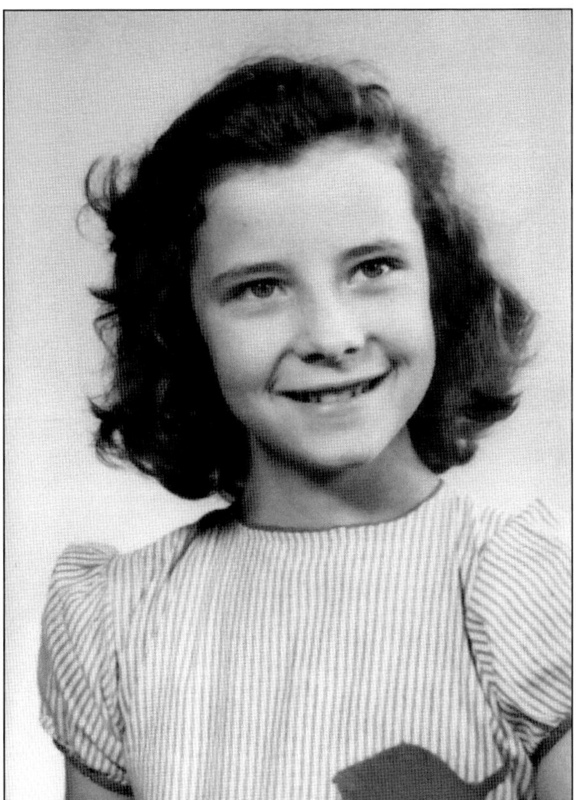

This is Carol Lucas Cummins when she was a fourth-grade student at Elkinsville School. Carol's mother, Marie, would often add a flourish to the clothes she sewed for her children. Note the oak leaf on this dress. Marie sent Carol and her brother Forrest out to find an oak leaf, which she then used as a pattern. (Lucas family.)

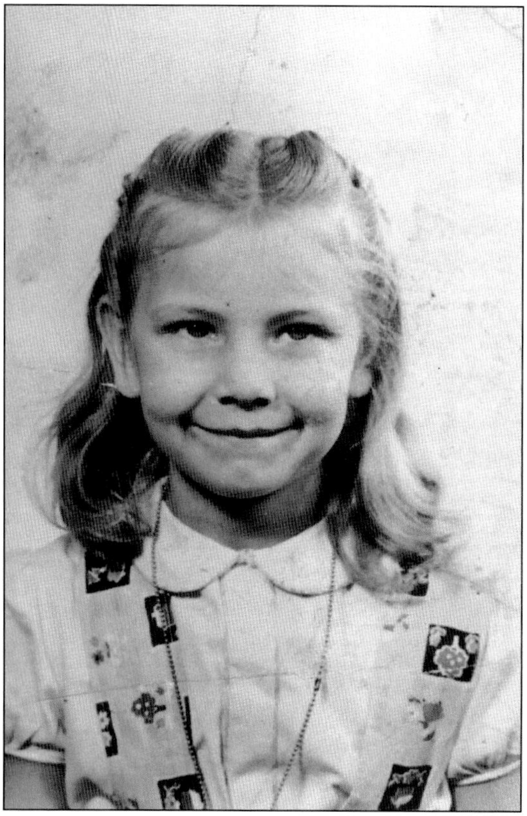

This is Connie Joan Lucas Schooler as a first grader in Elkinsville. Her sister Carol Lucas Cummins recalls how their mother sewed all their own clothes, using chicken feed sacks that she had saved. (Lucas family.)

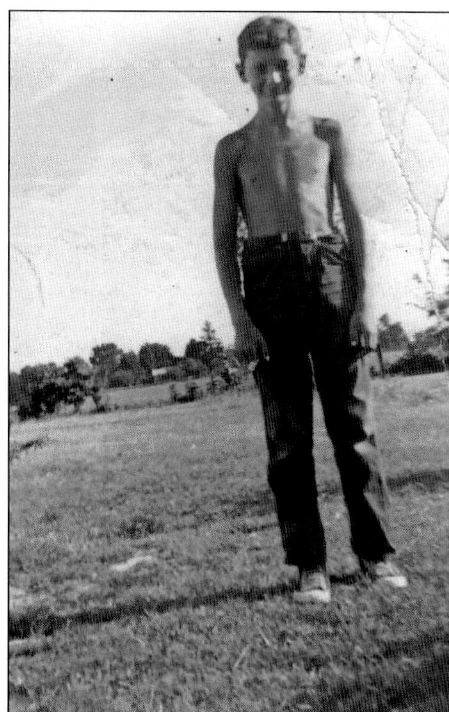

Posing here is Forrest Lucas as a young boy in Elkinsville. Though the Lucas family was poor, family was important to them, and even today, decades later, Forrest and his four sisters and their families still get together frequently. Forrest Lucas would go on to form Lucas Oil, and the new Indianapolis Colts stadium, Lucas Oil Stadium, is named after him. (Lucas family.)

Brenda Lucas Harris, daughter of Raymond and Marie Lucas smiles for her high school photograph. "There were people in Elkinsville who had enough to eat and those that didn't," recalls her sister Carol. In the winter months, the Lucas family lived off salt pork and sorghum. "Houses would be cold because no one had central heating. Grandma put sheets of newspaper under the bed and put root vegetables on them. My mother made sausage. The men would go out hunting with their coon dogs. Meat was not part of a family meal, it was more of a Sunday meal instead. The spring was a wonderful time, and my mother would go out and gather wild weeds that she cooked with bacon. They were delicious," says Carol. (Lucas family.)

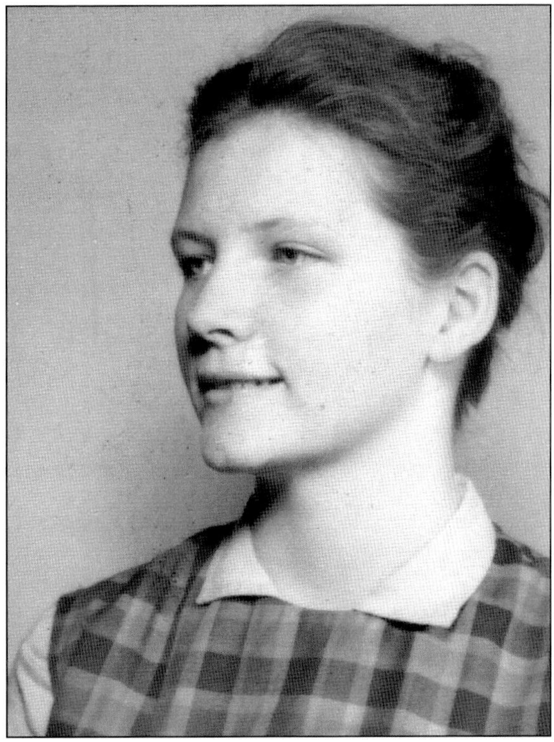

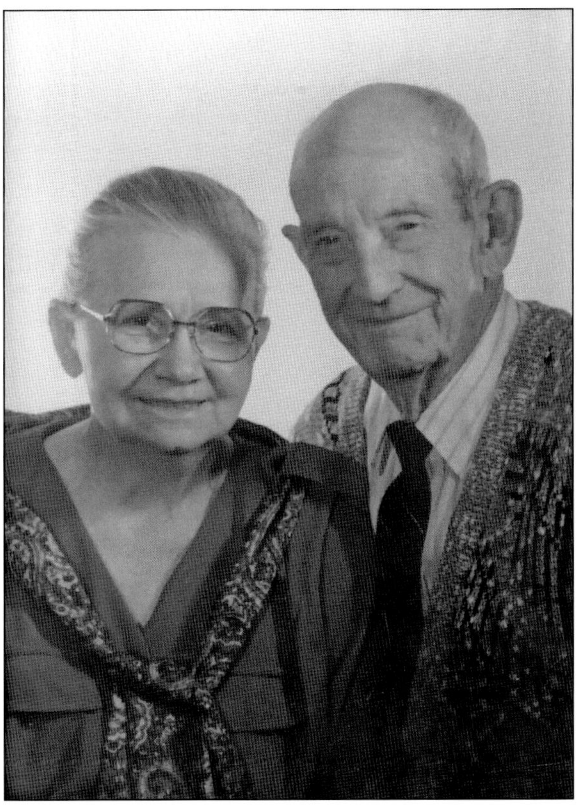

This is a photograph of Raymond and Marie Lucas honoring their 50th wedding anniversary. Their life in Elkinsville was hard, and the family was very poor, but both were very generous with time and what little money they had. Their son Forrest recalls how their father had them help others. "He'd call them widder ladies and sometimes he'd involve all us kids in those projects. He'd tell us that we're going town and dig a well for a widder lady or we're going to haul firewood for a widder lady." (Lucas family.)

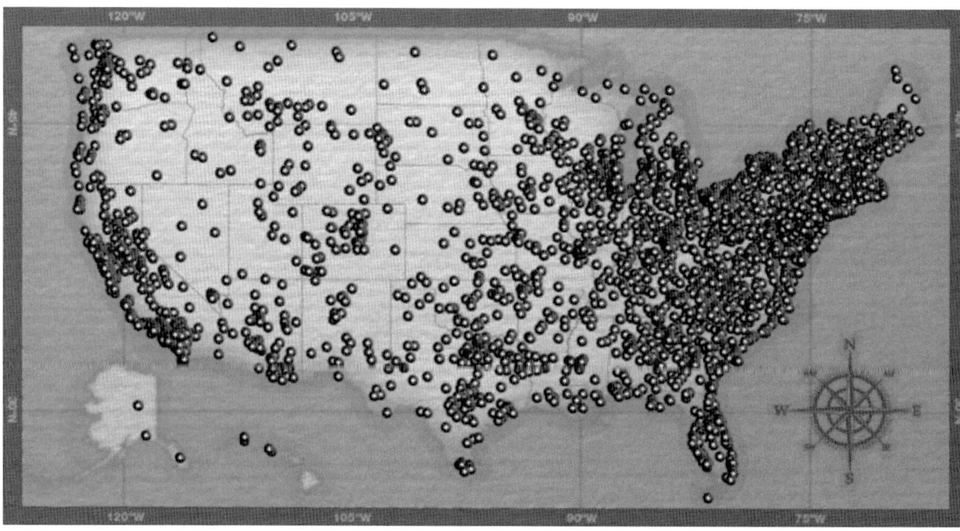